THE NEW
PRODUCTS
HANDBOOK

THE NEW PRODUCTS HANDBOOK

Edited by Larry Wizenberg

DOW JONES-IRWIN   Homewood, Illinois   60430

To my parents, Ethel and Izak Wizenberg

ISBN 0-87094-520-3

Library of Congress Catalog Card No. 85-71278

Printed in the United States of America

1 2 3 4 5 6 7 8 9 0 K 3 2 1 0 9 8 7 6

Preface

This book is about the important aspects of product development and new products management. Contributors to *The New Products Handbook* are practitioners—all authorities in their areas. Each of the chapters they have written sets forth their views, ideas, and approaches. They are meant to provoke your thinking—to enable you to experiment, develop strategies, consider options, and generally understand the techniques being used by innovative companies.

While there is no single formula for success, the fundamentals and nuances of launching new products are covered in depth. Hopefully, patterns will emerge that will increase the probabilities of success.

Our intended audience surely includes new products managers, marketing managers, and chief executives. The book should be useful to aspiring entrepreneurs and managers of small businesses, as well.

Special thanks must be given to the Editorial Advisory Board for their ideas and help in designing this volume. Some of them also contributed chapters of their own. We are honored to be able to acknowledge our indebtedness to our distinguished authors. Their dedication and cooperation made this project a pleasure.

Larry Wizenberg

CONTRIBUTING AUTHORS

ADAMEK, JAMES C., *Conway/Milliken & Associates, Chicago*
BAUM, HERBERT M., *Campbell Soup Company, Camden, N.J.*
BOBROW, EDWIN E., *Bobrow Consulting Group, Inc., New York, N.Y.*
BLYTH, JOHN STEVENSON, *Peterson Blyth Cato Associates, Inc., New York, N.Y.*
CAFARELLI, EUGENE J., *Center for Concept Development, New York, N.Y.*
DENTON, GRAHAM, *Initiatives Group and Product Initiatives, Toronto, Ont.*
FOX, JEFFREY, *Fox & Company, Inc., Avon, Conn.*
FRIEDMAN, MARTIN, *New Product News, Dancer Fitzgerald Sample, New York, N.Y.*
GILBERT, LYNN, *Gilbert Tweed Associates, New York, N.Y.*
HEHMAN, RAYMOND D., *BBDO, International, San Francisco*
HUPFER, HERBERT P., *Elrick and Lavidge, Inc., Chicago*
JAVED, NASEEM, *ABC DIAL INC., Toronto, Ont.*
KANE, CHESTER L., *Kane Bortree Associates, New York, N.Y.*
KUCZMARSKI, THOMAS D., *Kuczmarski & Associates, Chicago*
MARAN, ELAINE, *Yankelovich, Skelly & White, Inc., New York, N.Y.*
ROSENFIELD, DEBRA J., *Pfizer Inc., New York, N.Y.*
SPANNER, ROBERT ALAN, *Beckford, Spanner & Kelley, Palo Alto, Calif.*
STEFFLRE, VOLNEY, *New York, N.Y.*
VanGUNDY, ARTHUR B., *University of Oklahoma, Norman, Okla.*
WIZENBERG, LARRY, *Yankelovich, Skelly & White, Inc., New York, N.Y.*
WOOD, DAVID R., *Interbrand Corporation, New York, N.Y.*
YALOWITZ, MICHAEL S., *Synectics, Wyncote, Penn.*
YOUNG, ELLIOT, *Perception Research Services, Inc., Englewood Cliffs, N.J.*

Contents

ix

Part
I

Planning for New Product Development

Introduction to New Products Management

Larry Wizenberg
Yankelovich, Skelly & White
Editor of the New Products Handbook

The importance of new products management can not be overemphasized. As the lifeblood of nearly every business, new product development is the basis for maintaining profitability and market share in competitive markets. Sooner or later, most products are preempted by other products or else evolve into less profitable products due to increased competitive pricing and sales promotion pressures. New products are crucial because they can contribute the additional profit needed to sustain and increase company growth as the profit margin curve of existing products declines.

It is becoming increasingly difficult to gain trial and acceptance of new products because consumers and industrial buyers have tempered their thirst for novelty and change. During the 1970s, an era of new social values, people searched for a continuous injection of new things and new experiences into their lives. This paved the way for the trial of new products even when consumers were relatively satisfied with existing products and even when advantages were not dramatic. According to the Yankelovich *Monitor* life-style tracking study, the desire to experience it all, do it all, and have it all is waning. More than ever, new products will need to clearly demonstrate their advantages in order to gain consideration from the more pragmatic and savvy buyer.

An effective new products management program should focus on the development and launching of various types of new products responsive to the opportunities of the market-place. Few companies can rely solely on the limited notion of new products as those with unique patentable features that every customer wants and no competitor has. Viable strategies may range from a role as an originator of product concepts to a more passive role of replicating or modifying new offerings by others.

New product development includes gradations of new-ness ranging from unprecedented products, services, and processes that are marketed to gain widespread use, to those that are new to the company even if a similar product is marketed by another organization. As long as the problems and challenges in introducing a product have not previously been faced by management, it should be treated as a new product. This includes new categories to a company, new brands, and new packaging configurations.

Because the process of new product development involves a series of management decisions, it becomes more expensive to discard a product concept as we progress with each phase. The objective is to do a better job of eliminating concepts of limited potential before they reach the more expensive latter phases. The delicate balance involves not discarding concepts prematurely. Therefore, companies should clarify that the expressed goals and objectives are targets, parameters that are not to be rigidly followed but are to be used as a frame of reference.

The first phase of the new product development process is *idea generation*. This involves the search for product concepts to meet the company objectives. One of the challenges that we face is to instill creativity. Self-inflicted barriers to creativity should be broken in order to facilitate the search for a new order of meaning. Participants can be stimulated, asking them to view existing products in terms of potential substitutions, combinations, magnifications, miniaturizations, new uses, and new users. Also, they should be invited to reassess abandoned projects, analyze manufacturing process by-products, probe company personnel, customers, converters, and raw material suppliers, and anticipate social change (lifestyle trends).

The next phase is *concept screening*. This is an internal analysis to determine which ideas are pertinent and merit more detailed study. Screening is the systematic process of qualitative selection of product concepts based on management judgment. It is the process of collecting facts and opinions about the viability of each product concept. An estimate of potential profit, time, investment, and risk should be developed.

After the screening phase, an in-depth *business analysis* should be conducted. This involves a detailed appraisal of the product, potential competition, and overall marketing characteristics. Market and technical research, focus groups, and social trend data should be used to develop an understanding of the trends and characteristics of the market. This will serve as the basis for the eventual marketing program and product positioning.

The final phase prior to commercialization is *testing*. This involves laboratory and commercial experiments that verify or disaffirm previous business judgments. Tests might include user panels, laboratory test markets, perception research, and test marketing. These tools enable management to experiment with various elements of the marketing mix and can serve as a measure to forecast national sales.

When final plans for production and marketing are completed, we enter the *commercialization* phase. This is the actual launching of the product on a regional or national basis, monitoring acceptance and competitive reaction.

While there is no absolute formula for new product development, the techniques, strategies, and nuances contained in *The New Products Handbook* can enhance the probabilities of success.

1

New Product Planning
Setting the Stage to Win

Thomas D. Kuczmarski
Kuczmarski & Associates

Two essential ingredients are required to spark innovation and successfully manage new products: a blueprint and an entrepreneur. Companies successful at developing new products formulate new product strategies and nurture product champions. The winners link strategic focus with implementation and foster an entrepreneurial culture. That is, they are willing to risk not making a profit on a new product introduction. The real winners can swallow the risk and digest the uncertainty to fuel the lifeblood of future profits—successful new products.

Management's reluctance to accept the risk of failure is evident in the broad yet consistently conservative mix of new product types introduced. New products have centered around additions to and improvements in existing products. In a 1982 Booz, Allen & Hamilton survey of 13,000 new product introductions, these moderate risk categories represented 52 percent of all entrants. An additional 18 percent were cost reductions and repositionings. While 20 percent were products new to a company, only 10 percent were new-to-the-world products.

With truly innovative new products, there is a greater variability of return and outcome. But greater risk often brings greater profit. New-to-the-world products and new product lines accounted for two thirds of companies' most successful new products, even though they represented less than one third of all introductions.

The lopsided emphasis on "me-too" products is troubling. Nearly one half of companies have introduced no new-to-the-world products, and a quarter have not even introduced new product lines to the company. Companies that completely avoid the long shot in favor of the low-return "sure bet" are sacrificing the longer-term profit opportunities that will keep them in the race.

So what can management do? First, strike a better balance between the uphill battle for consistent quarterly earnings and the longer-term return from investments in high-risk categories. At present, management's focus on near-term profitability is the major obstacle to new product success. Second, management needs to create a corporate environment that encourages risk-taking and reinforces entrepreneurship.

Innovation is not a creative, unstructured, brainstorming activity. Instead, it should be viewed as a multidisciplinary and focused management process. Management can no longer afford the luxury of sitting around a conference table to blue-sky hundreds of ideas, which, in turn, are funneled through a costly screening and development process. Rather, company-specific strategic objectives and the roles that new products are to play should frame the focus required for idea generation and concept development.

On occasion, in the eyes of the less sophisticated new product manager, this approach may appear to stifle creativity and innovation. However, companies have a limited amount of capital and management time. Structuring innovation enables a company to optimize these two scarce resources, not minimize and dilute their impact. Building innovation should be a predictable and manageable experience—not a crapshoot dependent on luck.

NEW PRODUCT MANAGEMENT—A GRADUAL EVOLUTION

The companies most likely to succeed in the new product arena will be those that develop company-specific new product strategies. These strategies drive corporate objectives, link them to the new product development process, and build on internal capabilities that can be leveraged to exploit market opportunities. Furthermore, the new product strategy serves as an initial screen for idea generation and guides the management process.

Moreover, to succeed in new products, companies must capitalize on accumulated experience to achieve and maintain competitive cost advantages, and make the long-term commitment required to provide the necessary funds and requisite technical and managerial know-how. In addition, establishing a culture—a management leadership style, organization structure, and incentive reward system—conducive and tailored to new product strategic roles will be crucial for improving new product performance.

During the past two decades, the new product management process has undergone a gradual evolution in thinking and approach. In the 1960s, companies looked *internally* to create new products. They believed that management expertise, technological know-how, and production and distribution superiority would breed successful new products. Only now, from the vantage point of years of evaluation, can we see that effective management of new products requires the integration of multiple functional areas; but that is just the starting point.

The year 1963 was a very good year for the Polaroid Corporation. In that year, Polaroid introduced one of its biggest hits, the Color Land Camera, which provided virtually instantaneous photo processing. The introduction was a classic example of a company using one of its greatest internal strengths and capabilities—technological innovation—to create a new product that met a market need. By combining its sales and marketing know-how with its technology, R&D, and manufacturing acumen, Polaroid brilliantly capitalized on what it did best—going after a market need with a technological strength.

By the 1970s, the focus for new products shifted to identifying *external* consumer needs in the marketplace. With the advent of sophisticated market research techniques and segmentation analysis, companies searched for high-growth markets and niches that new products could satisfy. The driving forces behind new product development were becoming more complex.

In 1976, the Miller Brewing Company introduced Miller Lite because there was an identified consumer "need" for a low-carbohydrate beer that provided "Everything you always wanted in a beer and less." What had changed from the 1960s? Rigorous tracking of demographics, scanning of lifestyle trends, marketing research testing, behavior patterns analysis, and consumer segmentation uncovered the weight-conscious beer drinker. Companies had learned to look outward—first to identify high-growth markets and then to develop the products that would satisfy them. Polaroid's and Miller's successes attest to the fact that, during the 1960s and 70s, many U.S. companies were becoming better and better at identifying what the market—or more correctly, market segments—wanted, and at filling those needs.

Today and in the forseeable future, the underlying principle guiding new product development should combine both of these views. Matching external market needs with internal functional strengths allows companies to develop a new product portfolio that satisfies corporate strategic objectives.

Recently, the 3M Company introduced Post-It note pads. This new-to-the-world internally developed new product has been a marked success. Product conception was driven by an aggressive corporate objective of generating 25 percent of total sales revenues, within five years, from new products not yet in the market. This clearly places a focus and concentrated dose of management attention on the role of new products. Conceived within the womb of microadhesive technology, Post-Its featured a light-tack adhesive that was developed in the industrial minerals group. 3M then "fused" this internal technology with the external need for secretaries and executives to have attachable note and scratch paper that wouldn't ruin the document when subsequently removed. 3M had successfully matched the office need for efficiency with advanced technology. Combining externally driven needs with some internal economic or functional strengths offers companies the best possible groundwork for a new product launch. The gradual evolution of managing new products has sharpened and more highly focused the approach taken.

THE NEW PRODUCTS MANAGEMENT SCORECARD

The impact of these changes, especially the introduction of a step-wise process, has been substantial. But, before we further discuss how companies are interpreting and applying the lessons of the past two decades to the changing environment, take a moment to examine the new product program currently in place at your company. The questions below will serve as a guide for your analysis.

1. What are the explicit strategic roles that new products are to play during the next five years as determined by the corporate growth plan?
2. What is your company's financial gap (the amount of revenue and profits to be realized from new products as opposed to existing products or acquisitions)?
3. How are hurdle rates determined for different new products?
4. Describe the new product process in place in terms of the steps involved, its adaptability, and the length of its existence within the company.

5. What steps must be completed before idea generation begins?

6. How is new product performance measured against established objectives?

7. How are new product executives compensated?

8. Who is responsible for new product development? Is that responsibility clearly understood throughout the company?

9. What is the nature of top management's commitment to and involvement in the new product effort?

10. How is the new product effort structured within your company. How were those structures selected?

Now that you have formed a defined picture of your company's new product program, let's look at how other companies are approaching the new product process.

FEWER IDEAS CONSIDERED

Successful new product managers are integrating the lessons they learned from firms such as Polaroid and Miller—they are matching internal strengths to external market opportunities. The Quaker Oats Company provides an excellent example of this winning approach.

Recently, Quaker entered the snack food segment of the foods market with the introduction of Chewy Granola Bars. In line with the company's image of providing wholesome quality foods, the product was positioned as a healthful snack—in effect, a "health foods" candy bar. Quaker used its internal strengths of food technology and processing and its brand name identification and strong consumer loyalty to develop and introduce a product for which there was substantial demand. Why was the product such a success? Increased sophistication in the "up-front" planning and screening steps of the new product process was the key.

Quaker's success is representative of a major change in the new product process. Companies in general have significantly increased the amount of attention and financial resources given to the initial steps in the process. According to the Booz, Allen & Hamilton study, in 1968, for example, roughly half of all new product expenditures were made during the commercialization phase—the last step in the process. Now, commercialization-related expenditures account for only one fourth of the budget, while the portion of expenditures in the earlier steps of the process has more than doubled.

This imposition of professional management skills and the commitment of substantial financial resources to new product development have provided some important bottom-line fruit. The number of new product ideas considered for every successful new product introduced has dropped dramatically, from an average of 58 in 1968 to 7 in 1981, states the Booz, Allen & Hamilton study. That is, companies with a strong record of successful new product introductions are considering fewer ideas per successful launch. This implies that management is becoming more adept at screening out losers—products that either never make it to market or fail once they are introduced—much earlier in the process. In addition, the percent of total new product expenditures allocated to products that are ultimately successful has increased from 30 percent in 1968 to 54 percent today—probably because of the reduction in the number of ideas considered and the increase in resource allocations to early process steps.

CHANGING MANAGEMENT PRACTICES

Despite these improvements, many new product managers are looking for new, or at least better, approaches to managing new products more effectively. Rapidly changing technology, shifting market and consumer needs, shortened product life cycles, increased foreign competition, and the higher cost of capital have made the job of managing new products significantly more complex and demanding.

Successful companies have added an initial step to the

process: the development of a new product strategy that links corporate objectives to the new product effort and provides direction for the new product process. The addition of this step has changed the nature of the new product process. The first three steps—strategy development, idea generation, and concept screening and evaluation—are now more closely linked and much more iterative. The development of a new product strategy focuses the idea generation step by encouraging only those ideas that meet strategic objectives.

The development of a new product strategy necessitates that companies first identify the strategic business requirements new products must satisfy. The requirements then determine the specific strategic roles to be played by each new product. In essence, strategic roles define the purpose for the development of the new product.

Strategic roles are therefore linked both to the needs of individual industries and to the type of product developed. Industrial goods companies, for example, are more likely to find their most successful new products were developed to satisfy technological objectives. Consumer nondurable companies, however, are more likely to succeed with new products developed to satisfy market requirements. In addition, different types of new products perform different functions. Thus, all industries can boost their chances for success by matching strategic roles to the product type that performs the most appropriate function.

Once a new product strategy has been developed and new product ideas selected on the basis of the strategic roles they are to play, financial performance criteria can be established. And successful companies set performance standards relative to the required investment and associated risk of each new product.

The introduction of this more sophisticated new product process appears to be a main reason for the dramatic reduction in the number of ideas considered for every successful new product launch. The most successful companies consider fewer ideas than less successful companies. Ideas that do not meet strategic business requirements are screened out before idea generation even begins.

SUCCESS RATE

Despite the improved effectiveness of the highly sophisticated new product process, the success rate of commercialized new products has not improved, on average, in the past two decades. According to the Booz, Allen & Hamilton study, between 1963 and 1968, 67 percent of all new products introduced were successful based on company-specific financial and strategic criteria. From 1976 to 1981, 65 percent were successful.

The fact that the success rate has not changed in 15 years has important implications for managers in all industries. The challenge will continue as they look to new products to fuel future sales and profit growth.

Growth expectations are highest in industries with fast-changing technology, such as information processing and instrument controls. But even industries such as food and nondurables, where products are developed to satisfy market requirements, will demand that their new products contribute substantially to the company's profits.

Fortunately, several factors have been identified that can improve the success rate of a company's new products. The two most important are fit of the product with market needs and fit of the product with internal functional strengths. Developing a technologically superior product, receiving support from top management, and using a multiple-step new product process are additional factors.

The relative importance of each factor varies, however, by industry and product type. While the product's fit with market needs is the most important factor for success, technological superiority is important in developing new-to-the-world products, or improvements in and revisions to existing products, where companies seek to improve their position within an existing market. But the success of new product lines depends on how well a product fits with internal strengths. In developing new lines, a company is trying to enter existing markets in which production, distribution, and selling requirements are known and can be assessed relative to company capabilities. Finally, support of top management is considered to be a primary success factor and is one of the three most important factors in the successful introduction of new product lines and additions to existing lines.

SOME INGREDIENTS FOR SUCCESS

Companies across the board have made important advances in their approach to new products, but several characteristics can be identified that distinguish the real winners from their less successful competitors. These differences relate specifically to the extent of experience with new product introductions, choice of organizational structures, and management styles.

Experience in Introducing New Products

Companies experienced in new product introduction gain a competitive advantage because experience reduces the cost per introduction, thus improving new product profitability. The concept at work is the experience curve; that is, the more you do something, the more efficient you become doing it. More precisely, with each doubling of the number of new product introductions, the cost of each introduction declines at a predictable and constant rate.

New product development costs conform to this concept. For the 13,000 new products introduced between 1976 and 1981 by the 700 companies surveyed in the Booz, Allen & Hamilton study, the experience effect yielded a 71 percent cost curve. At each doubling of the number of new products introduced, the cost of each introduction declined by 29 percent.

Companies that adroitly exploit the benefits of experience can achieve competitive advantage. Much of the advantage stems from having acquired a knowledge of the market and of the steps required to develop a new product. This knowledge, accumulated over time, enables the experienced company to move more efficiently through the development process.

The positive effects of accumulated experience do not imply, however, that companies should introduce as many new products as possible for the sole purpose of gaining experience. Maintaining competitive advantage requires a consistent long-term commitment to developing new products.

Theoretically, a firm that cuts back on its new product program may put itself at a competitive disadvantage from which it may never recover. As an executive of a consumer durables company stated: "While our company has been successful in new products over the last 10 years, top management has recently narrowed the new product pipeline due to current business pressures. What will it take to get back up to speed once the valve is turned on again?" In actual practice, survey results show that successful companies remain committed to new product efforts for extended periods of time, thereby improving effectiveness and reducing the cost per introduction.

Organizational Structures and Management Styles

New product winners tie the structure of their new products programs to the specific needs of the products under development. The organizational structures used to guide these programs fall into two general categories: free-standing or autonomous units (such as interdisciplinary teams, separate new product departments, and venture groups) or functionally based units that are part of existing departments (e.g., planning, marketing, research and development, or engineering). Nearly half of the companies surveyed in the Booz, Allen & Hamilton study use more than one type of organizational structure to guide new product programs. More than three quarters of the most successful companies tie that structure to product-specific requirements.

Successful companies also choose management styles appropriate to meeting the needs of new product development. They further periodically revise and tailor those approaches to changing new product opportunities. In general, companies use some form of one of three approaches to managing new product development:

- *An entrepreneurial approach,* associated primarily with developing new-to-the-world products.
- *A collegial approach,* associated mainly with entering new businesses and adding products to existing product lines.
- *A managerial approach,* most closely associated with developing new products that are closely linked to existing businesses.

In the entrepreneurial approach, an autonomous new product group is established and reports to a general manager. It consists of an interdisciplinary venture team headed by an entrepreneurial new product manager capable of integrating diverse functional skills. Top management is strongly committed to and involved in the effort of developing new products. But less attention is paid to formal business planning than in either of the other two approaches, and there is less dependence on formal financial criteria to evaluate new product opportunities.

This less restrictive approach supports entrepreneurial behavior, thus creating a positive environment for risk-taking. Moreover, because new product managers in this environment enjoy incentive systems that reward success, they usually want to remain in the new product development function. And this situation results in greater continuity and accumulation of new product experience.

The collegial approach works like a fraternity. It is characterized by strong senior management participation in new product decision-making, strong top-management support for risk-taking, commitment to and support for a new product effort, and a formal new product process to guide the effort and ensure discipline. It is characterized also by a clear commitment across functional lines to provide whatever is necessary for success and to make decisions quickly.

The managerial approach consists of a hierarchical management structure that involves many levels of management and provides strong top-down direction to new product efforts. Companies that follow this approach stress functional leadership, have a strong business planning orientation, use a formal and often inflexible new product process, and rely heavily on formal financial criteria to evaluate new product opportunities.

Companies most likely to succeed in the development and introduction of new products in the future will have:

- *A Long-Term Commitment.* Top management must provide consistent commitment to new products and the necessary funding, and must possess the managerial and technical know-how necessary for innovation.
- *A New Product Strategy and Company-Specific Approach.* A well-defined new product strategy can form the core of a company-specific, tailored approach that links the new product process to company objectives, focuses idea/concept generation, and identifies the strategic roles new products must satisfy.
- *Accumulated New Product Experience.* Competitive advantage is gained through the reduced cost per introduction that results from the efficiencies of accumulated experience.
- *The Right Environment.* Companies must establish an environment, built on management style, organizational structure, and degree of top-management support, conducive to achieving company-specific new product and corporate objectives.

Successful companies in the turbulent decade ahead will be those that tailor their organizational structures and management styles to the type of new product opportunities they pursue. To succeed, companies must be willing to mount well-defined new product efforts that are driven by corporate objectives. Focus will help build innovation.

2

New Product Management and the Social Climate of the 1980s*

Elaine Maran
Yankelovich, Skelly & White, Inc.

New products have represented a top-priority agenda item for the health and growth of companies for over 20 years. Now in the mid 1980s, the process of bringing new products to the market, while never simple or fail-safe, has become increasingly complicated and challenging.

Today, regardless of product category or size of company, American business is accepting the reality and challenge of competing in a marketplace where unlimited growth can no longer be taken for granted. Likewise, consumers are accommodating themselves to the prospect of not "having it all,"

* Written with the assistance of Seth S. Levenson

as was assumed possible in the 1960s and 1970s; they too are committed to being "smart shoppers" whose goal is reducing costs without sacrificing quality. Management and consumers alike are recognizing that to be a "winner" in today's environment requires leveraging all available assets. For these reasons, as business examines options for growth, introducing new products continues to be looked at as one of the most important marketing strategies for management to pursue. Given this mission, new product management is relying more intensely than ever on both high-tech tools and high-touch researchers to assist in making appropriate decisions at the various stages of developing and marketing new products. The products and services of the firm provide the new products marketer with an overall integrated approach for developing definitive information quickly and cost-effectively, to meet this pressing need.

In this context, the perspective that YSW brings to all its client relationships and individual assignments derives from the knowledge and understanding of the general business environment and consumer climate based on its study of social change through the annual *Monitor* survey.

The *Monitor* research program—an annual measurement of U.S. lifestyles and social values—is the source and the springboard for the insights and marketing perspective of the firm. As Florence Skelly, chairman of the YSW Group, explains, "We are a firm that applies behavioral science research methods and consulting to identify, measure, and interpret social change and to help organizations (corporations, institutions, government) manage change effectively."

This extensive background in the business and consumer arenas has led to the development of such pioneering techniques as the Laboratory Test Market (the first test market simulation method), offered to the marketing community in 1968. Since its introduction, the Laboratory Test Market has been modified and applied, innovatively, for forecasting magazine circulation and audience characteristics, fashion accessories, and wearing apparel—as well as for conventional package goods, products, and durables.

Further, as part of the continued effort to speed up the new products decision-making process, the Idea Test Market was launched. This predictive tool, based on a behavioral model linked to the YSW Laboratory Test Market, enables marketers to advance a new product's timetable by determining its potential, in sales terms, while still in the idea stage of development.

This overview is intended to set the stage for the more detailed presentation of an integrated and cost-effective new product research program. This program is geared to five key stages in the new product development process that we've identified in our client relationships. As a general principle, however, its utilization does not depend on total particular client's needs. Participation does not, however, depend on going through the entire process.

I.   BRIEFING—GETTING STARTED

When the process starts at the first stage, it generally involves only senior members of the firm, who have the breadth, experience, and knowledge to work within the individual clients' new product strategy objectives.

First Step: Orientation/Corporate Input

An important part of the initial briefings and orientation is to arrive at a clear statement defining goals and strategic guidelines. Through interviews conducted with key executives, individual attitudes and opinions are consolidated to help shape objectives that reflect the corporate viewpoint.

Individual group interview sessions can be organized to collect employees' ideas about new products to determine if any merit further exploration.

Second Step: Information Consolidation/Monitor Work Sessions

In the second stage of the process, once we've gained an understanding of the corporate agenda and business requirements, the resources of *Monitor* are brought to bear for a focused view of the opportunities and hurdles for new products and services in the client's area.

Pertinent information, drawn from in-house data bases as well as secondary sources, is presented as input to identify potentially profitable areas and eliminate negative opportunity areas. For example, the following are illustrative of the areas in which updated information is crucial in analyzing marketing opportunities:

Consumer demographics: migration trends, urban/suburban population shifts, female/male occupation trends, age.

Microeconomics for the public: per capita income in middle/upper-class households, savings versus spending patterns.

Shifts in consumer social values.

Shifts in consumer lifestyles: time spent at home, leisure time activities, shopping behavior.

Shifts in retail distribution: blurring of existing outlets, rise of new types of outlets.

YSW proprietary services, *Monitor,* and T.R.A.C. (Technologies Research and Consulting) are, of course, important resources for both a global view of the climate for new products and for narrowing in on the most opportunistic areas that are compatible with the requirements and expertise of the client company.

II.   IDEA DEVELOPMENT—CRYSTALLIZATION OF PRODUCT CONCEPTS

In addition to the two different types of input described above:

Ideas/concepts from within the corporation

Patterns/developments (which suggest ideas/concepts external to the corporation

another source that frequently is built into the program is the consumer him/herself.

First Step: Proprietary Research for Consumer Input (when appropriate)

To make this as productive as possible, we suggest a series of pinpointed qualitative explorations among key life-style and life-stage groups.

This approach, while qualitative in nature, does aim for synthesis and consensus. The approach is called Idea Generation/Consensus Groups. To increase the quality of the output, the sessions (conducted by a highly experienced staff moderator) are structured along any one of the following lines, depending on which is most relevant. Accordingly, the point of departure for idea generation may be:

Brand name leveraging.

Technology transference and/or new applications for current technology.

Needs created by new technology.

Reconstruction of experiences for needs/wants investigation.

The underlying objectives in terms of the method of conducting these groups are to stimulate thinking of a wide array of new product ideas and to reach agreement within the group as to the ideas that represent real solutions to problems or are, at least minimally, better (in terms of time, effort, or money) than existing products.

Typically, these Idea Generation/Consensus Group sessions are conducted with 15 to 20 qualified consumers at a time in two or more locations until a sample of 100 or more is obtained.

Second Step: Translating Input into Business/Product Ideas Susceptible to Evaluation

In effect, for the process to work, responsibility has to be assigned for taking concepts (rough ideas) and putting them into forms that can be tested.

This can be accomplished by collaborating with the client task force and possibly the advertising agency in conceptualizing the ideas for testing.

III.   SHAPING THE IDEA—LEADING TO REFINED CONCEPT(S) FOR PRELIMINARY ESTIMATE OF MARKET POTENTIAL

There are several distinct cost-effective approaches to evaluate and forecast sales potential of concepts and products.

Stimulus/Response Concept Evaluation Groups: For Complex Ideas

This approach takes into account the need for consumers to "work through" new product or research ideas that are innovative or complicated. Specifically, to have the opportunity to raise questions and hear others respond to these questions. (In effect simulating the effect of word-of-mouth or networking.)

The approach is proven effective for evaluating high-priced new durable products (i.e., personal computer, interactive video) and for new service concepts (i.e., new distribution systems for financial services).

The step-by-step procedures followed in the conduct of these groups permit variations of the concept to be systematically tested with the same group of respondents. (In this way, the concept can be shaped and refined in one step.)

Another feature of the approach is the ability to collect quantitative as well as qualitative data. We obtain a measure of interest based on individual recording on a self-administered questionnaire and diagnostic feedback from the group dynamics.

The end product of Stimulus/Response Concept Groups is a penetration forecast at three levels:

Optimistic.

Realistic.

Conservative.

Additionally, a report covers, in detail, the marketing and consumer issues affecting the acceptance of the new product

or service and the product or service elements that are clear
and satisfactory and those that need changing or modification.

Typically, sessions are conducted with groups of 20 to 25
in multiple locations. Samples of 100 or more are accrued
for each assessment.

Idea Test Market (ITM): Estimate of
Sales Potential

This system is particularly appropriate for testing more
conventional packaged goods and durables and, as such, is
the offspring of the YSW Laboratory Test Market (LTM) data
base and estimating model.

Background on the ITM.   The ITM was developed to avoid
some of the gross inaccuracies of conventional concept testing. These inaccuracies came to our attention in the LTM,
when many products which presumably tested well at the
concept test stage fell down badly when tested in the Laboratory Test Market.

Many of those inaccuracies, in our judgment, were largely
due to the fact that conventional concept tests, despite various refinements, are ultimately based on consumers' statements of purchase intention. The research literature has am-
ply documented the imperfect relationship between
purchase intention and subsequent behavior. Our intent in
constructing the ITM was to develop a concept testing
method that would not rely on purchase intentions and that
would offer direct estimates of trial/sales potential.

The extensive LTM data bank was analyzed to isolate a
set of variables that could successfully predict LTM trial
rates. These variables became the basis of a system that
would predict LTM trial rates using only concept statements
as stimuli. Accordingly, the development of ITM entailed a
two-step process:

1.   Development of predictive variables.
2.   Validation.

The model that ultimately evolved for the ITM uses a set of evaluative criteria or variables known to predict LTM purchase, the basis for LTM estimates. (Importantly, the LTM estimates have had a 92 percent validation rate over the years the service has been in effect.) Because the ITM is thus geared to the LTM system, the same types of concrete estimates can be made from the ITM.

In short, the ITM, unlike conventional qualitative concept research, is designed to provide decisive answers very quickly for new *concepts* before any development, advertising, or packaging costs are incurred. And in today's rapidly changing, competitive social/business environment, ITM is a valued tool for eliminating the losers early and for realistic go/no go decision-making by new product managers.

How It Works.   Based on personal, individual interviews conducted at several locations with qualified samples of 150 to 300, the ITM is applicable for testing a concept only or for conducting a concept and product placement test.

Qualified respondents see the concept in the form of a statement, a concept board, or a storyboard. Reaction to the concept is measured on a six-point rating scale related to these six critical dimensions:

1. Current product-related dissatisfactions.
2. Perceived new product benefits.
3. Absence of salient negatives.
4. Perceived uniqueness.
5. Perceived versatility.
6. Value for money.

Diagnostics, personal classification, and category usage information are obtained through supplementary questions.

The final step, if combined with a product use test, involves placing the product and setting a date for a follow-up interview after a suitable period of testing for at-home usage. In the follow-up interview, the information obtained follows the concept assessment format. Specifically, reaction to the product is measured on the same battery of evaluative

criteria. And likes/dislikes are reported in terms of fulfillment of expectations.

The ITM report contains the following information:

1. ITM potential trial rate.
2. ITM adjusted projected trial rate.
3. Performance of concept on full series of evaluative criteria.
4. Delineation of strengths and weaknesses of concept versus appropriate category normative data.
5. LTM statistical model overlay, if utilized, for share or
   volume forecasting, applying an assumed repeat purchase rate and marketing inputs.

The ITM service is flexible from a design point of view. For
example, it can be structured to enable a marketer to:

1. Screen up to six different ideas with a simple sample
   for the basic projections—but no diagnostics.
2. Assess, in greater depth, up to three different ideas.
3. Evaluate a single concept in the context of alternate
   product elements—such as price, package design, home,
   varieties or flavors, etc., and/or alternate positioning
   strategies.

IV. MARKETING PLANNING—FOR PRODUCT LAUNCH

Reactive, Custom Research for Checking Tactics

As indicated earlier, while YSW's role in a new product
program changes from assignment to assignment, the firm's
services are, by design, integrated with the process.

In the period after the decision is made to invest in the
development and marketing of the "winning" idea and its
launch as a fully formed product, there is frequently a need
for various types of tactical research checks. Proprietary re-

search projects might include product use tests, name tests, package tests, pricing tests, communications tests, etc.

Laboratory Test Market: Final Check of Marketing Mix

A General Description. YSW pioneered test market simulation research methodology in the early 1960s. Since 1968, when the system was formally introduced, over 1,700 tests have been conducted in nearly all packaged goods categories and for a broad range of nonpackaged goods products. The Laboratory Test Market has served marketers developing entirely new product categories, marketers launching new brands in established categories, and marketers developing new strategies for established brands.

Theoretical Framework. The Laboratory Test Market is a simulation technique that forecasts sales potential for new products, relaunched products, and line extensions quickly, efficiently, and in secret. As such, the technique is designed to recreate the key elements of the marketing process and to capture consumers' purchase behavior—under controlled time and space compression.

To accomplish the above, procedures are implemented to:

1. Create awareness of products through advertising and/or other stimuli.
2. Provide consumers with an opportunity to make purchases in a realistic buying situation—using their own money.

In this strategic climate, the Laboratory Test Market is positioned as the test market substitute for determining the sales impact of marketing alternatives. In the realistic context of the Laboratory Test Market, various marketing alternatives can be assessed and the results read more accurately than in a real market test. For this reason, marketers use the Laboratory Test Market to experiment and study the sales impact of different options related to price, package put-ups, advertising strategy, etc.

The results of the LTM experiments, analyzed in combination with the information supplied by the client or marketer with respect to advertising weight, consumer promotion allocation, and distribution levels, provide the key informational inputs for sales projections.

The Laboratory Test Market Procedure.   The LTM is essentially a time and space compression of the critical elements impacting product acceptance under normal marketing conditions.

The research steps consist of the following:

1. Research is custom designed according to the test product's particular marketing needs.
2. Qualified consumers are recruited to a facility.
3. A background/demographic questionnaire is administered.
4. Consumers are exposed to product category commercials, including the test product commercial.
5. Consumers are given the opportunity to purchase the test product and/or competitive products in a real store environment (trial) using their own money.
6. Focused group discussions are conducted and questionnaires are administered to discover the reasons for acceptance or rejection of the products (diagnostics).
7. Purchased products are used under normal, at-home conditions.
8. Call-back questionnaires are administered to determine usage patterns, frequency, and repeat rate.
9. Extended use tests are conducted if "wear-out" is a possibility.

The LTM has evolved into a sophisticated, economical, and fast-working marketing tool that permits today's marketer to introduce LTM-tested products many months earlier than ever before possible—by bypassing the test market for checking the sales impact of product and marketing variables. (Naturally, LTM studies are conducted with complete confidentiality to guarantee that product introduction will not be revealed to competitors.)

In short, LTM can aid today's marketer by:

1. Estimating relative pricing, packaging, and positioning more cost effectively than in a test market.
2. Estimating the potential of brand extensions.
3. Estimating increments in share to be derived from changes of product or tactics for brand relaunch.
4. Analyzing brand strengths and weaknesses vis-à-vis competitors.

Moreover, with over 1,700 test market simulations performed to date, LTM normative data represent the largest body of behavioral new product norms in the United States. This information, coupled with the extensive collective new product experience of our staff, yields powerful and insightful diagnostic aids.

In addition, we employ the Yankelovich *Monitor* (social trends tracking study) to provide a general environmental perspective to each specific new product evaluation.

V. MONITORING THE IN-MARKET PERFORMANCE OF THE PRODUCT

The YSW commitment to new product development and management extends beyond the launch stage, recognizing that in this cost-conscious climate, time is a critical factor in assessing the state of health of the product—and ultimately profits and payout of investment.

Test Market Adjuster (TMA)

Marketers need early feedback on a new product's performance to determine whether performance is on target with predicted performance and to take action quickly if corrective action is indicated. The TMA is a service designed to relate consumer information that is indicative of the in-market performance of new products, and marketing information on a wave by wave basis, to arrive at projections for the test market period.

Using a quantitative evaluative model that measures product performance against a predesignated set of criteria, TMA answers questions such as: Is trial as predicted? Are the distribution numbers right? Are awareness levels what they should be? Thus, the TMA permits early detection and solution of problems, if uncovered, in terms of:

Distribution/point-of-purchase conditions.

Advertising/media utilization.

Promotional activities.

Price/pricing.

Competitive activity.

The YSW Statistical Model

The YSW Statistical Model is an interactive stochastic model that serves as a decision aid to the marketing manager in the development of a marketing strategy for a new product introduction.

In addition to early forecasts of marketing performance for a new product, the model also provides diagnostics for refinement of the marketing plan.

The model is designed to work with a limited amount of consumer data, such as would be provided by a Laboratory Test Market or real world market tracking data for TMA applications.

CONCLUSION

The overall system as described above, serves to illustrate how YS&W, Inc. research services are integrated in the new product development program.

As we've structured it, the market research function is relatively broad ranging. It involves: 1) identifying promising trends, 2) spotting and shaping opportunities, 3) assessing market potential early and in quantitative terms, and 4) providing marketing guidelines to optimize the success of the launch.

The underlying objective of the market research endeavor is to provide the new products manager with relevant and reliable information, quickly and cost effectively, to increase the level of confidence at decision points. Most importantly, it helps the manager to avoid wasting time, money, and human resources by pursuing failures.

3

Realities of New Products Management
What to Do—What to Avoid

Herbert M. Baum
Campbell Soup Company

Successful management of new products is the absolutely, positively overnight way to advance your career. If I were to identify the highest degree of difficulty in the marketing business, it would be new product development. As Stanley Katz, chairman of LKP Advertising, says "If you can perfect the skills which assure success in introducing *new* products, then surely you can market established products successfully. If you can jump six feet with some regularity, then you can surely clear the bar at five feet."

The more sophisticated a company's management, the more likely it is to view the successful development of new products as a postgraduate course that requires a depth and breadth of experience. It's important to have lots of experience, out in the marketplace with your neck on the line, to succeed in marketing new products.

You have to know in your bones what worked and what didn't work—and be able to *feel* what didn't work then but what might work now. Simply stated, it is my belief that new product development is not the type of work for new people or junior people.

The other essential ingredient for new product success is *continuity*. New product success is a marathon not a relay race. Nothing threatens the success of a new product as much as making changes in the team mid-stream. From the very inception of the idea through its development, testing, and marketing—and right through the first year of the product's life—the same team must be in place.

Like a baby, a new product requires the emotional commitment of the parents who conceived it to bring it to birth and raise it until it is able to walk by itself.

Sophisticated managements are also likely to view managing new product development as the ultimate testing ground for potential CEOs. Next to the top job, it requires and demonstrates the broadest range of management expertise in sourcing, technical development, commercialization, manufacturing, sales, finance, packaging, and working with the advertising agency. The new product venture integrates in microcosm the infinite complexities of running the whole corporation. You are being asked to start a business from scratch.

Where else can you gain more concentrated, intensive experience in seeking, avoiding, and taking risks? Where else must you make so many critical decisions And, here's the clincher, where better can management evaluate your true potential for the top.

Now that you are convinced that your new product responsibility is a breakthrough opportunity (not, as in some companies, a setback), what are the key elements of a new product management approach? Here are the five rules that have worked best for us at Campbell Soup Company.

I. GO FOR THE HOME RUN

At the same time that both Nielsen and Dancer, Fitzgerald & Sample are telling us that the number of new product introductions is setting records, SAMI is telling us that the number of new product introductions that reached $1 million in sales in their first year dropped to 58 in 1982 from 86 in 1981 and 103 in 1978. To quote our Market Research director, Tony Adams, "The net net is there's a lot of *junk being thrown out on the marketplace* as many manufacturers try to jump on the new products bandwagon. It's going to make it tougher for the well-thought-out new entries to gain shelf space and get trade attention with so much mediocrity around." I don't know about most companies, but Campbell Soup Company would not consider $1 million as success no matter how hard it is to get there. What we consider successful is the $175 million success of LeMenu Frozen Dinners and the $100 million success of Prego Spaghetti Sauce. That is what we mean by a home run. We are not opposed to crisp singles, or better yet, long doubles, but what we mean by a new product home run is a new brand that can stand on its own and eventually foster its own line and brand extensions. The demographics may be trending single, but the economies of marketing work better for brand families—the bigger the better.

Line extension and brand extension may be much easier to pull off than a new brand, and they are certainly a whole lot cheaper to pull off than a new brand, but let me inject a major caution. There is a grave downside risk in line and brand extensions. Don't be greedy. Nothing must be allowed to pull down the quality image of a healthy brand. You can't take risks with the corporate jewels. Line extensions and brand extensions must be managed just as meticulously and aggressively as new brands. It just takes less money. So all right, you agree with me—your goal is the home run, and you're trying to blast it out of the park. You're more than willing, but how do you get able?

II.   BE SURE OF THE CONSUMER: THE CONSUMER IS THE MOST IMPORTANT MEMBER OF YOUR NEW PRODUCT TEAM

The most important ally you can have is the consumer, if you know how to work with him or her. And I'm not talking about a one-night stand like a focus group, I'm talking about a relationship. Who is this consumer we're talking about? David Ogilvy would tell you she is your wife. And I assume your wife is a consumer. But the consumer is more *talked* about than truly served; more *misunderstood* than listened to.

Let me briefly list some misconceptions about the consumer.

1.   The consumer is not an abstraction.

2.   The consumer is not a mass.

3.   The consumer is not defined primarily by age, income, or marital status.

The consumer is a number of living, breathing, distinctly different individuals who can only be grouped into a target market because of a common concern, problem, need, hope, or behavior.

What key trigger can unite a large enough group of individuals to make a market for your product that transcends not only demographics but geography as well? The United States is still the richest and largest of the domestic marketplaces, but we are no longer rich enough or strong enough to protect that domestic marketplace from foreign invasion. Look what the Japanese and the Europeans have done to the American automobile marketplace, the audio marketplace, the camera marketplace, the watch marketplace, the instant noodle marketplace. Long ago our foreign competition had to learn to build worldwide franchises that would transcend national borders, like the Mercedes franchise, the Sony franchise, the Rolex franchise, the Chivas Regal franchise. We have a lot of catching up to do.

4.   The consumer is no longer defined by where he/she shops.

The same woman or man on the same shopping trip will buy private-label cheese in one aisle and Pepperidge Farm Bread in the next. The same shopper in the same week will shop both K mart and Neiman-Marcus.

5.   The consumer may not be the one who consumes the product.

The shopper may buy the peanut butter and the dog food and the apple juice and most of the men's cologne but may not be the primary user. The most sensitive and often overlooked determination that must be made in the marketing process is to make sure you know whether it is the purchaser or the user who's the primary influence on the brand decision. It's just too expensive, most of the time, to market aggressively to multiple audiences. Most cereal and toy companies focus on the child. Children's vitamins have to sell the mother. Many marketers kid themselves that they can do all family appeals on all family shows attentively watched by both parents and children. When is the last time you saw that scene in your own living room? It is wishful, lazy thinking. A choice of focus must be made, and yet, you can't afford to ignore either end of the purchase equation. In our own case, we have found out that children like our Campbell's Chicken Noodle Soup even more than their mothers think they do. And while our focus is firmly on mother, we are running more supportive advertising to children.

6.   She may not be a she.

There are very few single-sex categories any more. Now men are important in the purchase of food, furniture, china, sheets—the so-called women's products. Women are important in the purchase of automobiles, insurance, financial services—the classic men's products.

Now that I've discussed what the consumer is not, let me make sure I identify who the consumer *is*.

1. The consumer is your boss.

You may think your CEO is your boss. He may think his board and stockholders are his boss. But in the consumer products business, it is the consumer who is the boss of all of us.

Advertising, if consumers think it's good enough and there's enough of it to catch their attention, can force trial, but then the consumer is both judge and jury. If the product doesn't fulfill the promise you have made for it in your advertising, that's the end of it. No quality or amount of advertising can sell that product the second time if it isn't any good.

2. Be sure you respect how tough and demanding today's consumer really is.

More mature, better educated, far more skeptical than their predecessors, consumers manage their own time and money as carefully as businesspeople manage theirs within the corporation. Within a personal framework, the consumer allocates resources just as many of us do in business. Nearly every purchase is a *considered* purchase. That's why the product has to either deliver the highest quality or the lowest price. The middle is not where the action is. Only the best or the cheapest can make it.

3. The consumer is not married to you.

No matter how many years they have been loyal members of your franchise, you can lose the consumer tomorrow. If somebody can make a better ketchup than Heinz, or a better mayonnaise than Hellman's, or a better cereal than Kellogg's Corn Flakes, or a better soup for the money than Campbell's, the consumer will try it and stay with it until somebody else makes it even better or makes it just as good but cheaper. Parity products are *doomed* before they get out of the starting gate. There are four conceivable strategies for success.

a. Better than—
b. Cheaper than—
c. Different than—
d. New . . . really new!

When you think of it in this way, the consumer and the marketer are on the same side, looking for the same goals. You can collaborate to find something better, cheaper, different, or new. It can be a very creative partnership providing *you* understand who does what. It's *your* job to come up with the new ideas. The consumer won't do it for you. It is the consumer's job to confirm or deny your ideas. You propose; they dispose. Fortunately, this is a process and not an event. The first time around, they will tell you what they like and don't like about your idea. Listen hard, modify your ideas, and take it back to the consumers. Work with them intensively, not only in focus groups, but in the home through home-use tests and in the store. Rehypothesize and revalidate with the consumers. Know when to stop. Quantify what you learned qualitatively. Then go for it. But be sure to *keep* talking to consumers even after that test market success. Check them out every six months. Either they or your competition could be changing on you. Check it out before it hurts.

III.   BEFORE YOU GO FOR THE HOME RUN, MAKE SURE YOU HAVE MONEY AND STAYING POWER: BIG GUYS CAN'T BE BLUFFED

Even with the baby boom's baby boom, most markets are flat. A new product's share probably has to come out of somebody else's share. That competitor—depend on it—will do anything to save his own share. He may run four 45-cent coupons on a 59-cent item in a three-month period to foul up your reading of a test market. He may load up the category's consumers even if he has to *give* the product away. It is cheaper to stop you early in a new product test and discourage you from rolling out than to compete with you nationally.

Save your product, yourself, and your company by making the accurate assumption that the competition will be ferocious and will stop at nothing to discourage you from starting, continuing, or finishing the job. You must be just as ferocious. Be smart enough to assume you will be burned in the test market experience if you go for the home run. Test simultaneously in a controlled laboratory environment. (Editor's note: Refer to chapter 10 on simulated test markets.) If that comes out successfully, be willing to spend and keep on spending. Underspending in the volatile marketplace is the unspeakable crime. You have got to be number 1 or 2 to make it big. Market leadership doesn't really cost in the long run—it pays.

On the other hand, don't be afraid of the big boys. They may be the most vulnerable because they are the most complacent. They have been sitting on those big brands so long. By definition of their age, those big brands could be reaching the end of their life cycle. They may be committed to a passé technology. They don't have the freedom that you may have to break out into a new package form or a new technology. They may have lost their nimbleness. Necessity is the mother of invention, but necessity might just have ceased to operate for the big boys. This is your opportunity.

IV. KNOW YOUR ECONOMICS

As a corporate manager you will be asked to share the responsibility for allocating the corporate resources. You should be sure that you have a viable financial proposition for the long haul. Here are some things I've learned that may help you.

Spend money up front. Let the competition know you're serious.

Don't insist on breaking even the first year. That's the way you strike out.

At Campbell Soup Company we use a tool called a Minimum Business Proposition to analyze the effect of key marketing, production, and financial factors on the long-term financial attractiveness of any major venture.

The main elements of the MBP are:

1. We explore the sensitivity of return on investment to many factors: projected volume (and its associated inputs—trial, repeat, and package rate), growth, start-up and ongoing marketing expenses, responsiveness to marketing, price, price-volume relationship, attrition to other product lines, capital investment, working capital, cost components (production, ingredients, selling, etc.).

2. We take a long-term view. An investment is not evaluated on its first-year return on investment but on its average ROI over the projected life.

3. We subjectively evaluate the likelihood of occurrence of a situation (or combination of situations) that will cause a less-than-acceptable ROI. We do many scenarios.

The MBP has proven its value to us. It told us, even before we entered the marketplace, that Prego would be a winner and suggested V-8 Ketchup would be a loser.

The Minimum Business Proposition tells us—if our assumptions are correct—what the net effect of the business proposition will be. More importantly, it tells us what minimum level of business we need from our test situation (nationally projected) in order for us to be economically viable. It's a go/no go tool.

Unless you are absolutely convinced that you have a better than even chance for a home run, have the courage to get out. More great new product ideas have died from underfunding than from underthinking. What is the point of having 50 new product horses at the starting gate if all of them are too starved to run more than $1/16$ of a mile? In today's ferocious competitive environment, there is no way to delay the truly tough decisions. Senior marketing management *has* to back its winners *early* and back them to the hilt. Most companies have more new product ideas than they can afford to fund. The hard, tough choices must be made early and then stayed with for the full fight for market position. A successful new product needs a champion, but every champion needs a success. Take the 1 in 10 shot, not the 10 to 1. Above all, don't fool yourself that you can take 10 shots; not one of them will have enough money behind them to make it.

V.   THE PRODUCT IS HERO

It's my fifth point, but it's my central theme and the most important. Quality really doesn't cost; it pays. The product you bet on had better be that much better than anything else out there. How much better? We insist on a preference rating of at least 1.6 to 1 versus the prime competition. Who decides how much better? Only the consumers. Once you get the quality, keep the quality. Once upon a time it may have been possible to reduce the cost of goods without the consumer noticing but not with today's tougher, demanding consumer. They will notice. And today's time-constrained consumers may not take the time to complain, they'll just switch. Be the lowest cost producer you can be but never at the cost of quality.

I'd like to close by quoting Campbell Soup Company Chief Executive Officer Gordon McGovern.

> Quality is more important than cost. How can we get our people to understand, believe, and then act with the knowledge that top quality brings the best cost? The Japanese are re-teaching us lessons from our childhood. We must bring our culture into one of zero defects and 100 percent quality and service. The consumer is ready for improved performance. Delivering it is the true secret of new product success.

4

Success and Failure in a Competitive Environment
Making It with New Products

Martin Friedman
Dancer Fitzgerald Sample

This chapter could have been easily titled "The Agony of New Product Development." This theme would be quite appropriate because in no other phase of product marketing do manufacturers break their hearts and tear their hair more than in the development of new products. No single marketing area has caused more pain and, conversely, produced more joy than giving birth to a successful new product.

In the 20 years I have been editing *New Product News*, I have reported the introduction of just about 19,500 new food and drugstore items, consisting of over 36,000 flavors, colors, or varieties—not including health foods, health nonfoods, and gourmet products, which we started reporting

44

last year because they became more important in supermarkets.

That breaks down to about 35 new consumer packaged goods offered to Americans every week, although most were available in selective geographic areas in test market situations.

Our listings are good but probably not complete. Each week we scan 80 best-food-day/night newspapers from all across the country and each month read over 60 trade journals and 30 consumer magazines. Plus, I spend lots of time wandering around supermarkets buying new products and attending various trade conventions, which manufacturers use to showcase their new items.

However, in spite of this extensive market coverage, it's easy to miss a new flavor of ice cream from a local supplier, a new bread variety from a local bakery, or a new product that some manufacturer is surreptitiously panel-testing in Eau Claire. Nevertheless, I believe that *New Product News* truly has revealed the significant new products that have been introduced in the past two decades.

The new product trend over the past 20 years has been decidedly up as more and more companies continue to discover that the old adage, "innovate or die," must prevail. They must introduce new products to retain or increase sales, to maintain consumer interest, to keep trade support, to sustain recognition by the financial community, and to enhance all the other components that keep a company healthy and strong. In the last five years, we only saw a decline in new products during the 1977 business slowdown. However, the recent trend has been nothing short of overwhelming. During the first eight months of 1983, as compared with 1982, new product introductions increased from 954 to 1,205—a more than 26 percent increase. This was a continuation of a new product surge that began in the midst of the recession. It is our conviction that most manufacturers do not adjust their new product development to the business cycle. Due to the long lead time required, they must continue to test even during recessions so that they will have new products available when good times return. This is a policy that most sophisticated marketers seem to

pursue, and perhaps it accounts for the phenomenal increase in new items we reported in 1982 (see Table 1).

Also, most supermarket products retail under $1.50 so
recessionary influences may not affect them to a marked
degree. In fact, there are some who believe that when you
can't afford a new car or home, you may use your reduced
discretionary income to try new food products.

What do all these numbers mean? How many new products were successes? How many were failures—rejected by
consumers and no longer on supermarket shelves?

As we try to answer these questions, we quickly face
some tough problems with definitions. What *is* a "new"
product? For our purposes, a "new" product is defined as
an addition to the consumer product line of a manufacturer
which is either a new brand, a new extension of an existing
brand, or a new flavor, color, or variety of a brand. Basically, *New Product News* defines a new product as something the company is making for the first time. However,
this definition has a built-in problem. A new brand of General Foods coffee, such as Brim, and a new flavor of General
Foods Jell-O, like their milk chocolate pudding, were both
new products, yet there is a multimillion-dollar differential
in their sales and profit impact.

There is also a major problem in defining the "success" or
"failure" of new products. In our view, success can only be
profitability, and here we're talking about overall company
profitability, since many new products cannibalize business
from within. Since few, if any, manufacturers disclose their
individual product profit figures, it's virtually impossible for
me to judge whether a brand is a success or failure. So, next
time you hear some self-styled expert tell you that only 10
percent of new products succeed or 85 percent of new products fail, you'd better look closely at his statistics and definitions.

Nevertheless, some research may offer valid insight. A
few years ago, DFS's Research Department combined *New
Product News'* entries with A. C. Nielsen sales figures for
1970–77 to determine which products were successful. A
summary of their report said, "New food products introduced during 1970 through 1977 were scrutinized for items

Table 1: New Products Introduced in 22 Selected Grocery and Drugstore Categories, January 1964 to December 1982

Category	64	65	66	67	68	69	70	71	72	73	74	75	76	77	78	79	80	81	82	Total
1. Baby food	6	3	9	10	8	9	3	3	2	6	4	1	3	2	2	5	5	2	5	88
2. Baking ingredients	44	30	35	35	32	20	23	23	25	30	31	18	17	29	29	23	22	18	40	524
3. Beverages	62	51	45	75	51	42	43	45	39	49	32	35	51	72	89	80	66	67	61	1,055
4. Breads, cakes, cookies	20	23	22	30	24	21	29	25	38	39	47	63	45	49	66	72	70	76	81	840
5. Breakfast cereals	10	11	10	11	11	16	8	11	19	13	19	14	14	11	11	7	10	14	11	231
6. Candy and gum	37	22	27	25	26	35	66	35	36	31	54	81	98	102	101	86	93	87	90	1,132
7. Canned fruit, vegetables, juices	14	15	29	22	24	37	34	22	21	17	24	33	24	21	25	26	27	34	52	501
8. Canned meat and fish	17	11	7	17	9	17	15	24	14	13	8	10	24	14	10	12	12	15	15	264
9. Dairy foods	28	34	31	38	45	41	32	36	40	41	55	62	45	47	54	69	68	81	91	938
10. Desserts, sugar, syrup	19	21	23	22	15	15	18	18	13	21	16	9	7	14	15	7	14	8	10	285
11. Fresh meats and fish	15	8	18	11	12	8	3	7	6	7	13	16	27	43	50	35	37	37	48	401
12. Frozen foods	72	81	120	145	123	112	100	120	165	163	179	186	205	200	176	150	184	183	207	2,871
13. HBA	121	89	93	125	121	137	136	110	86	117	139	203	245	270	254	274	298	338	369	3,525
14. Household supplies	65	72	62	65	79	87	55	51	49	65	70	66	69	87	63	65	76	66	85	1,297
15. Low-calorie foods	28	34	31	39	34	33	19	10	17	25	27	28	32	29	29	37	42	42	60	596
16. Macaroni, potatoes, rice	27	18	21	20	22	23	15	19	27	24	24	11	19	19	20	20	15	16	30	390
17. Paper products	16	14	12	21	9	12	18	29	21	14	21	19	11	14	6	12	17	17	19	302
18. Pet products	17	23	22	7	30	28	23	26	46	26	35	26	43	39	31	32	31	24	33	542
19. Sauces, spices, condiments	48	47	42	55	62	68	64	64	50	54	58	61	62	45	71	64	85	66	71	1,137
20. Snacks, crackers, nuts	16	21	28	41	35	48	38	21	33	23	42	38	40	67	69	54	67	89	102	872
21. Soups	13	17	10	12	17	6	8	12	10	13	10	9	27	24	9	19	11	6	13	246
22. Tobacco products	20	22	26	35	19	25	24	25	17	11	23	34	20	20	17	15	18	31	17	419
Total	715	667	723	861	808	840	774	736	774	802	931	1,023	1,128	1,218	1,197	1,164	1,268	1,317	1,510	18,456

Source: Dancer Fitzgerald Sample, *New Product News.*

which achieved at least $15 million in retail sales anytime during 1970–78. For the 6,695 introductions of dry/frozen and refrigerated human food and pet foods evaluated, only 93 products met this criterion." That's a success rate of around 1½ percent—and 25 percent were pet foods! And remember, we measured success as $15 million in sales. These days it's easy to spend over $15 million in advertising and promotion just to launch a product, so we don't know how much of the $15 million was profit. Other key findings in the study may be of interest.

As expected, the large food firms had the greatest number of successful new products. General Foods led the way with 15, followed by Ralston with 10.

Most of the new product successes did not create new categories but instead were entries in already very large categories—canned and dry dog food, coffee, powdered soft drinks. Some brands did create new categories—Stove Top Stuffing Mix, Cup-A-Soup, and Hamburger Helper.

Most of the successes were line extensions or flanker brands. By the way, line extensions represent new sizes, flavors, and the like where the items use an existing brand name in the firm's present category, such as Duncan Hines Pudding Cake Mixes. If the company introduces a new brand into a category where it already has a position it is called a flanker brand—like Purina Tender Vittles. In the food area, very few could be considered truly new products, that is to say, the result of breakthrough food technology, like freeze-dried coffee in the 1950s. Apparently, consumers are more responsive to evolutionary products in the short term.

Most of the successes came from firms already in the product category, for example, Brim Coffee/General Foods, Meow Mix Dry Cat Food/Purina, Puritan Oil/Procter & Gamble. Some were through acquisition—Celeste Pizza/Quaker, Gorton's Fish Sticks/General Mills. This suggests that firms should stick close to categories they know and innovate where they have an established position. Imitation is rarely the best product development strategy, but cases exist where similar or "improved" products did produce dollar successes—Nestle's Souptime following Lipton's Cup-A-Soup and Betty Crocker's Big Batch Cookie Mix following Nestle and Quaker entries. However, as evidence of the short life cycle of new products, Souptime is no longer available, and Big Batch Cookie Mix sales are way below introductory year levels.

Now, before you think that companies are crazy for even trying one new product a year, let us throw in a few disclaimers to our own study. First, there are many new products, especially new flavors, colors, or varieties, that make money with less than $15 million in sales. Second, the study did not include health and beauty aids, including such big money winners as Agree Shampoo, Aqua-Fresh Toothpaste, and Tylenol. Nor did it examine cigarettes like Philip Morris' Merit and Reynolds' Vantage or soaps and detergents such as Irish Spring, Coast, and Dawn. Also, many new brands considerably topped the $15 million figure, with Folger's Flaked Coffee pulling in $139 million, Quaker's Tender Chunk Dog Food $100 million, and Hawaiian Punch Drink Mix $60 million. It has been reported that Frito-Lay's Tostitos produced $140 million in sales in its first year, and *Ad Age* called the brand the most successful new product in the past 10 years. So the 1½ percent success figure is subject to lots of interpretation.

Another look at the success versus failure equation can be found in SAMI's New Product Study released last year. According to their tracking, products introduced since 1970 make up 19 percent of all warehoused grocery store brands with $1 million or more sales. Furthermore, 21 percent of the 1,445 brands with annual volume exceeding $10 million have been launched since 1970. According to Allan B. Miller of SAMI, "These numbers dramatize the important role new products play in filling the ever-changing needs and tastes of consumers. Without new product innovations, manufacturers run the risk of relinquishing their leadership to private label and generic brands which thrive when new product activity wanes."

Facing the high failure rates I've mentioned, you're probably wondering why manufacturers bother to aggressively pursue new product development. While there's no question that new product marketing is frustrating, inexact, costly, and difficult, its rewards of satisfaction and profit often far outweigh its difficulties.

One look at most manufacturers' annual reports will show that they continue to believe in new products as the life-blood of their future and will keep developing, testing, and marketing new products. A Booz, Allen & Hamilton study of product development practices at 700 major companies in a diverse selection of industries reported that new products will account for 31 percent of their profits over the next five years compared with 22 percent over the past five and that new products will be responsible for 37 percent of total sales growth compared with 28 percent in the earlier period.

Why will some companies enjoy very successful new product track records whereas others will pile failure on failure? I think there are some important reasons why products succeed or fail.

As in most business situations, the first key factor is that management must be willing to allocate financial, person-nel, and time resources to the pursuit of new products. It isn't enough to stand up to stockholders and say, "We be-lieve in new products." Top management must be ready to truly support the firm's new product effort even if it reduces short-term profits.

Too often we have seen an unwillingness to pay new product people the kind of salary and bonus that goes to the stewards of profitmaking, on-line brands. Too often new product staffs are second-rate because the hot shots in the company want to be working on existing products. If man-agement wants a successful new product program, they must put nothing less than the best people in place.

Another reason why new products succeed or fail is be-cause of consumer and product research. It is extremely dif-ficult to get a group of people together and have them truly respond to new product ideas. Focus-group sessions are great for giving you ideas or direction. But you can be very wrong if you introduce new items based on this kind of re-search. What people say they like or want or need must be followed up by some evidence of behavior. Will they do what they say? Will they buy what they swear they need? You must be prepared to do extensive purchase testing, in-home usage testing, and finally, market testing before you can feel remotely confident that you have a winner.

Surprisingly, product testing has been found to be more of a problem than you would expect it to be. What looks and tastes perfect in the lab or pilot plant turns out to be a product disaster under mass-production conditions. Some examples of this include a new flour that didn't reveal that it absorbed moisture on the shelf until millions of women discovered it fouled up all their Christmas baking recipes, a great new soup that for two months went out of a brand new, automated factory without salt, or an aerosol soft-drink syrup that had a slow leak out the bottom so that the cans stuck hard to the shelf. You may have your own horror story. The point is, you can't be too careful in checking out the new product. Just because you have made something similar for years doesn't automatically mean you know how to mass produce that new product. You must check, test, and then check and test again with retailers, with consumers . . . in the home . . . in the market.

Obviously, budget is a key determinant of success or failure. It's nice to think of making money right away on your new product, but I'm afraid that's very unrealistic. One of the most successful companies I know thinks nothing of 36- and even 48-month payouts.

It is unreasonable to expect that in today's highly competitive climate you can make money on a truly new product in the first year or two. Note that I said truly new product. You should be able to make money fairly quickly with a line extension or new flavor.

Companies differ dramatically in their new product systems. However, most will utilize the following, very rough, critical path:

The first step in new product development is to unearth raw new product ideas. These can come from anywhere— your technical staff, your marketing people, consumers, new product development companies, and even your advertising agency. This stage should take about two months and cost roughly $20,000.

After refining the mass of new product ideas you have generated, you must shake out the obvious losers and develop concept statements for the most promising products. Concept statements are merely attractive, tightly written and visualized statements of the product's attributes and benefits. These concept statements are then taken to focus groups of potential consumers for qualitative research to ascertain positive or negative reactions and develop hypotheses for later quantification. This stage should take two or more months and cost roughly $50,000.

The concepts that rate highly are then refined further and presented to consumers again—this time with rough advertising and packaging and with more depth analysis by the interviewers. The objective here is to try to gauge feelings for true buying intentions and repurchase interest of the consumers. However, if your concept research in Stage 2 looks especially promising, the less time and money you will have to invest in this predictive quantitative research (but to skip it could increase your risks). This stage should take another two months and cost about $40,000—a minor price to pay to reduce risk in keeping the ultimate bottom-line profitable.

Now, hopefully, you have a group of product concepts with widespread, strong consumer appeal. The green light then says "go" to the next stage, which is product development. If you haven't got any good prospects or sufficient prospects to meet your volume/profit goals, then it's "no-go"—and back to Stage 1 again.

In Stage 4, you unleash your R&D people to work out products that fulfill the successfully tested concepts. Actually, a professional new product marketing man will keep his R&D people apprised of what's happening from the beginning and encourage their contributions throughout the entire process.

Product development should take about four months and cost $80,000. However, don't try to push your research people into unrealistic time frames. Sometimes equipment must be handmade, and more time is required.

Assuming your lab technicians come up with products that taste pretty good, even to your own family, it's then time to move into home-use tests—that is, to try out the newly developed product on real consumers in real-life usage situations.

There are research companies that can find the guinea pigs for you and handle the testing. This stage may cost about $60,000 and take another two months in the schedule.

If the consumers get deathly ill or burn your products in effigy, then you'd better go back to Stage 1. However, if you do produce a big winner or two, you're ready for test marketing. Actually, you should have begun your test market planning back in Stage 4, so you're ready to go if you've produced a winner.

The subject of test marketing is too complicated to adequately cover here (it is covered in depth in Chapter 10), so all I'll say is that I believe in the value of test marketing in minimizing overall marketing risk and in its ability to point out the flaws in your marketing programs. I believe you should plan to test in about 3 to 4 percent of the United States in order to generate valid test results. Such a program will cost about $300,000—mostly for introductory advertising and promotion—and should last a minimum of six months.

If there's still a green light in terms of meeting your goals, after test marketing you're ready to move into a regional expansion or, if you have the funds, a national launch. The calendar I have outlined lasts 18 months and costs over a half-million dollars. Obviously, many products have been introduced with far lower testing expenditures—others with far higher. My proposal here is an ideal one, which imposes strict research disciplines. Your budget may not permit this luxury. However, every step you eliminate further increases your risk of failure, so my message here is to proceed cautiously.

Now that you are ready to move nationally, how much will it cost? May I suggest that if your profit expectations are realistic, you have a better chance of launching your new product with an adequate budget. And, let's face it, you need money to introduce new products. With 30-second, prime-time commercials costing $80,000 to $100,000 (and as high as $365,000 for 30 seconds in the Super Bowl), you really can't think about marketing a broadscale-appeal new consumer product with less than $10 million national ad budget for the year. Anything less than $10 million and you won't be heard above the noise level in the marketplace. And add to the $10 million in advertising a healthy budget for trade and consumer promotion of probably another $5 million to force distribution. The retailer isn't going to put you on his shelf for nothing, and today's price-conscious consumer isn't going to try your product unless you reduce his or her initial cost with a substantial coupon or refund price reduction. Initially, your advertising/promotion ratio may be 50-50 to help create abnormal trade excitement before you return to a more typical split of 65 percent advertising/35 percent sales promotion. So if you hope to produce a $15 million sales success in your first year and you need $15 million in advertising and promotion, it's reasonably obvious you can't expect to make money in year 1.

Yes, you're expected to pay some pretty fancy dues to enter the new product club, but you can and, in fact, must reduce your risk by extensive test marketing. There are some highly adventurous souls out there who try to go national without testing, but not too many have the resources or guts to try a national introduction on a really new item. Some go national because they believe they have a unique item and want to preempt the market. But for most companies, test marketing remains a necessity. It cuts your risks. It enables you to adjust and refine your programs so you're better able to resist any competition that follows you on the market. It allows you to more accurately predict your final sales and costs and profits. In our view, professional test marketing is the mark of a successful new products company.

While the tone of this chapter is hopefully realistic, it may discourage everyone from ever working with a new product again. Obviously, few smart marketers have accepted this philosophy. New products continue to grow and produce incremental sales and profits for manufacturers. Remember that every successful brand on the supermarket shelf was a new product at one time. The new product gamble is a risky one, but it's still worth the agony.

Part II

New Product Development Strategies

5

Idea Generation

The Focus Group as a "Consumer Laboratory"

Chester L. Kane
Kane Bortree Associates

You want to market a new product or service that people will buy. How can you reduce the risks involved? The focus group is one of the traditional methods used by new product marketers to help reduce their risks. Focus groups function as an aid in predicting which products and what "positioning" will appeal most to consumers. They are expected to help answer questions that assist marketers in determining, for example, whether consumers want a proposed product or service because it is cheaper, faster, easier, better quality or attractive as a status symbol.

The key to how well focus groups succeed in providing this information lies in how, why, and by whom they are conducted. These factors determine the extent of their value. When used as a qualitative research tool—a kind of "consumer laboratory"—focus groups are invaluable. If conducted in a scientific manner, the approach is to explore consumer attitudes and opinions through a systematic process of careful experimentation using a sequential series of groups. The focus group permits consumer interaction in a way that is not possible with quantitative research, and it is the "true life" element of the focus group encounter that adds the important qualitative dimension to statistics.

Focus groups may be used successfully to generate ideas for new products, and they are especially effective in pinpointing the appeal of a new product idea to consumers. For products in "image" categories, focus groups can be used as an aid in developing an image before the product actually exists. They are equally effective in helping to position new products as they are in repositioning declining brands.

This chapter will explain specifically how to tap the potential of the focus group in new product development. It will outline the conditions necessary for effective use as a qualitative research tool. It will show how focus group results can become "projectable" when focus groups are used to generate ideas, not merely to gather data. It will also demonstrate how results can be better interpreted, valid consumer responses can be obtained, and genuine insight can be gained.

GENERATING IDEAS

Since focus group findings are not statistically projectable, they should not generally be used as the sole basis for "go/no go" decisions or commitments to launch a product nationally. However, they can be projectable in the sense that, when they are conducted by skilled specialists in order to develop a new product concept or positioning and if they are conducted in a prescribed way, the results are highly likely to be corroborated in quantitative testing.

Such disciplined groups, scientifically structured in a sequential series to build on the information obtained in each preceding group, have consistently produced strong concepts and positionings, which greatly increase the chances for test market success. During the course of a concept generation program where a number of concepts are developed, at least one is virtually guaranteed to exceed quantitative success norms considered projectable for the category, thus signaling sufficient potential in the marketplace for a launch.

A systematic approach such as we are advocating was used to develop ideas for a new shampoo product. The concept eventually recommended for quantitative testing began as two "triggers" or benefit-oriented statements used to stimulate consumers to respond with greater honesty and spontaneity. Triggers encourage creative thinking by focusing attention on benefits, not products per se.

Both triggers were exposed to nonusers, heavy users, and others in a series of focus groups. As the series progressed, it became evident that a significant number of consumers liked both triggers. Through skillful listening, observers learned that women with shoulder-length hair or longer felt they had an oily hair problem near the scalp and a dry hair problem near the ends.

During the course of the focus group series, the triggers evolved into a modified concept, which was then exposed to more groups. Visuals were added in the refinement stages because the cosmetic category depends largely on eye appeal. In subsequent rounds of focus groups, alternative concepts were presented, and a working name was introduced.

Ultimately, this concept was recommended to the marketer: "My hair has a split personality. It's oily near the scalp and dry near the ends. But now there's a revolutionary new shampoo that actually takes care of both problems: new Duo shampoo . . . New Duo—for hair with a split personality."

While the success of this concept in itself was not projectable, the consistently positive reaction to it in the series of groups conducted was a good indicator of the very high score subsequently achieved in a quantitative test. On the standard five-point buy scale for the shampoo category, this concept exceeded the norm by 40 percent. The successful product later became the leader in the shampoo category. It also played a significant role in revitalizing its company's personal care division, replacing a long-declining brand. Such actionable results have led many marketers to conclude that a dollar spent upfront in idea generation is worth 10 times the test-market dollar.

While it is not appropriate to base launch decisions solely on focus group findings, it behooves the new product marketer to allocate funds early on in the development process for a rigorous series of focus groups conducted by skilled specialists in order to generate concepts. Ideas generated in this way more often lead to successful quantitative tests; thus, focus groups used to generate ideas, not just data, are a genuinely significant part of the new product development process.

BETTER INTERPRETATION OF RESULTS

How groups are conducted, of course, is extremely important to better interpretation of results. They must be planned, structured, and managed in a way that constitutes a conducive environment. As we have already indicated, the use of a sequential series of groups is a vital aspect of the process. In addition, several elements combine to create the kind of environment that produces actionable findings, not mere statistics: (1) careful screening, (2) advance formulation of hypotheses, and (3) the use of professional interpreters.

The first step necessary to better interpretation is careful screening. It is possible and beneficial to screen consumers for focus group participation not only by demographic and psychographic segments but even by specific attitudes. Such careful screening takes into account discriminators that are relevant to the market.

Self-esteem, for example, has been found to be a prime discriminator in segmenting the women's market. Especially for image products, a more accurate reflection of behavior can be obtained by screening for qualities and levels of self-esteem than can be obtained through traditional segmentation based on demographics, psychographics, and lifestyles. To segment "working" and "nonworking" women, for example, doesn't necessarily create a valid division since either group is likely to contain women with both traditional and modern values. Furthermore, many women today are in transitional stages, and it is helpful to take this into account in screening.

Next, groups should be viewed as a forum that attempts to corroborate beliefs, and it must be recognized that hypotheses about issues and behavior must be formulated in advance of the group. Such hypotheses form the basis for planning and structuring the group discussion, which will confirm or dispel the beliefs, thereby determining the direction for the next group. Thus, the formulation of advance hypotheses is an important step toward achieving better interpretation of results.

For example, groups were held recently to help reposition for American consumers an insecticide that had been marketed in Europe. Experience led the project team to hypothesize that the product form (a thin, felt-tip dispenser, much like a magic-marker pen) was likely to be perceived as ineffective. With this in mind, the marketing team was able to create positionings for discussion that were designed to dispel the notion of inefficacy.

When the issue prevailed and the group discussions consistently corroborated the hypotheses, alternative product forms were sought. A thicker nib (perceived as more effective) proved to be the answer. When tested, that product form achieved a very high "definitely will buy" score.

Finally, because interpretation of focus group findings is subjective, dependent largely on the ability of the interpreter to "listen with a third ear," the use of skilled professionals is essential to obtain meaningful results. Experienced listeners make an important difference in better interpretation of group discussion. For example, experience has shown that women logically discussing facial moisturizers say they prefer the product to be packaged in plastic because it's more convenient, not breakable, etc. In reality, there are a number of mass-marketed moisturizers packaged in plastic that are all overshadowed by the giant in the category, Oil of Olay, which is packaged in glass.

Interpreters listening with "a third ear" understand that moisturizers are an image category and that consumers respond emotionally as well as logically. Skilled specialists in new product development, taking this into account, will challenge the consumer preference by exposing concepts and visuals using glass containers to indicate quality and prestige. They know that, despite what is said, emotional reaction is likely to be strong.

VALID CONSUMER RESPONSES LEAD TO GENUINE INSIGHT

To obtain genuine insight from focus groups, responses should not necessarily be taken at face value. There are many reasons why people don't simply say what they mean or mean what they say. Some people are inarticulate. Others are reticent and inhibited. If they are confused, they may answer inappropriately. People with a need to dominate may influence the responses of others in the group. A skilled moderator employs techniques to control these situations so that a conducive environment is established and valid responses can be obtained.

Moderators use special techniques for the reticent, inhibited, and less articulate to draw them out and help them to say what they mean. For example, projective techniques, such as the "unfinished scenario" and the "celebrity image transfer," are particularly useful when the focus group is discussing an image category (such as cosmetics or liqueurs) and the issues are emotional. These techniques encourage consumers to be more articulate about their self-images and feelings, creating a more fruitful discussion to guide and stimulate the project team.

The "unfinished scenario" encourages more honest communication because consumers are not asked to talk about themselves or their own feelings. Instead, they are requested to finish a brief story or "scenario" about a fictitious person.

Both users and nonusers are given an opportunity to identify with certain characters in scenarios presented. Each scenario is developed with a specific issue in mind, e.g. aging, status, etc. From the responses and ensuing discussion, the skilled observer gains insight to important issues such as self-esteem.

"Celebrity image transfers" ask consumers to create 10-word profiles of various celebrities whose personality types are commonly known, e.g. Mary Tyler Moore, Sissy Spacek, etc. Consumers match brands with pictures of these celebrity types and in so doing reveal their own brand preferences and self-images. Through the transfer process, a desirable "brand personality" emerges.

In the liqueur category, for example, the celebrity image transfer technique was used to get a well-defined idea of the images of several brands and to identify gaps in the category. Consumers were asked to match a preselected list of celebrities to a preselected list of cordial brands and drinks. Some of the choices were: Meryl Streep with Kahlua, Burt Reynolds with the Rusty Nail, Humphrey Bogart with cognac, Woody Allen with Amaretto, and Marcello Mastroianni with Stregga. However, for Mean Joe Green there was no appropriate match. In the group discussion, it developed that no cordial was perceived to be extremely masculine. Thus, a new product, "Devil's Choice," was recommended, with the positioning: "Get To Know the Devil's Choice. Demon Rum Black Liqueur. 110 Proof. Strong But Smooth." These and other techniques aid the skilled moderator in gaining genuine insight into consumer motivations.

SUMMARY

Focus groups are a valuable qualitative research tool when used in the right way for the right reasons. They can be used successfully to develop ideas and "images" for new products, to position them, and to reposition declining brands. In order to tap the potential of the focus group, it must be used scientifically as a consumer laboratory. By that we mean that its purpose must be to explore consumers' beliefs and the hypotheses that have been developed, to experiment with possibilities, and to build new hypotheses. Mere data collection only scratches the surface. It is also essential to conduct a sequential series of groups designed to build on each other.

One criterion for the conduct of focus groups that provide actionable results is the use of skilled professionals to determine how to screen participants, how to moderate, and how to interpret discussion. In addition, it is necessary to employ special techniques in order to obtain more valid consumer responses. Groups planned and managed in this disciplined way lead to better interpretation, significant, genuine insight, and more successful new products.

6

Organizational Creativity and New Product Development

Arthur B. VanGundy
University of Oklahoma

The complexity and turbulence of most business environments make it impossible to predict with certainty which new products will be successful in the future. Even with all the sophisticated quantitative tools available, we are still somewhat limited in our ability to know how consumers will react to a new product. Although some of the guesswork has been eliminated in many areas, there still remains much to know about often fickle consumer preferences.

Further compounding the problem is the time lag between product conception and market introduction. Lags spanning several years are not uncommon in most industries. In the auto industry, for example, almost a decade can elapse before a new model is introduced that is considered to represent a radical change from earlier models.

Very few managers would disagree that organizational creativity is needed to help adapt to an uncertain future. Unfortunately, I suspect that many high-level executives provide little more than lip service when it comes to developing, managing, and maintaining organizational creativity. There are many organizations where systemwide efforts have been made to develop environments conducive to creative functioning. However, these organizations are the exception rather than the rule.

Organizational creativity tends to be a little like the weather: everybody talks about it, but little is done to change it. Unlike the weather, however, there is much that can be done to make organizations more creative and responsive to their environments. The resources available to most business organizations can be used to enhance creative behavior once a targeted program is begun. However, such a program requires more than talk.

IMPORTANCE OF
ORGANIZATIONAL CREATIVITY

A first step toward organizational creativity is recognition that there is a need to become more creative. Not all organizations require the same degree of creative performance. And the need for creativity will even vary between different organizational levels. However, once the need is identified, action can be taken.

A simple analogy can be made by comparing individual and organizational creativity. Depending on the goals they have set for themselves and the type of work they do, most individuals will have different views about their need to become more creative. Quite often, these differing views arise from how they see themselves. Many people have simply decided that they are not creative. I believe that we all are creative but vary in the degree to which we have developed our creativity potential.

The same holds true with most organizations. Not all organizations have objectives that require a finely tuned level of creative performance. However, most organizations can benefit from some increase in their creative abilities. And, perhaps most important, all organizations have the potential to become more creative.

In most organizations, the motivation to create stems from a variety of factors. The uncertainty perceived to exist in the external environment can be a major stimulus to creativity. When the market is highly volatile, you have to be prepared to make many creative responses. Clearly articulated organizational goals, backed up by required resources, can be a second stimulus to organizational creativity. The achievement needs of individuals who desire to express themselves creatively would be a third stimulus. A fourth stimulus is peer pressure that often exists within work groups. If creative expression is emphasized within groups, individual motivation levels can be heightened. However, an overall organization climate that is conducive to creativity usually is required to foster group climates conducive to creativity. Interdepartmental competition frequently operates as another stimulus. Constructive competition can serve to motivate groups to enhance their creativity. Finally, a sixth stimulus is intercompany competition. Keeping up with the Joneses is often as effective a corporate motivator as it is a social motivator. If an improvement can be made on an unsecured market niche, a company may be stimulated to develop a more creative (and thereby more attractive) product.

If companies can be motivated by one or all of these factors, they will be in a better marketing position. Competitive advantage will be strengthened, and market niche leadership will be more attainable. In some cases, organizational survival may even be at stake. Nevertheless, a creative organization is more likely to exploit opportunities and produce innovative products more frequently than a less creative organization in a similar market environment.

MANAGING ORGANIZATIONAL CREATIVITY

All of these advantages associated with organizational creativity are the good news; the bad news is that becoming more creative as an organization is easier said than done.

Many barriers must be overcome. A partial list of such barriers includes such things as:

1. A climate of conformity and preoccupation with tradition (the "not invented here" syndrome).

2. A lack of slack resources to innovate (e.g., time, people with appropriate skills, money, and relevant and timely information).

3. A climate that fosters "killer phrases" rather than deferring judgment on ideas. Most of us are culturally conditioned to see only the negative aspects of a new idea.

4. Fear of failure and risk-taking. An organization that goes strictly by the book often will suppress creative thinking and penalize failure and risk-taking.

5. Overemphasis on competition. Although a moderate amount of internal or external competition can stimulate creativity, too much competition can produce stress levels counterproductive to creativity.

6. Short-range thinking and lack of or inadequate strategic planning. An emphasis on short-term goals and objectives coupled with a lack of effective long-range planning does little to foster the reflective atmosphere needed for creative thinking.

These barriers can be overcome with proper management of creative processes within organizations. Rather than being reactive, organizations concerned with new product development may need to be more proactive and forward looking. As Wiggins (1972) stated in discussing organizational innovation, "consciously organized opportunity ought to replace necessity as the mother of invention" (p. 35). Managing and controlling these opportunities is a key ingredient in organizational creativity.

Perhaps the most essential consideration in managing creativity is to start from a clear-cut philosophy of organizational creativity. Such a philosophy needs to be translated into specific plans and policies. Intangible factors, such as moral support for creativity, are also important. However, major emphasis needs to be placed on integrating the creative aspects of new product development with corporate objectives.

Business organizations cannot afford to be creative just for the sake of being creative. New product ideas must be congruent with overall corporate objectives as well as with more specific objectives within product areas. Ensuring this congruency means that a front-end market analysis must be conducted prior to development of any creative new product ideas. The market area must be specifically identified and targeted to take best advantage of the creative process. Ideas can exploit opportunities but only if the opportunity search is organized and managed.

The managers responsible for developing and exploiting new product opportunities will need to initiate a variety of activities consistent with short-range and long-range corporate plans. According to Kanter (1982), these activities involve three primary phases: (1) project definition, (2) coalition building, and (3) action.

Project definition involves acquiring and evaluating information relevant to the product area. This requires interacting with a variety of sources and gathering as much information as possible. Effective listening skills are important during this phase as is the ability to keep an open mind. It probably is most important, however, to seek information from persons outside the manager's primary functional area. An R&D manager, for example, may need to talk with other managers in product design and marketing. Finally, project approval must be obtained from the required sources.

Coalition building has as its objective the acquisition of power and resources to help ensure that the project can be carried through to completion. Acquiring power during this phase does not mean that managers should spend their time buttering up their bosses or asserting their authority. Rather, power needs to be based more on horizontal relationships. During this phase, managers should first contact a number of people at the same level and garner their support for the project. Such support often can be obtained by stressing how they all will benefit. When necessary, top level executive support also may be needed, although direct support is not always required. Simply blessing a project may be all that is needed. This blessing will, in turn, help develop a solid team of supporters.

Once a coalition of supporters is formed, the action phase can begin. This phase involves four primary management tasks. First, the manager must handle interference or opposition that might jeopardize the project. Second, the manager must maintain momentum and continuity. It is very easy for initial enthusiasm to die out over time as more routine tasks are given a higher priority. Third, the manager must use secondary redesign activities to keep things moving along. Plans and structures often need altering to keep a project alive. Finally, the manager must use external communication to inform supporters of progress being made on the project. In addition, communication involves sharing awards and recognition to stimulate pride and motivation.

Although these three phases—especially coalition building—represent important aspects of managing creativity, they are somewhat general for new product development. One of the most universally accepted new product planning models is the one developed by Booz, Allen & Hamilton (1968). This model consists of six stages: (1) exploration, (2) screening, (3) business analysis, (4) development, (5) testing, and (6) commercialization.

All of these stages involve using creative thinking and problem solving to various degrees. Organizational creativity, however, usually will have the greatest impact on the exploration stage. This is the stage where ideas are sought using either internal or external sources. For example, ideas can be gathered internally from R&D, systematic application of formal creativity techniques, and suggestion systems. Some external sources include consumer research, new product consultants, customer suggestions, distributors, and demographic trends.

From the research in this area, it appears that most new product ideas originate from external sources. Although it may be logical and rational to rely on a market-driven model for new product ideas, there are those who maintain that such an approach is not likely to increase competitive advantage. For example, Foster (1984) believes that a more sustainable competitive advantage is likely to result from a "technically driven approach that meets a market need not yet well defined" (p. 62).

I would argue that both internal and external sources need to be used. Internal sources alone may lead to more innovative ideas, but the resulting products may not gain widespread market acceptance. External sources have the advantage of being more responsive to market needs. However, assessment of market needs must be conducted in a systematic and organized manner. To do anything less is likely to lead to products low in innovativeness and consumer acceptance.

It is for these reasons that I recommend the use of both internal and external idea sources. However, more emphasis should be placed on internal sources than currently is the case. A greater emphasis on internal sources does not need to suffer from weak consumer acceptance if the internal search is preceded by a market analysis. The goal of such an analysis is not to generate specific product ideas. Rather, the purpose of a front-end analysis is to determine the most likely product area and needs. Internal sources can then take over to develop specific product concepts during the exploration stage.

IDEA GENERATION TECHNIQUES

Most companies rely very little on formal creativity techniques for generating ideas internally. For example, Johansson (1975) surveyed 218 Fortune 500 companies and found that only 24 percent offered training courses in creativity. When asked about their use of 12 techniques, Kepner-Tregoe and Brainstorming were reported to be used most (37 percent), followed by Function Analysis (33 percent), Work Simplification (28 percent), and Morphological Analysis (18 percent). In a similar study conducted with 126 West German companies involved in product development, Geschka (1973) reports that Brainstorming was used "sometimes" or "often" by 83 percent of the respondents, while Morphological Analysis was used by 28 percent. More recently, Geschka (1983) found that the same companies reported a greater awareness of these techniques than indicated in the earlier survey. From 1973 to 1980, the companies' awareness ("Detailed Knowledge") of Brainstorming increased from 17 percent to 41 percent, and awareness of Morphological Analysis increased from 7 percent to 16 percent.

Very little published research exists about the use and knowledge of creativity techniques in the corporate environment. However, from the studies just cited, it can be concluded that relatively few companies use formal idea generation methods. Moreover, the use and awareness of techniques is limited to only a small portion of the available methods. More research in this area clearly is needed given the well over 100 techniques available for idea generation in new product development (see, for example, VanGundy, 1981a, 1982, 1983).

To illustrate the variety of techniques currently available, I will briefly describe nine individual methods and six group methods that probably are less well known than Brainstorming. All of the individual approaches can be adapted for group use, but only one of the group methods can be used by individuals (Picture Folders). Because the descriptions are brief, the reader interested in more information should consult the references provided.

INDIVIDUAL TECHNIQUES

Analogies.   (1) Develop a list of several things or processes that are similar to a product or the problem a product is intended to solve (e.g., if the product is a door lock, you might think of things in nature or technology that use the principle of securing something and prevent it from being opened or moved), (2) select one of your analogies and describe it in some detail, (3) look over the descriptions and use them to help prompt new ideas, and (4) select another analogy and repeat steps 2 and 3 (deBono, 1970; Gordon, 1961; Prince, 1970; VanGundy, 1983).

Attribute Association Chains.   (1) List major product features and attributes (if you want to develop a new product rather than a modification or extension of an existing product, list attributes of the general product area), (2) generate a list of free associations for each attribute identified (e.g., handle might cause you to think of lever, which might lead to stick, which might lead to tree, and so forth), (3) examine each association generated and use it as an idea stimulus (VanGundy 1983).

Exaggerated Objectives.   (1) List major product (or product area) objectives (e.g., you might want a radio to be portable, lightweight, modular, pocket-size, etc.), (2) exaggerate or "stretch" each objective (e.g., you might stretch portable to "can't be moved" or "can be moved with the touch of a finger"), (3) use the stretched objectives to suggest new products or improvements (Olson, 1980; VanGundy, 1983).

Morphological Analysis.   (1) List all major product attributes in a column down the left side of a piece of paper, (2) going across the paper from each attribute, list major subcomponents or alternative attribute forms (e.g., an attribute of a radio might be its shape; alternative forms might include round, square, oval, cylindrical, etc.), (3) select one subcomponent or alternative form from each of the attributes listed and evaluate the resulting product, (4) continue to select different combinations of subcomponents or alternative forms until several new product ideas have been suggested (VanGundy, 1981a, 1983; Zwicky, 1969).

Product Improvement Checklist.   (1) Develop an extensive list of random words (e.g., modify, substitute, combine, rearrange, freeze, twist, protect, concentrate, bubble, roller skates, shutters, etc.), (2) quickly read over the list while trying not to think of the product to be improved, (3) read over the list a little more carefully and see what ideas might be sparked by each word, (4) repeat steps 2 and 3 at a later time (VanGundy, 1983).

Semantic Intuition.   (1) Develop two sets of words related to the product area (e.g., for a vacuum cleaner, you might list "rug, dirt, dust, floor, walls, and furniture" as things that are cleaned and "motor, handle, bag, cord, brushes, and beater" as parts of a vacuum cleaner), (2) select one word from the first set of words and combine it with one word from the second set, (3) use the combination to suggest new products or improvements (e.g., "floor-vacuum" might suggest a vacuum system under the floor for use with a specially designed carpet or "floor-cord" might suggest a retractable cord built into the floor of each room in a house), (4) repeat steps 2 and 3 until all possible combinations have been examined (Schaude, 1979; VanGundy, 1981a, 1983).

Stimulus Analysis.   (1) Select 5 to 10 objects unrelated to the product, (2) choose one of the objects and describe it in detail (e.g., if you select a bicycle, you might describe it as having two wheels, a chain drive, human powered, inflatable tires, consumes no petroleum fuels, and uses gears to adjust to different speeds and terrains), (3) examine each description and see if it might suggest a product improvement or new product, (4) repeat steps 2 and 3 until all objects have been analyzed and new ideas written down (Schaude, 1979; VanGundy, 1981a, 1983).

Theoretical Limits Test.   (1) Identify major product attributes, (2) select one of the attributes and think of extreme uses or attribute features (e.g., make thinner bicycle tires), (3) analyze the consequences of pushing the attribute to an extreme and list any new products stimulated (e.g., extremely thin bicycle tires might suggest developing disposable tires), (4) repeat steps 2 and 3 (Quinn, 1967).

Wishful Thinking.   (1) List 5 to 10 "what if" questions about the product or general product area (e.g., What if windows could automatically adjust the amount of sun permitted to enter? What if cracked windows could repair themselves? What if windows could allow air to enter during warm weather?), (2) examine each "what if" question and write down any practical ideas suggested (Rickards, 1974; VanGundy, 1981a, 1983).

GROUP TECHNIQUES

Collective Notebook.   (1) Select 10 to 20 participants, (2) distribute notebooks to participants and include a statement about the general product area, (3) ask the participants to write down at least one new product idea each day for two weeks, (4) have the participants exchange notebooks with one other participant and continue to write down at least one idea per day for two more weeks, (5) collect the notebooks and categorize the ideas (Haefele, 1962; Pearson, 1979; VanGundy 1981a).

Gordon/Little.   (1) Withhold the specific product area from a small group, (2) develop a highly abstract description of the product's purpose and ask the group to think of ways of accomplishing this purpose (e.g., if the product is a toaster, you might ask the group to "think of ways to change something," since toasters change bread), (3) ask the group to write down all of their ideas, (4) ask the group to think of a slightly less abstract way of accomplishing something related to the product (e.g., "now think of ways to change the surface of something,) and write down their ideas, (5) ask the group to think of an even less abstract way of achieving the product's purpose (e.g., "Think of ways to heat a surface") and write down their ideas, (6) reveal the product to the group and ask them to develop modifications or new products using their previous responses as stimulators (e.g., if a way to change something was to ask it to change, a modification might be a voice-activated toaster) (Taylor, 1961; VanGundy 1981a).

Picture Folders.   (1) Have a small group spend 10 minutes brainstorming new product ideas, (2) give each group member a folder containing 10 pictures unrelated to the product area (or use slides), (3) have the group members describe aloud what they see in the first picture and write down all the descriptions, (4) have the group members use the descriptions to stimulate new product ideas and write down any ideas suggested, (5) instruct the group to select another picture and repeat step 4, continuing this process until all the pictures have been described and ideas generated (this version of Picture Folders is a modification of the Battelle-Bildmappen-Brainwriting technique described in VanGundy, 1981a).

Pin Cards.   (1) Distribute a stack of index cards to a group of five to seven people seated around a small table, (2) instruct the participants to write down one idea on a card and pass it to the person seated to the right, (3) tell the person who receives the card to examine the idea for possible modification or stimulation of new ideas and write down any modified or new ideas on separate cards, (4) have the group members continue this process for 20 to 30 minutes, (5) collect the cards, pin them to a bulletin board (or lay them out on a table), and organize them into categories, (6) if time permits, discuss the ideas and write down any new ideas suggested (VanGundy, 1981a).

SIL Method.   (1) Have a small group silently write down new product ideas (each person writes down ideas without discussing them) for about 10 minutes, (2) ask two of the group members to read one of their ideas, (3) instruct the other group members to develop ways of integrating the two ideas and write down the new ideas, (4) ask a third member to read an idea and have the group integrate it with the idea from step 3, (5) continue reading and integrating ideas in this manner until all ideas have been exhausted, (6) ask the group to review all of the ideas and develop any modifications or new ideas that may emerge (VanGundy, 1981a).

Split-Brain Comparisons.   (1) Form two groups of about five to seven persons each, (2) instruct the first group to brainstorm a list of practical and logical new product ideas, (3) instruct the second group (separated from the first group) to generate a list of wild and crazy ideas, (4) after about 45 minutes of idea generation, ask the groups to convene, (5) ask each group to read one idea, (6) have both groups identify the positive features of the "wild and crazy" idea and attempt to use these positive features to improve the "practical and logical idea", (7) repeat steps 5 and 6 until all ideas have been examined and a final list of new product ideas has been developed (VanGundy, 1981b).

The group techniques described above do not represent the most widely used and known methods. Noticeably absent are Brainstorming and Synectics. I decided to exclude Brainstorming because it is so widely known and used; I did not include Synectics because of its complexity and requirement for a fairly skilled group leader. The techniques described require very little in the way of special training or skills and should be more immediately useful.

ORGANIZATIONAL CLIMATE AND CREATIVITY

Although formal creativity techniques can be useful in helping to generate new product ideas, they are not a panacea. Creativity techniques alone are not likely to lead to a more creative organization. They can help provoke new ways of looking at products and reinforce creative thinking as an aid to innovative product development. However, techniques will be optimally effective only when an organizational climate exists that is conducive to creative thinking and stimulation.

Like the weather, a desirable climate should contain a balanced amount of different factors. For instance, some worker participation in decision making may be conducive to creativity but too much participation may result in nonproductive anarchy. The right amount of any given climatic factor must be determined by each individual organization. What is right for an established, family owned business with a limited product line may not be right for a public organization with a more diversified product line.

Another consideration in examining organizational climates is the role of the CEO. The person at the top usually sets the tone for the entire organization. Managers at different levels also will play some role in establishing a climate, but it is the CEO who can take the lead and exert the greatest influence.

A creative climate cannot be mandated, however, like production schedules. Organizational climates must be nourished and prodded to develop and be sustained. But they will not develop because they are ordered to develop. Attitudes of people in an organization contribute to what makes up a creative climate. If the people in an organization believe that the climate is conducive to creative thinking, they will more likely engage in this type of thinking.

The role of management in developing or maintaining a creative climate is to provide the necessary conditions and ingredients. In the academic literature, a variety of managerial prescriptions has been identified as important for fostering organizational creativity (VanGundy, 1984). I have selected 12 of these prescriptions and will briefly describe them next. However, it should be noted that these prescriptions are by no means exhaustive. Furthermore, there may be some overlap among the prescriptions, since many aspects of creative climates are interrelated.

1. Provide Necessary Resources.   Just as a product requires resources to be manufactured, a creative climate requires resources to be developed and sustained. Such resources include time, skills, money, and information. Time to be creative is very important, since new ideas cannot be produced under conditions of extreme time pressure. Bright ideas usually require periods of incubation. Skills are important, since the value of many ideas is determined by the skills possessed by the people who are knowledgeable about the product area and have the ability to champion ideas and carry them through to implementation. Information plays a major role in new product development in many ways. New product personnel need to be informed about competitor products, suppliers, market feasibility, and technological aspects of the product area. If any of these resources are in short supply, new product projects will have less chance of success.

2. Disseminate Ideas and Problems within the Organization.   Many problems can be defined and ideas generated better when people from outside the original work unit are involved. The selective sharing of problems and ideas can often bring diverse viewpoints on how to define a problem or suggestions for modifying an idea. The openness required to accomplish this sharing also will help contribute to a general climate of receptivity to new ideas. Of course, all problems and ideas cannot be shared. A decision will have to be made as to which problems and ideas could benefit most from wide dissemination.

3. Emphasize Professionalism. Some research suggests that organizations with a high degree of professionalism will be more innovative than organizations with less professionalism. Employees involved in new product development should be viewed as professionals who possess a prescribed body of knowledge about specialized areas. However, many organizations stress status difference to such a degree that the independance of thought and action associated with professionalism often is not given a chance to emerge.

Moreover, professionals should be provided opportunities for growth and development, such as executive sabbaticals, training in new skill development, and attendance at conferences and seminars. These conferences and seminars do not always need to be related directly to the new product field. New ideas frequently can be obtained from attending meetings somewhat unrelated to one's area. For instance, a marketing manager might benefit from attending a seminar on graphic design or communication techniques.

4. Acknowledge Employee Needs for Autonomy. Most employees perform at their peak when they are internally motivated and primarily self-directed in their behavior. We all have different needs that help motivate us, but someone constantly looking over our shoulders usually is not one of them. Employees should be encouraged to perform well, but a moderate amount of pressure usually is all that is needed. Overmanagement is likely to backfire and be seen as contributing to a repressive atmosphere. A feeling of freedom to try new ideas is likely to occur only if employees feel that they have some degree of independence and control over their own motivation.

5. Consider Loosening up the Formal Organization Structure.   Rigid, unchangeable organizational structures are most appropriate when the primary tasks are relatively routine in nature. The ill-structured tasks encountered by new product people rarely lend themselves to inflexible organizational structures. Instead, cooperation between units frequently is a requirement. Sometimes this cooperation can take the form of informal contacts with other units, and sometimes temporary teams may need to be formed. The important thing is that managers retain a willingness to work with others outside their units and to form and disband temporary teams whenever necessary. I should note, however, that structural looseness does not mean anarchy. A project manager will need to be identified and recognized, and the responsibilities and authority of all team members should be clearly spelled out.

6. Encourage Open Group Processes.   All groups concerned with new product development should be encouraged to clearly separate concept generation from concept evaluation. Perhaps most important, however, is that group members feel free to express themselves during discussions. Groups can provide an ideal setting for reducing the risks often associated with individual creativity. There can be strength in numbers if all group members believe that their ideas will receive a fair hearing and not be rejected outright.

7. Establish Appropriate Communication Channels.   The free flow of ideas within an organization requires open and responsive communication channels. Organizational units that can contribute toward the development of a new product must be functionally interconnected to facilitate rapid dissemination of information. In most cases, such channels can be developed by designating specific individuals from different units to act as temporary linking pins for dealing with particular product areas.

8. Use Decentralized Authority Structures.   As much as possible, decision-making pertaining to the creative development of new products should be delegated to the level of the innovation area. Requiring a maze of bureaucratic decision-making procedures can stifle most creative projects. Consequently, bureaucratic procedures should be reserved for more routine problem-solving situations. However, any authority delegated must be backed up by appropriate support in the form of material, information, or whatever is required to get the job done. Watered-down authority will be of little value in developing and especially implementing creative ideas.

9. Provide Opportunities for Workers to Fail.   All creative people have failed at some time during their careers. If we do not have the opportunity to fail, we will never learn how to benefit from our failures. Unfortunately, many organizational climates tend to punish failure. When this occurs, the motivation to create will be repressed, and, in the long run, the entire organization will suffer. Of course, the amount of failure tolerated must be monitored and restricted to specific types of situations and limited in the number of occurrences. Failure obviously should not be viewed as the primary route to organizational creativity.

10. Provide Training in Creative Thinking and Problem Solving.   Contrary to some popular thinking, basic creativity tools can be learned. Although we all possess the ability to think creatively, some of us are more creative than others.

   People who are less creative than others frequently can benefit from formal training in creative thinking principles and application of the creative problem-solving process. Such training should stress avoidance of "killer phrases" (e.g., "It will never work here," "We already tried that," etc.), testing of all assumptions made about problem situations, acceptance of divergent and "off-the-wall ideas," looking for the positive features in all ideas no matter how impractical they may appear, and separation of idea generation from idea evaluation.

11. Recognize Worthy Ideas.   Many experts believe that people are motivated most effectively from within themselves. Others, however, believe that external factors also can play an important role in human motivation. The truth probably lies somewhere in between: most people are motivated by a combination of internal and external factors.

If worthy ideas are informally or formally recognized, some recipients may shrug it off. But I suspect that the majority of workers will respond more positively. If nothing else, it is encouraging to know that your ideas are valued. It costs very little to pat someone on the back or tell them you appreciate their contribution. Formal recognition of ideas also can be important in the form of certificates, plaques, merchandise, or cash bonuses. The bottom line is that most people desire and appreciate recognition. And, when recognition is given uniformly, it can help motivate people to increase their output of creative ideas.

12. Exhibit Confidence in Workers.   Recognizing ideas is one way to indirectly show workers that you have confidence in their ability. At a more general level, however, exhibiting confidence in workers should be part of an overall management philosophy that believes in the creative potential of all workers. If you tell people that you believe in their ability to think creatively, they will be more likely to believe that they can think creatively. Their behavior, in turn, should reflect this belief. This is what is known as a self-fulfilling prophecy. People who are told they are creative often begin to act creatively. On the other hand, people who have little confidence shown in their creativity often act as if they are not creative. Management can then point to the workers and say "See, the workers here are not very creative." If you want your organization to be creative, believe in each person's creative abilities and tell them you believe in them. You have nothing to lose and a more creative climate to gain.

REFERENCES

Booz, Allen & Hamilton. *Management of New Products.* 4th ed. New York, 1968.

de Bono, E. *Lateral Thinking: Creativity Step by Step*. New York: Harper & Row, 1970.

Foster, R. N. Cited in B. Little, "Significant Issues for the Future of Product Innovation." *Journal of Product Innovation Management* 1 (1984), pp. 56–66.

Geschka, H. "Introduction and Use of Idea-Generating Methods." *Creativity and Motivation in Industrial R&D*, Working Group No. 14, European Industrial Research Management Association, 1973.

———. "Creativity Techniques in Product Planning and Development: A View from West Germany." *R&D Management* 13, No. 3 (1983), pp. 169–83.

Gordon, W. J. J. *Synectics*, New York: Harper & Row, 1961.

Haefele, J. W. *Creativity and Innovation*. New York: Reinhold, 1962.

Johansson, B. "Creativity and Creative Problem-Solving Courses in United States Industry." Survey funded by the Center for Creative Leadership, Greensboro, N.C., 1975.

Kanter, R. M. "The Middle Manager as Innovator." *Harvard Business Review*, July-August 1982, pp. 95–105.

Olson, R. W. *The Art of Creative Thinking*. New York: Barnes & Noble, 1980.

Pearson, A. W. "Communication, Creativity, and Commitment: A Look at the Collective Notebook Approach." In *Proceedings of Creativity Week I, 1978*, ed. S. S. Gryskiewicz. Greensboro, N.C.: Center for Creative Leadership, 1979.

Prince, G. M. *The Practice of Creativity*. New York: Harper & Row, 1970.

Quinn, J. B. "Technological Forecasting." *Harvard Business Review* 45 (1967) pp. 89–106.

Rickards, T. *Problem-Solving Through Creative Analysis*. Essex, U.K.: Gower Press, 1974.

Schaude, G. R. "Methods of Idea Generation." In *Proceedings of Creativity Week I, 1978*, ed. S. S. Gryskiewicz. Greensboro, N.C.: Center for Creative Leadership, 1979.

Taylor, J. W. *How to Create Ideas*. Englewood Cliffs, N.J.: Prentice-Hall, 1961.

VanGundy, A. B. *Techniques of Structured Problem Solving*. New York: Van Nostrand Reinhold, 1981a.

———. "Comparing Little Known Creative Problem-Solving Techniques." In *Creativity Week III, 1980 Proceedings*, ed. S. S. Gryskiewicz. Greensboro, N.C.: Center for Creative Leadership, 1981b.

———. "A Typology of Techniques for Generating New Product Ideas." Paper presented at the Sixth Annual Conference of The Product Development and Management Association, Philadelphia, 1982.

————. *108 Ways to Get a Bright Idea and Increase Your Creative Potential.* Englewood Cliffs, N.J.: Prentice-Hall, 1983.

————. *Managing Group Creativity, A Modular Approach to Problem Solving.* New York: AMACOM, 1984.

Wiggins, W. "The Innovational Revolution." In *Climate for Creativity,* ed. C. W. Taylor. New York: Pergaman, 1972.

Zwicky, F. *Discovery, Invention, Research Through the Morphological Approach.* New York: Macmillan, 1969.

7

Optimizing New Products Research

New Initiatives for New Products

Graham Denton
Initiatives Group and Product Initiatives

We need new initiatives for new products. And there is one fundamentally good reason why that is so—because 8 out of 10 new products still fail. Why?

Many new products have failed because they were too new. An interesting thought, but let's remember that Leonardo Da Vinci's airplane was laughed at. Closer to our day and age, it took 12 years for Kellogg's to establish that a cold breakfast was an OK way to start the day. And although the technology for the video phone has been around for over 20 years, the idea has been too new for consumers. They just don't want to be seen by the other party when making a phone call.

Today, however, most new products fail because they are not new enough. According to Marketing Intelligence Service, a new products intelligence company in the United States, 90 percent of all new products introduced in North America in the last 15 years were not really new. They were new sizes, new packaging configurations, new formulations, new flavors, but not *new products*. They didn't offer people a significant point of difference.

Here's an example of what happens when we fail to offer people that significant point of difference.

> Cue Toothpaste. It was a perfectly good product. The only problem was that Cue had no significant point of difference from Crest, which was already a market leader for P&G. Our main reason for launching Cue was to threaten Crest, which as it turned out, had little to worry about since we wound up losing $15 million in just one year.
>
> David R. Foster, past president
> Colgate-Palmolive Company

A successful new product always offers consumers a *significant point of difference*. What is a significant point of difference? How can you be sure your new product offers one? Here are five basic guidelines that ensure a significant point of difference. Let's look at them.

1.   A significant point of difference is one that consumers can *recognize*.

That sounds obvious, but too many new products are based on technical differences measurable in the laboratory *but not obvious to the consumer*. An example of this is the cake mix Moist & Easy from Procter & Gamble. Moistness is the critical factor in cake mixes. Moist & Easy was technically more moist than the competition, Betty Crocker's Snackin' Cake. However, in consumer blind testing, most did not notice the difference. Despite this, P&G launched the product. Now, some seven years later, Moist & Easy has been withdrawn in America and folded into the Duncan Hines flavor line in Canada. It's a failure. Consumers could not recognize its point of difference. So we say new products must be thoroughly and sensitively researched to make sure consumers recognize the point of difference *and that it matters to them.*

This leads to the second guideline.

2. A significant point of difference is one that consumers *need or want.*

What *do* consumers need or want? Think about it. They want benefits like:

- Quality, as implied by brand names they've learned to trust.

- Improved performance, as with the first soft margarines, which were much easier to spread, especially straight from the refrigerator.

- Value, as with the generic or no-name supermarket products.

- Convenience, as with sheet fabric softeners that work in the dryer obviating the need to catch the rinse cycle with a liquid.

- Solutions to problems, as with the first fluoride tooth-pastes, which significantly reduced dental cavities.

- And new services, as with one-stop muffler repair shops.

If your new product isn't needed or wanted, it won't be significant. However, consumers don't *know* what they need or want. That's especially true when it comes to new products.

Therefore, we have a third guideline.

3. A significant point of difference must go hand-in-hand with a *chord of familiarity.*

The chord of familiarity should highlight the point of difference, or newness, by contrasting with it. For example, the underlined word in the following list is the chord of familiarity for each of these once-new products.

- Liquid <u>soap</u>
- Spray <u>cleaner</u>
- Disposable <u>diapers</u>
- Diet <u>soft drinks</u>
- Space <u>shuttle</u>

- Paper <u>towels</u>
- Light <u>beer</u>
- Nondairy <u>creamer</u>

Consumers are more perceptive to a new product when they can see some chord of familiarity, something that links it to their past experience.

And now the fourth guideline.

4. A significant point of difference must have credibility *that is confirmed on delivery.*

Consumers must believe the new product will deliver the significant point of difference it promises. If *they* don't believe, they won't make that first purchase. Then if *you* don't deliver, they won't make a second purchase.

The significant point of difference for Ultra Max Shampoo could be simply stated as a shampoo specially formulated for people who blow-dry their hair. Ultra Max got trial because consumers found the point of difference credible. But as soon as they realized that it was no better than their regular shampoos for blow-drying, they stopped buying. Ultra Max offered a point of difference that was credible but not delivered. Therefore, it wasn't significant, and Ultra Max failed.

The fifth guideline relates to presentation.

5. A significant point of difference must be *communicated in every aspect of presentation.*

Presentation encompasses every element that could express the point of difference. That means name, package, price, the product itself, appeal, and ultimately promotion. Presentation defines the consumer proposition of a new product, communicating the point of difference and *establishing the brand identity.*

Indeed branding, or the presentation of an idea, can even *create* a new product's point of difference. Here are three examples where that happened:

- L'Eggs Pantyhose—a unique presentation in terms of package, name, and distribution through racks. The pantyhose were no better and no worse than any other brand, yet they were a huge success.

- Clinique Cosmetics—a totally new presentation for cosmetics: skin care rather than skin beautification. An appropriate, therapeutic name and packaging to match resulted in an incredibly successful brand.
- Tic Tac Mints—a new name and pack that put more mints in more pockets at a higher profit than any of us would have thought logically possible.

Branding is crucial *because people buy brands not products*. People don't buy shaving cream. They buy Gillette Foamy, Old Spice, Noxema, or even a can of generic shaving cream. In fact, we've become so inured to brands that even generic brands are brands in the consumer's mind. That's why it is critical to develop *new brands*, not just new products—new brands that offer people *a significant point of difference*.

To recap, a significant point of difference is one that:

1. Consumers can *recognize*.
2. Consumers *need or want*.
3. Goes hand-in-hand with a *chord of familiarity*.
4. Has *credibility that is confirmed on delivery*.
5. Is communicated in *every aspect of presentation*.

Now all good rules are obvious. And, if it's that simple, why do 8 out of 10 new products still fail? I say still fail *deliberately* because, if we look at any one of the past 15 years, the report card would have been the same—80 percent of new products don't succeed. Yet there have been over 100,000 new product launches in North America in the past 15 years. By now, we should all have sharpened our sights. We should have learned some lessons. We should have reversed those odds. We haven't.

We continue to need new initiatives for new products— new initiatives not only in terms of *what* represents a significant point of difference, but also in terms of *how* a point of difference can be significant to consumers.

In order to do so we have to understand that a new product's point of difference can *appeal* to consumers in four ways. These appeals are best illustrated by looking at how people are "aware." Since the time of Plato, it has been widely believed that people are "aware" in four ways. This understanding of the four kinds of awareness was used by Jung in his teaching on human psychology. He gave the four functions of the mind specific names: thinking deals with logic and rationale, sensation is the direct perception of phenomena, feeling is concerned with emotions, and intuition is the ability to sense the intangible in a situation.

Because we are *aware* in these four ways, we are open to four kinds of appeal. This means that *brands* can appeal in four ways. And *new* brands have four potential ways to be distinct from the competition.

1. Appeal to rational thinking.
2. Appeal to sensations.
3. Appeal to emotions.
4. Appeal to intuition.

Consumer products normally employ a combination of appeals but are usually led by one primary appeal. Because some brands focus more on one kind of appeal and some another, we need more than one model to understand how new brands can be successful.

Rational Appeals.   It is sometimes said that man is a rational animal, and certainly there are many "rational" brands on sale. Rational brands are those with tangible points of difference that are demonstrated in a logical way. Crest helps prevent cavities. Tide washes whiter. Bounce is more convenient because you don't have to rush for the rinse cycle. But rational appeals also crop up in other markets. The appeal of low-tar or mild cigarettes is fundamentally rational.

Appeals To Sensation.   Consider, for a moment, the world of food marketing. Virtually all food brands appeal to the senses. For many it is the primary appeal the brand has to make. If the ketchup didn't taste good, there would be little reason to buy it. Freshen-Up, a liquid-center gum, offers a mouth feel sensation with its liquid center. Pringles, a formed potato chip, made little appeal to the senses. Perhaps this is one reason for its failure to set the snack food market on fire.

Sensation-based brands are not limited to food. For example, Coast, a high-fragrance soap, employs a sensation-based point of difference with its high-impact fragrance.

Emotional Appeals.   We react to the world with more than logic. We react with emotions. We make value judgments and become deeply committed either for or against something. It's great to get an emotional commitment from your consumer.

New York Life, a life insurance company, creates an emotional aura around the insurance it sells. We see the values we cherish (family, children, future financial security) held up for approval. And virtually everyone in the target audience endorses these values and feels to some extent committed to the same aims as the advertiser. Paco Rabanne, a male fragrance, projects quite a different type of emotion. Here, an open approach to sexuality reinforces the sensual possibilities of a male fragrance. Yet a light-hearted fantasy prevents any embarrassment among the target audience.

Intuitive Appeals.   We react to the world in even more ways than with sensation, logic, and emotion. Much of what we do is intuitive. Intuition is the skill that aids judgment. Without intuition, none of us could hire a secretary, choose a restaurant for dinner, or find a path through a maze of conflicting information. Somehow we just *know* that we should be following a certain path.

There are lots of intuitive brands. These are brands that we know instinctively are brands for people like us—brands that fit our lifestyles. Intuitive brands are the stuff of everyday; they help us convey something about ourselves to the world at large. Intuitive brands are different from the emotion-led brands that stir us and touch a chord that moves us deeply. If you like, the emotion-led brands are introverted, and the intuitive-led brands are extroverted.

Marlboro advertising conveys the point about intuitive-led brands. The cowboy, the West—the mythology says it all. Another intuitive example is beer. What is the difference between Miller Lite and Natural Lite? Apart from minor differences in formulation, the main difference is that different people feel comfortable with different brand images.

Intuitive brands enable consumers to say something about themselves. The consumer identifies with an intuitive brand. He makes a personal statement when he uses it, and this is a great asset for a brand.

Four different appeals mean four different ways in which a point of difference can be significant to people.

To recap, a significant point of difference will be one that appeals to:

1. The rational.

2. The senses.

3. The emotions.

4. The intuition.

Now how do we make *certain* that the new product is offering a significant point of difference that appeals to people? How do we "hear" the consumer's final say before investing millions of dollars on a new product? That is, how do we increase our odds of being right? These questions are key for new product market research.

Unfortunately, research *fails* to produce the right answers all too often. It says go when the right answer is stop. It says stop when the right answer is go. New products need new initiatives in market research as much as in anything else.

There are five maxims to keep new product research *honest*. Let's see how the first works in a hypothetical example.

This new three-ply toilet tissue is extra soft and strong, and costs $1.44 for four rolls.

This is a typical new product concept statement—a typewritten statement on a card. It achieved favorable consumer reaction in Canada and the United States. But the product failed in each country after considerable expense in test market. Research gave the wrong answer. It said *go* when the right answer was *stop*. How could the research have been designed to give the right answer?

If a 3-D presentation had been made alongside competition, consumers would have seen the new product as too expensive. The new product gives fewer sheets per dollar. And in this market, economy matters as much as softness and strength.

So the first maxim is:

1. Test new products alongside competitive products.

But what do you test? Companies often fail to identify the key variables in the proposition and test the wrong things. For instance, if you're developing a new cigarette, taste and satisfaction are only part of the story. You need to test the *image* of the new product vis-à-vis competitors since this is where the point of difference will lie. If you're developing a perfume, the accompanying fantasies and user image are more important variables than the fragrance itself. If you're developing a new cereal for children, taste is not the most important variable. Fun and size impression are. These are the variables you must test.

And so the second maxim is:

2. Identify and test key differences—key differences that relate directly to the significant point of difference.

Our third maxim concerns respondents and our example is taken from candy bar research. If you do research among a conventional mix of heavy and light users of candy bars, you will find they want a new taste sensation. But think— there's an important difference between what heavy and light users want. Light users want a new taste sensation. However, heavy users want value or a longer lasting candy bar. And in this market, like most others, 20 percent of users, the heavy users, account for 80 percent of the volume. Heavy users generally want something *quite different* from light users. All too often researchers recruit *all* users and drown the critical opinion of the heavy user.

So the third maxim is:

3. Know and test among your target market (usually *heavy users of key competition*).

Find your target market and pay attention to what the heavy user has to say. But how do you find the key competitors and the key points of difference? You listen to consumers. You listen to and interpret what the consumer has to say about your new product, its competition, and the category. You cross-examine.

You

4. Get to the *bottom of consumer motivation.*

Consumers can't analyze their motivation. They can't put their motivations into order of importance. That's the researcher's job, and it's best approached indirectly.

For example, let's assume you want to find out why people use muffler shops instead of local gas stations. If you ask a direct question like "Why do you go to Midas Muffler?" you get an easy, logical answer like "Because they're quick and efficient." A logical answer like this makes the respondent feel good because he or she has answered the question. It makes the researcher feel good because it's simple to pass on to the client. But it's the *wrong* answer.

However, if you ask an *indirect* question of the same people, such as "What were your feelings the last time you took your car for repair at a gas station?" you may get an answer like "I was afraid," "They put a hammer through the perfectly good muffler," "It was a rip-off." Through this type of comment, you discover the real advantage of the muffler shop is predictable cost or honesty.

The principle of direct questioning is applied to *quantitative* as well as qualitative research. So you dig deeper. You ask respondents to rate the local station on various attributes like friendliness, price, and honesty, and you cross-analyze the answers by those who *do* and those who *do not* use a muffler shop. You find agreement that the local station is friendly and has good prices. But views differ on the question of honesty. Thus you discover that the real advantage of the muffler shop over the gas station is the perception of honesty.

Now the fifth consumer research maxim:

5. Use *realistic consumer stimuli.*

Speak a language the consumer understands. Too many good ideas are lost because of the way they are presented to consumers. You wouldn't speak Chinese to an Italian and expect him to understand. Similarly, let's not speak to the consumer in marketing or research jargon. Don't show unresolved hypotheses. Let's show things that look like ads or television commercials, or sound like radio spots.

We often develop proposition boards that look like print ads. They express the idea but don't sell it. The format provides consumers with something to relate to—something familiar. And in this way, we test alternative approaches, especially emotional and intuitive ones, with greater ease.

That's why we show consumers comprehensive three-dimensional package designs too. Consumers can't visualize a finished, branded package. So we can show them one or more often a whole range. But whatever we show consumers, it's in a form they recognize and in a language they understand.

Now to remind you of the five research maxims:

1. Test new products *alongside competitive* products.

2. Identify and test *key differences*.

3. Know and test among your *target market* (usually heavy users of key competition).

4. Get to the bottom of *consumer motivation*.

5. Use *realistic consumer stimuli*.

For 15 years, we've lived with an unacceptable failure rate when it comes to new products. What we need is new initiatives for new products. New initiatives in terms of *what* represents a significant new product. New initiatives in terms of *how* the new product is significant. And new initiatives in terms of *researching* the new product with consumers.

8

Technology Management and New Product Development

Michael S. Yalowitz
Synectics

It is surprising that many managers fail to adequately consider the key element underlying business growth today. Too little attention is generally devoted to understanding the role *technology* plays in shaping the future of industry. In fact, while most executives manage their corporation's financial, manufacturing, marketing, and human resources, they leave technology management in the hands of the research and development department, at best, and often to no one specifically.

Instead of managing technology to ensure their futures, an increasing number of firms will find their futures managed by technology—generally, technology developed by competitors with more aggressive technology management practices. At the very least, if technology is not actively managed, a company will fail to recognize new opportunities, particularly those outside their traditional industries. At the very worst, technology will leap in from other industries altogether, threatening the existing businesses. Remember carbon paper?

Even if you are not in an obviously high-technology industry, you may be as vulnerable, and perhaps more vulnerable, to the influence of technology as a computer or chemical firm. Technology affects not only the products and services you sell, but the way you sell, distribute, and service those products. Technology affects the way you conduct fundamental business proceedings. Word processors are common. Computerized invoicing and financial tracking are widespread. In turn, these technological cost advantages dictate how competitive your firm is. In fact, it is the non-technology service businesses that will be most vulnerable to the impact of technology during the next decade. A 1983 report completed at the Massachusetts Institute of Technology indicates that "white-collar" technology investments will have three times the productivity impact as equivalent investment in manufacturing technology. As a result, technology will shape your future whether your company is a service business, a manufacturing concern, or a high-technology products firm. If the impact in nontechnology businesses is this significant, you can imagine the importance of technology elsewhere—particularly in the development and introduction of new products and services.

To successfully manage and control a firm's future, one must integrate technology variables closely into the planning process because the firm's technology position defines its market opportunities and threats much more potently than other business variables. A technological focus provides a way to understand the firm's focus and resources and to capture opportunities outside of your traditional markets. In fact, technological skills, whether applied to products, services, or the conduct of basic business functions, will define a firm's strategic options. As a result, technology should be viewed as a vital corporate resource, incorporated into the planning process, and aggressively managed. The challenge is to (1) recognize that technology is a critical corporate asset and (2) use it to shape the company's future— particularly in terms of new product management.

THE IMPORTANCE TO NEW PRODUCT DEVELOPMENT

Companies who do not actively manage their technological resources face three threats:

1. Traditional competitors whose technology permits advantages in terms of costs or productivity. This is particularly true in business and nontechnology consumer businesses.
2. New competitors who bring technology from other industries.
3. Lost opportunities for growth through the failure to apply your own technology skills to new areas and product categories.

While the third threat is costly, the first two are deadly to any company. Products and services based on stagnant and declining technologies generally offer fewer options to managers regardless of whether decisions involve features, pricing, position, or distribution. As a result, it is most important that you base new products and services on emerging technologies while using products and services based on older technologies for profit-taking and market positioning.

ARE YOU MANAGING TECHNOLOGY?

How do you know if your company is not managing technology effectively? If a firm faces the following situations, it may be the result of an emerging technological gap:

Increasingly narrow market segments.

Loss of market share, particularly in specialized segments.

Emergence of new, small, aggressive competitors using radical approaches.

Emergence of technology-based competitors from other industries.

R&D spending directed toward process or productivity not product improvements.

Lowered leverage of R&D expenditures and a perceived decrease in R&D effectiveness and creativity.

Cost disadvantages relative to competitors, particularly smaller competitors.

Movement of suppliers or customers into your traditional sphere.

If these are increasingly a concern, it is clearly time to begin a technology management assessment.

By the way, there are also favorable hints that your firm is not managing technology actively. If companies outside your traditional industry contact you to provide a product or service that varies slightly from your usual ones or if present customers ask you to extend your expertise to other areas, it is likely that a variety of applications and markets exist. A technology management assessment would be helpful to permit your firm to develop new products and services based on growing rather than declining technologies. Technology management will permit you to "export" products and services based on old technology to other markets and to "import" products and services based on new technologies into your existing target markets.

WHAT IS STRATEGIC TECHNOLOGY MANAGEMENT?

To do this, you will want to be able to predict the direction of technology so your firm can respond appropriately—just as you track other business variables in order to respond to them. Strategic technology management consists precisely of this process: identifying your firm's technological foundation, resources, and skills; assessing your product or service technology position relative to the market's requirements and to competitors; and identifying and taking corrective actions in order to achieve corporate goals. These steps are outlined next.

WHAT ARE THE STEPS FOR A PRODUCT-TECHNOLOGY ASSESSMENT?

1. Identify Alternative Technologies on which Products and Services Can Be Based

In addition to the technology on which your present products and market position are based, you must develop clear definitions of the competitive technologies that are likely to emerge, are emerging, or have already penetrated into your traditional sphere of participation. Technologies in use in other industries where your firm's skills and resources may be applied must also be identified. In this manner, you can identify areas where your firm's technology can be applied to new products and services in other industries and where technology from other industries can be imported to enhance your next generation of products and services in your traditional areas of interest.

Your sources to find these competitive technologies include: emerging competitors, new competitors from other industries, distributors, and customers (particularly those who are integrating vertically). Technologies that are maturing in your supplier industries as well as those that have fully penetrated other horizontal segments are other natural candidates.

Review them in an exploratory manner for their applicability to your industry and target markets. Certainly, you cannot expect to make detailed analyses at this point. However, you may be able to eliminate some technologies based on significant major impediments such as cost, time to acquire, or customer reluctance to adopt.

2. Profile Competitive Technologies and Conduct a Technology Forecast

After identifying competitive technologies in your traditional industries and in those industries you suspect you might expand into, develop comparison profiles of these technologies and forecast their future to determine which are growing, which are stagnant, and which are in a state of decline. Be sure to include the technology on which your firm's current products and services are based. A technology forecast really involves predicting the length of time during which products based on a specific technology can stay competitive with other technologies. For example, how long can print magazines compete with electronic publishing? How long can chemically based diagnostics compete with immunoassay techniques? How long can firmware-based electronic video games compete with software-based home computer games?

Figure 1 illustrates several technology curves. In addition to determining each technology's life span, identify the rela-

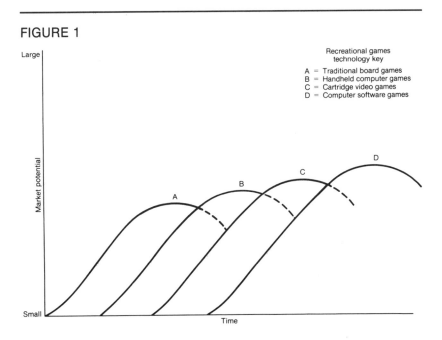

FIGURE 1

tionship between each technology curve as well as how they are linked in time. Developing these technology forecasts requires that you understand the factors behind the growth and decline of each technology curve, including market requirements, distribution, and regulatory and economic factors. In conjunction with this, develop profiles of the technologies identifying their strengths and weaknesses in order to determine the environments, applications, and markets in which each can flourish.

In this fashion, it will be possible to "position" individual markets or segments on each technology curve in order to decide which markets are good short-term candidates for products based on the technology, which are potential targets at a later time, and which will never be penetrated. It will reveal when technology skills should be imported and when your firm's existing product-technology base will be adequate.

Where do you get the data to enable you to develop these technology forecasts and profiles? Much of it involves solid market and product research using traditional data collection techniques. Quantitative and qualitative surveys, discussions with users, suppliers, and distributors, and secondary research are all required.

3. Profile Market Requirements Relative to Technology Profiles

After the development of the technology forecast and comparison profiles identifying the specific strengths and weaknesses of products based on competitive technologies, markets and operating and application environments where the various technologies may be successfully applied should be identified. These profiles will define the requirements of the environments in which products based on existing or competitive technologies may seek market opportunities. To do this, the following questions must be answered:

Who are the potential users?

What major business functions and applications are presently being performed and how can they be expected to change?

How are they currently accomplishing these business functions and applications?

What are each segment's priorities in terms of improved functions and increased productivity?

How can products based on alternative technologies accomplish similar or improved business functions and applications?

How acceptable are the various product technologies as replacements for existing materials?

What are the market requirements for these products, including function, application, price sensitivity, distribution, training, ease of use, quality, and shelf life? How well do alternate product technologies meet each of these requirements?

What is the perceived market advantage of these product technologies?

What considerations are important in terms of integrating products with systems already in use by customers?

In this fashion, emerging opportunities may be identified both within and outside your traditional markets and for products based on your existing technology base or on competitive product technologies as you determine each technology's potential in various markets.

An analysis similar to that illustrated in Figure 2 can be used to identify the relative advantages and disadvantages of products based on competitive technologies in terms of various marketing parameters ranging from price to distribution costs to storage and inventory. Note that products based

---

FIGURE 2:   Product Technology Comparison

Requirement	Technology 1	Technology 2	Technology 3
Physical characteristics Price Distribution Inventory Training Shelf life Ease of use Quality			

on various technologies differ in terms of nontechnological performance characteristics too. For example, it is certainly easier to ship inflatable rubber life rafts than metal ones. This analysis should be completed for each market of interest. Naturally, the importance of the various factors will vary from market to market.

This profile task offers several distinct benefits. First, it ensures that your new thrusts rely on the advantages of your technology. Second, it permits you to seek growth areas based on the weaknesses of competitive technologies. Third, it offers an opportunity to seek markets outside your traditional industry. Fourth, it tells you when products based on your existing technologies may be vulnerable to products based on emerging technologies.

4. Match Product Technologies to Individual Markets

Identify segments using well-entrenched, competitive technology and processes because these segments represent poor growth targets based on your existing technology. Identify segments where installed products and applications technology are waning because these segments present future growth opportunities for alternate technology. This technology positioning will be based on a variety of criteria ranging from each segment's technological orientation, productivity improvement requirements, applications, and other criteria outlined in the prior step. Naturally, you will want to include your traditional markets of participation in this analysis.

5. Examine Strategic Technology Options

After positioning technologies, markets, and products relative to one another and identifying your own product, use the technology management matrix to select the appropriate new product or service strategic options depending on the company's technology position. This must be done for each market and product area individually.

FIGURE 3

Product Position	Technology Position		
	Same Technology	Different Technology	
		Older Technology	Newer Technology
Behind competitors	Take traditional strategic actions Assess marketing strategy and target markets Enhance product features Improve operational efficiency	Evaluate viability of your technology Implement newer technology Divest products based on older technology	Evaluate availability of resources to sustain technology development and full market acceptance Continue to define new applications and product enhancements Scale back operations
Ahead of competitors	Define new applications for the technology and enhance products accordingly	Take advantage of all possible profit	Define new applications for the technology and enhance products accordingly

As illustrated in Figure 3, different strategic actions are available depending on whether your firm's products are based on similar or different technologies vis-à-vis competitors and whether your position is based on the older or the newer technology. Note that a broader array of options are available to firms whose technology base is stronger than competitors'.

Although the relationship between competitive technologies largely determines market opportunities, actions can be taken to prolong the competitiveness of older technologies given that the phasing of the two curves is not drastically different. However, little can be done to make a severely declining technology competitive with a rapidly emerging technology. Our experience with clients over the past several years shows that the range of options available to management decreases as the distance between technology curves increases. If your product's technology is significantly behind that of competitors, you should either make the technological leap to the competitive process, abandon the market altogether, or, as a short-term strategy, identify and pursue those segments that are laggards in terms of adopting new technologies.

On the other hand, if your technology is significantly superior to competitors', different strategies are required as you seek to identify and convert the "cream" customers, particularly market innovators who are imitated by more conservative market segments. Often, the broadest range of options are available to companies whose products are based on emerging technologies. However, even this position has its special problems.

WHAT CAN STRATEGIC TECHNOLOGY MANAGEMENT PROVIDE?

This type of technology management approach to new product development offers several major benefits. First, it alerts you to threats from both traditional and emerging competition and helps you recognize the full spectrum of competition from within and outside your industry. Second, it helps to identify the company's technological assets in terms of whether they are emerging, mature, or declining, while determining the extent to which these technology assets presently meet market requirements and their prospects for the future.

Third, technology management matches these assets to specific market opportunities and identifies new products and services based on these technologies, including product opportunities that lie outside traditional areas. Fourth, it permits you to pinpoint missing technological assets and resources and identifies corrective actions required to ensure continued success. Also, it allows you to define the range of strategic options available and identifies appropriate strategic actions relative to current and intended market position. Finally, it provides a focus to coordinate dispersed traditional business planning activities and permits the company to identify and develop a market technology image, particularly in relation to competitors.

HOW SHOULD YOU ORGANIZE FOR TECHNOLOGY MANAGEMENT?

First, it is easiest to define how you should *not* organize for technology management. It should not be left in the hands of research and development. Nor should it be the job of marketing alone. Input is required from marketing, sales and research, *and* development. Most of all, careful listening to the marketplace, including customers, distributors, and suppliers, is required. Second, product technology management should become part of the continual product and strategic planning process. Many companies who were technology innovators have lost their technological advantage.

Technology management is a complex and sometimes artful process. Sensitivity to it will enhance your new product development efforts and reveal opportunities for existing products.

Part
III

Research and Evaluation Considerations

9

Screening New Products

Eugene J. Cafarelli
Center for Concept Development

The purpose of this chapter is to discuss ways that concepts can be evaluated as to their appropriateness or "fit" with the firm.

There are a number of assumptions and issues that it would be best to state early on so that the reader can put what is written in the proper perspective. Briefly they are:

1. For a concept to make it into serious development, it must undergo a *strategic screen*, a *business suitability screen*, and a *customer or consumer interest screen*. Only concepts that qualify for all three should merit the allocation of the firm's resources. This chapter will concern itself only with the first two. Other chapters address the latter

111

issue, but I want to emphasize that obtaining an estimate of the (sales) volume potential of a concept (which is one of the goals of concept research) is extremely important from a "concept screen" point of view also because it is not uncommon for concepts that look like good businesses at the screening stage to have insufficient customer interest to make the volume worthwhile. *Our screening in this chapter will allow for estimates for volume potential. This works fine as long as some harder numbers are substituted at a later phase* so that the screening can become more refined at that point.

2. This chapter is concerned with screening concepts. Actually, to be more precise, it is better to think of this as screening potential business propositions or business alternatives for the firm. Therefore, it doesn't really matter whether you are working with a concept-driven system (such as a toiletries marketer might normally use) or a technology-driven system (as, for example, a medical diagnostic instrumentation marketer might utilize). In reality, in all cases, you are dealing with a business proposition, and you merely need to convert the new piece of technology or invention into a concept or statement that illustrates the type of business or businesses it is capable of supporting. Then, no matter which way you approach this, you wind up in the same position—with a number of concepts that are to be screened.

3. I have also assumed that you will be screening a relatively large number of concepts.

Note that screening systems work best when you are looking for alternatives—hopefully a number of them. The "numbers" turned out by any system are useful only in their *relativeness* to other alternatives and to the normative data of past history.

There is a kind of "law of large numbers" in concept work that suggests, quite logically, that the more concepts you look at the more likely you are to wind up with one or two good business propositions. The whole idea of a concept screening system is to allow you to do that in an efficient manner.

THE NEW PRODUCTS CHARTER/GUIDELINES— THE "STRATEGIC SCREEN"

The first step in a concept screening is to make sure that it meets the *strategic objectives* of the firm.

As noted previously, the strategic plan is interpolated, for the sake of guiding new product development in the correct strategic direction, in a new products charter or set of guidelines. Generally, charters and guidelines contain very similar information—some corporations prefer the paragraph style of the charter, others prefer the point-by-point exposition of the guidelines. The author prefers the latter style for its clarity of communication and will use it for the remainder of this chapter. However, if the reader is active in a corporation preferring the former style, this same data can easily be placed in a series of paragraphs.

In thinking about guidelines, there is always the issue of degree of specificity . . . degree of definition of parameters. Many corporations prefer a looser or broader set of guidelines. The argument here is that new product development is basically an entrepreneural activity. Loosely defined parameters give the new product development function more operating room, more areas in which to start. The argument goes on that it's always easiest to identify inadequate opportunities later and that this approach casts the widest possible net for business opportunities.

Despite this persuasive argument, the author prefers a more tightly defined set of guidelines. It has been his experience that, too often, projects that appear to meet the guidelines do not fall within management's perception of the company's goals. However, by the time this is discovered and discussed, considerable time, effort, and resources may have been placed into evaluating and developing the proposition. It is felt that since new product development is in the process of allocating scarce resources, it is better to do so against those opportunities that have the best chance of management approval. This goal is assisted by tighter, more well defined guidelines.

Preparation of the Set of Guidelines

Guidelines should contain all the parameters within which the corporation will feel comfortable with its new product opportunity. In the main, these define the "business" that the company is really in by indicating the key aspects of that business. Generally, guidelines should cover the following five areas:

1. R&D constraints.
2. Manufacturing constraints.
3. Product policy constraints.
4. Marketing and sales constraints.
5. Financial constraints.

The following document is a sample New Product Guidelines statement that is typical of that of a middle-sized firm. Of course, this is a sample only, and you should expect that yours might differ dramatically depending on your type of industry and stage of its growth.

The XYZ Company: New Product Guidelines

The following outline serves as a guideline for developing new products within the XYZ Company.

Financial
1. Product contributes a minimum 5 percent after-tax profit after a maximum 36-month payout.
2. Minimum volume potential: $5–$15 million.
3. Requires low capital investment/start-up costs.

Manufacturing
1. Eventual use of existing manufacturing facilities.
2. Requires no complicated new technology.
3. Broad-based raw material source. Ingredients and packaging elements are relatively cost stable and readily available.

Product
1. An anticipated long life cycle. No fad characteristics. No pronounced seasonality.
2. Has unique characteristics.
3. A high-quality product and image.
4. A branded food product, utilizing one of our brands or a brand name that we can acquire.

5. Not heavily regulated by consumer/government groups.
6. Employs established corporate brand names where feasible.

Sales/Distribution
1. National distribution potential.
2. Uses current distribution network/sales coverage.
3. Offers above-average margin to the trade.
4. No extensive sales servicing required.
5. Primary benefit easily communicated.
6. One unique advertisable element.
7. Category not dominated by major manufacturers.
8. Minimal likelihood of immediate competitive response by major manufacturer.
9. Potential for line extensions/flanker products.
10. Institutional sales potential.

LOOKING AT CONCEPTS AS POTENTIAL BUSINESS PROPOSITIONS—THE "BUSINESS SCREEN"

Once the concepts have passed the strategic screening, you now face the decision of selecting those few that you are going to investigate more carefully. This further investigation might involve consumer research, some R&D to develop prototypes, or whatever. But before you reach this point, what you need is an accepted procedure for evaluating the potential worth of the new product ideas while they are still in the concept stage. Such a procedure should provide as objective an analysis as possible for the proposed new product and should direct itself to all of the key variables that comprise the marketing of a product: the potential volume and profit, an analysis of competition and the marketplace, the expected cost of entry, the cost and involvement of production, and the fit of the product into your company's way of operating. This procedure should result in the concepts being sorted into groups with specific characteristics—such as development time and cost, ROI, and the like.

This requires a procedure that combines hard data (such as market size) with a number of subjective determinations (such as market vulnerability). This procedure cannot be avoided if you are to fully evaluate the opportunity (indeed, the combination of hard data with subjective judgments is

the basis for Baysian statistics). The key point, however, is
to make these subjective determinations explicit and to
quantify them so that they do not assume a disproportion-
ately important role in evaluating new product ideas.

Once you have developed this procedure (it is important
that it be agreed to by the entire firm so that the results are
accepted by all departments), it is possible to assign priorities to products and even discard those with unacceptable
prospects. If it is properly handled, you will always have a
bank of ideas that you can plug into your development system as opportunities arise.

The following New Product Concept Evaluation System
was developed for use by a package food products firm. It
is not appropriate for all industries but can serve as a model
for the development of one appropriate to your firm. You'll
note that points are assigned to reflect the company's atti-
tude toward each factor, so that some factors are worth a
maximum of +5, others less; conversely, some can only
contribute negative points (−5). In any event, these points
are eventually added for each concept so that one summary
number can provide the basis for assigning priorities among
concepts.

New Product Concept Evaluation System

1. Market Factors

(This section includes: the size of market, growth trend of market, a
determination of competitive strength and vulnerability, and an evaluation of the strength of the proposed new product concept.)

a. Size of Market

Translated to manufacturing dollars, the size of the market under
consideration is rated positively—relative to its increasing size:

	Criterion Value
Market size over $150 million	+4
Market size $50–$150 million	+3
Market size $25–$50 million	+2
Market size less than $25 million	0

b. Trend of Market

The marketing assumption on trend is that business is more easily
gained by a product if a market is growing than if a market is
static or contracting:

	Criterion Value
Excellent annual growth rate (10% or over)	+4
Good growth rate (5–9%)	+3
Growth rate about equal to population (2–4%)	+2
Static market (growth over past 2 years)	0
Severely declining market (−10% or more annually)	−1

c. Brand Potential

The potential of a particular product is determined basically by two factors: the strength or vulnerability of the anticipated competition and the soundness/strength of the new product concept.

(1) Market Vulnerability

Although often subjective in nature, an attempt must be made to evaluate the proposed market and the anticipated competition. Specific criteria, such as very heavy advertising and promotion expenditures for brands in the category, long-term domination, recent failures by other companies attempting to enter the market, all provide background for determining vulnerability. The assignment of points in this section will nearly always be the result of consolidation of various judgments:

	Criterion Value
Competition/market appears very vulnerable based on evaluation of existing product performances, product positionings, or advertising/promotion support levels.	+5
Mixed consensus by Marketing as to entrenchment of anticipated competitive products. (This "no-man's land" will be scaled anywhere from +3 to −3 based on combined judgment.)	+3 to −3
General agreement that competition is heavily entrenched and/or has been unmoved by recent attacks by other companies.	−5

(2) Strength of Product Concept

The strength of the proposed product concept is probably the most judgmental in nature of all the proposed criteria. Because it is at least equal in importance to any other single element in marketing a new product, every attempt should be made to judgmentally rate this quality as high as practical, giving the concept the benefit of any doubt or disagreement:

	Criterion Value
General agreement that proposed product is a strong product concept.	+5
General agreement that it is a good concept.	+3 or +4
Mixed agreement that it is a good concept.	0
Concept represents no unique advantage in the proposed category.	−5

2. Product Formulation/Performance

The proposed product, as conceived, should be evaluated as well as possible versus existing products performing the same primary consumer function. This criterion will be reevaluated after the product is actually formulated and, of course, again after it is consumer-tested.

Criterion Value

Proposed formulation versus existing products:

Product represents a true breakthrough in technology and/or consumer benefits	+5
Product is somewhat above parity	+2
Product at parity with products already on the market	0
Below parity product	−1

3. Cost of Goods

Initially, cost of goods percent should be projected on the assumption that retail and trade pricing will be directly competitive, unless purposely designed to be higher or lower as an integral part of the brand's strategy. The cost of goods percentage dictates the eventual potential income that can be made available for profit and/or advertising and promotion support. A high cost of goods percentage puts a product at a definite disadvantage in the marketplace and, if such exists, should dictate an automatic reevaluation of the proposed retail pricing structure.

Based on approximately competitive retail-pricing, cost of goods percentages should be weighed accordingly:*

Cost of Goods	Generic Food Categories	Special Foods Categories
Under 15%	—	+5
15–20%	+5	+3
21–25%	+3	0
26–30%	+1	−1
31–35%	0	−3
36–45%	−3	−5
46% or over	−5	—

4. Company Distribution/Marketing Ability

This criterion should be an objective evaluation of whether or not the proposed product fits within the company's current or planned sales abilities and distribution patterns or whether extensive restructuring would be needed. Rating depends on combined judgment, scaled from +5 to −5.

5. Profitability/Marketing Investment/Volume

It is an important, practical consideration not to project a product's volume and profitability further into the future than marketing awareness will normally permit. On this basis, a proposed product should be

---

* Calculated as a percent of *gross* sales (before selling expenses, etc.).

evaluated in terms of profitability, marketing investment, and volume on a short-term projection of the first 12 months in national introduction (the third year of a package goods brand in today's changing marketplace should represent a mature level of sales and profits).

a. Profitability/Marketing Investment

The same relative scale is applicable when projecting profitability (gross profit) and marketing investment (advertising, promotion, and market research):

	Marketing Investment (per each $1 million net invest. in marketing exp.)	Break-Even (marketing investment = profit)	Gross Profit Pretax (per each $1 million gross variable margin after direct expenses)
1. Short-term (first 12 months)	−1 additional	+2	+1 (additional to +2 for breaking even)
2. Long-term (year 3 national)	−5 additional	0	+2 additional

b. *Volume*   *Criterion Value*

Aside from basic minimum volume requirements which may arbitrarily be set on new products by the company, there should be an independent projection of the proposed dollar and share of market objective based on known established trade policies on accepting new products. In the case of the food store trade, the ground rule for maintaining shelf position for a generic-category food product is a turn rate (velocity) of approximately one case (dozen) per month per major store.

Any projected new product sales rate, which, when divided by the correct number of anticipated outlets, results in a velocity of less than this minimum should be penalized in this evaluation.†   −5

Using the Accumulated Criteria Points to Develop Standards

Based on the accumulation of the preceding criteria value points, approximate standards can be established for use in determining priority for a proposed product:

---

† If above average turn carries special benefits (to the marketer) with it, plus points can be assigned to this area also; generally this is not the case.

	Top Priority Product Range	Average to Good Product Range (Average—+9 to +15; Good—+16 to +23)	Low Priority Product Range
Preprofitability section points‡	+24 to +33	+9 to +23	+8 to −17
Total points	+26 or better	Average—+11 to +17D Good—+18 to +25 +11 to +25	+10 to −17

‡ In cases where sales volume estimates are particularly arbitrary (e.g., where you are dealing with positioning concepts) or where they are difficult to estimate, you can utilize preprofitability scores for setting priorities; later, when you have potential volumes, you can finish this evaluation.

Source: This system is excerpted from a book I prepared for John Wiley & Sons and is excerpted with their permission. Eugene J. Cafarelli, *Developing New Products and Repositioning Mature Brands* (New York: John Wiley & Sons, 1980).

SETTING PRIORITIES

This process, in effect, goes a long way toward the establishment of priorities. Those products with high potential scores (or potentially good investments) usually become high priority and so on.

The additional factors to add into the establishment of priorities are, of course, (a) development and proposed marketing timing and (b) potential development investment.

All new products with high priority obviously cannot go into test, or expand nationally, simultaneously. Also, heavy R&D costs must be programmed to meet the resources of the firm. Timing, therefore, should be factored with potential.

The result should be this kind of priority ranking.

Action Categories

Group A-I. Products assigned to this priority group represent the highest possible marketing interest. There is immediate activity necessary on all areas on behalf of these products. These products can also be developed within normal product development lead time. Products in this group should be reported on at least every two weeks.

Group A-II. Products in this group also represent highest marketing interest but are anticipated to require longer development times due to areas of unknown information, manufacturing complexities, and so forth.

Group B-I. Products in this group represent high potential but also represent eventual high investment. These projects will be pursued on a regular basis but not with immediate urgency (the intent is to reduce the level of risk by further development so that the probability of success warrants the large investment).

Group B-II. This priority grouping includes products that are not of high priority but that merit being carried in the program because of possible eventual marketing.

Group S. All products dropped or suspended at any stage of development will be kept in this grouping for the record.

Of course, the number of concepts that you pursue depends on how ambitious your program is, the resources of your firm, and the like. However, once you have categorized your concepts, you should be able to move to the next step with some assurance.

An operational hint: when you are dealing with a large bank of concepts, it is sometimes easier to stop the evaluation of each concept at the preprofitability level. This allows you to speed up the evaluation process and usually does not represent a large risk since, more often than not, you are dealing with concepts that fall in the same or similar product categories.

However, the profitability section should not be dropped when you are dealing with a bank of concepts that exhibit strong differences. Invariably you will find:

> different investment levels
> different payback potentials
> different sales volume estimates

In this case, the profitability section becomes important in the evaluation process and cannot be avoided.

Regardless of your decisions, after your concept refinement research, you will be able to produce a sales potential estimate. At this point, you need to reevaluate those concepts still under consideration. *This will be your final priority setting before submitting concepts to the R&D process and the advertising development process.*

It is often useful, when trying to understand the system, to see an example. The following case utilizes this system (I have made it a food company since we used that industry in showing how the values of the system can be set).

The case involves the Middle South Milling Company, which started an ambitious program of new product development. They had a "portfolio" of 82 concepts. The questions facing the new product development manager were those addressed in this chapter:

Which of these concepts make the best business sense for Middle South Milling?

Which concepts merit further expenditures in consumer research and product development?

CASE: THE MIDDLE SOUTH MILLING COMPANY

All 82 concepts could be divided into four groups on the basis of the product category they fell into: cookies, powdered beverages, cereals, and snacks. Taking one from each:

1. **Cheesecake Puffs.** This is a puffed cookie. The shape is like a small cream puff. The crust tastes like graham crackers. The filling is creamy and tastes like cheesecake. These could come in several flavors: creamy cheesecake, cherry cheesecake, and so forth.

2. **Profruit.** This is a powdered beverage. It is made of natural fruit crystals, fructose, and powdered protein. It can be mixed with milk or water. It comes in three flavors: orange, grape, and cherry.

3. **Puffed Granola Cereal.** This would be a granola-like cereal that would be "puffed" much like some wheat or

rice cereals currently on the market. It would be positioned as a "natural" cereal (sweetened with honey and molasses). It could be marketed as a single-flavor brand, or it might come in a variety of flavors (e.g., cinnamon, vanilla and almonds, etc.).

4. **Puffed 'n Stuffed Snacks.** These would be similar (in shape) to the Cheesecake Puffs just described, but the crusts would have the taste of snacks like corn chips, potato chips, and the like, and the creamy insides would taste like dips (e.g., sour cream and onion). They could be packaged in a variety pack or as a line of products.

Let's make a preliminary business judgment on these ideas by putting them through our evaluation system.

Cheesecake Puffs

Market Factors
Size of Market
Market over $150 million . . . . +4
Trend of Market
The previous year had a 16% growth . . . . +4
Brand Potential
(1) Market Vulnerability
General agreement that market is enterable by new brands/
flavor . . . . +2
(2) Strength of Product Concept
General agreement that this is a good concept . . . . . . +3

Product Formulation/Performance
Agreement that, with our technical/manufacturing facilities, we
could produce a product that is somewhat above parity . . . . +2

Cost of Goods
With the decisions that (a) we want to be in the regular cookie
section (not the specialty food section) and (b) we want to be
competitively priced, it was estimated that our cost of goods
would be 25% . . . . +3

Company Distribution/Marketing Ability
The company has a system of good food brokers, 20% of whom
already have a cookie client, and thus we would have to add
some brokers if we marketed a line of cookies—therefore, our
distribution system is not perfect for this proposed product (but
the correction does not constitute an insurmountable problem) . . +2

Profitability/Investment/Volume

According to our best guesstimates, we will break even at the end
of year 1 (national) (+2) and will be generating a $2 million gross
profit by the end of year 3 (+4) . . . .   +6
Volume—sales estimate indicates no velocity problem . . . . . .   +0

Total Points—Cheesecake Puffs . . . .   +26

Profruit Powdered Fruit and Protein Drinks

Market Factors

Size of Market
    Market over $150 million . . . .   +4
Trend of Market
    The growth is established to average 15% a year . . . .   +4
Brand Potential
    (1) Market Vulnerability
         Agreement that segments of market can be entered al-
         though market is competitive . . . .   +2
    (2) Strength of Product Concept
         General agreement that this is an extremely strong concept   +5

Product Formulation/Performance

Product represents a true breakthrough in technology and/or consumer benefits . . . .   +5

Cost of Goods

The product will be premium priced.
The cost of goods should be 20% . . . .   +3

Company Distribution/Marketing Ability

The channels would be the same as our regular products, although this is a new section of the store and this might present us
with a few initial problems. . . . .   +4

Profitability/Investment/Volume

Break-even should be reached by the end of year 2. By the end of
year 3, we anticipate that we will be generating $3.5 million in
increased profits . . . .   +7
Volume—sales estimate indicates no velocity problem . . . . . .   +0

Total Points—Profruit Powdered Drinks . . . .   +34

Puffed Granola Cereal

Market Factors

Size of Market
    Market over $150 million . . . .   +4
Trend of Market
    The growth rate of the most recent year was 11% . . . .   +4

Brand Potential
(1) Market Vulnerability
General agreement that the cereal market can be entered
by a new brand . . . .   +3
(2) Strength of Product Concept
General agreement that product concept is strong because
(*a*) granola cereals have experienced an above-average
(for the cereal category) growth, and (*b*) puffed cereals
have been established sellers for some time . . . .   +5

Product Formulation/Performance
Agreement that we can produce a product that is above parity—
but which would not represent a true breakthrough. . . . .   +2

Cost of Goods
The cost of goods is estimated at 18–20% . . . .   +3

Company Distribution/Marketing Ability
Since our firm already markets a cereal product, we would not
anticipate any problems in introducing a new one . . . .   +5

Profitability/Investment/Volume
We estimate that we will not break even until year 2 and will be
generating a $2 million gross profit at the end of year . . . . . .   +4
Volume—estimate indicates no velocity problem. . . . .   +0

Total Points—Puffed Granola Cereal . . . .   +30

Puffed 'n Stuffed Snacks

Market Factors
Size of Market
Market over $150 million . . . .   +4
Trend of Market
Sales growth was 3% . . . .   +2
Brand Potential
(1) Market Vulnerability
General agreement that the market is somewhat vulnerable
to new entries . . . .   +3
(2) Strength of Product Concept
General agreement that this is a fairly strong product con-
cept. . . . .   +4

Product Formulation/Performance
Product represented a true breakthrough in consumer benefits . .   +2

Cost of Goods
The decision was reaffirmed that we do not want to be in the specialty food category. This means that we must be priced near the
market, which leads us to a relatively high cost of goods (30–
35%) . . . .   +3

Company Distribution/Marketing Ability
Snack foods get to retailers (e.g., supermarkets) one of two ways: (a) through local trucks whose driver then stocks the shelf and (b) through the standard channel (manufacturer to warehouse to retailer). We would be forced to use the second channel, which is less desirable; therefore, we would rate ourselves as having only average abilities in this area . . . .   +2

Profitability/Investment/Volume
A preliminary estimate indicates that we will be "out" $1 million at the end of year 1 (−1) and, at the end of year 3, will be generating $3 million in gross profit (+6) . . . .   +5
Volume—estimate indicates no velocity problem . . . .   +0

Total Points—Puffed 'n Stuffed Snacks . . . .   +25

An Expanded Factor List

The author realizes that for many firms the foregoing system will not be correct. The firm may desire the evaluation of more factors. Certainly, depending on the industry, different factors will come into prominence. The following is an expanded factor list that should meet your needs. Conceptually, it is not much different than what we've just done but will allow you to construct a system to suit your particular situation. All you need to do is assign a rating scale (such as the following) and you can begin:

```
      0 ←————————————————————→ 10
      Low         Average        High
```

I. Concept/Product
    A. Performance. How well does it work?
        1. Effectiveness. Does it do its intended job well?
        2. Reliability. Does it perform consistently, dependably, and safely?
        3. Simplicity. How efficient and uncomplicated is it?
        4. Convenience. Physically, how easy is it to install, use, store, and/or repair?

    B. Salability. How well will it sell?
        1. Appearance. Is it physically and/or functionally attractive?
        2. Uniqueness. Does it have important exclusive features and talking points capable of supporting strong promotion?
        3. Economy. How does its cost (to buy, install, operate, maintain, etc.) compare with its competition?
        4. Timeliness. Is this an opportune time for it?
        5. Understandability. Can its functions and merits be easily and quickly understood by potential users?
        6. Tradability. How well adapted to the proposed trade is it?
        7. Buyability. To what extent does the buyer feel a conscious need for it at the point of sale?

C. Defensibility. To what extent can the company maintain its exclusivity and defend it against direct competition?
   1. Legal. How firmly are its important features protected by patents, copyrights, trademarks, licenses, titles, franchises, or other legal means?
   2. Newness. Does it have much of a jump on competition from the standpoint of development time?
   3. Proprietary. Does it enjoy special advantages, such as captive supplies, captive sales, process secrets, brand preference, or a strong line of companion items?

II. Company Factors
   A. Marketing. Does the company have what it takes to market this item effectively?
      1. Experience. How well does the company know the market and understand how to reach, sell, and service it?
      2. Support Services. How does the company compare with average competition in order handling, warehousing, delivery time, freight expense, complaint adjustments, sales analysis, and so forth?
      3. Technical Service. How does the company compare with average competition in terms of technical sales support?
      4. Market Coverage. How completely does the company presently cover the market?
      5. Entrenchment. How strong is the company's present trade and customer loyalty in this field?
      6. Dependency. To what extent does the company's applicable marketing strength depend on just a few individuals or accounts.
      7. Volume. What was the company's volume in associated items last year, related to total sales?
      8. Penetration. What is the company's approximate share of the total market for associated items?
      9. Management. Is the company well situated for this item in terms of sales management?
   B. Technology. To what extent does the company have the technical know-how required for success here?
      1. Design. How does the company's design competence compare with competition?
      2. Engineering. How does the company compare with competition in terms of engineering and problem-solving capabilities?
      3. Materials. How well does the company know the materials involved in this item?
      4. Techniques. How competitive is the company in terms of fabrication methods, systems, and process techniques?
   C. Production. Can the company produce the item competitively?
      1. Labor. How does the company's present labor situation compare with competition?

2. Facilities. How does the company compare with competition in terms of plant efficiency, equipment, automation, flexibility, and so forth?
3. Purchasing. How does the company compare with competition in terms of accessibility and prices of raw materials, supplies, and services required?
4. Dependency. To what extent is the company's production capability dependent on just a few individuals?
5. Capacity. Does the company presently have the capacity to produce this item?
6. Location. How competitively located is the company?
7. Management. Is the company's production management well suited to handling this item?

III. Environment Factors

A. Market. Is there a strong market for this item?
   1. Potential Volume. How large was last year's national market for similar items that are realistically displaceable by this item?
   2. Proportion. How large is the anticipated market volume in proportion to the company's current total sales volume?
   3. Fertility. What share of this market volume would the proposed item displace at a saturation level of marketing effort (not limited by cost) in all areas?
   4. Growth. How much is the market expanding each year?
   5. Stability. How constant is the demand?
   6. Outlook. How great and enduring is the future demand for such items?

B. Competition. What kind of competition dominates this market?
   1. Size. How large is the typical competitor compared with the company?
   2. Specialization. To what extent are other firms specializing in this item to the exclusion of companion items?
   3. Entrenchment. How deeply entrenched in the trade are the competitors?
   4. Pricing. How favorable is the traditional price behavior in this market?
   5. Entry Reaction. What kind of competitive counteraction will your entry into this field probably cause?

C. Suppliers. Is the industry well situated for supplies and services?
   1. Materials. Are the required supplies and components readily and consistently available in the desired qualities and quantities at reasonable prices?
   2. Equipment. Is the required equipment always readily available?
   3. Services. How well supported is the industry in terms of available services—information, transportation, printing, equipment, repair, finishing, and so forth?
   4. Dependency. To what extent are the industry's costs and op-

erations dependent on uncontrollable supply and/or service factors?

D. Government. How might government be expected to affect this venture?
1. Regulations. How burdensome are government controls or rulings likely to be?
2. Taxes. To what extent will special tax considerations affect this venture?
3. Programs. To what extent will current or imminent government programs directly or indirectly affect the venture?
4. Politics. How is the political situation expected to influence this venture.

IV. Venture Factors
A. Support. How strongly supported is the venture?
1. Chief Executive. To what extent does the chief executive sponsor the proposal?
2. Management Group. Does the operating management group support the proposal?
3. Trade. To what extent do the company's key agents, distributors, and dealers support the proposal?
4. Customers. To what extent do customers (or key prospects) endorse the venture?

B. Investment. Is this a good investment?
1. Size. What is the total venture cost as a percentage of net worth?
2. Commitment. What percentage of the total venture cost is already committed?
3. Maturity rate. How long will it take for sales volume to reach substantially full development?
4. Risk. How would the investment risk be classified?
5. Return. What is the estimated annual rate of return (on a present value or discounted cash flow basis)?
6. Salvageable. If the venture should fail, what portion of the total investment could be salvaged or converted to cash?

C. Strategy. How well does the proposed venture serve the company's overall interests?
1. Consistency. To what extent is the venture consistent or compatible with the company's goals, policies, obligations, and image?
2. Appropriateness. How appropriate is this venture as a company undertaking?
3. Improvement. To what extent will this venture improve the company and strengthen its overall position?
4. Preemption. To what extent would pursuit of this venture preempt other promising opportunities open to the company?
5. Necessity. To what extent is this venture really necessary for the company?

6. Intuition. Intuitively, how do you feel about the overall chances of success in this venture?

(If you were to use all these factors, you might want to prepare a New Product Evaluation Form like the one that follows.)

Note: For a good discussion on the development of these factors and the use of such a system, see W. R. Park and J. B. Maillie, *Strategic Analysis for Venture Evaluation: The Save Approach to Business Decisions,* (New York: Van Nostrand Reinhold, 1982).

New Product Evaluation Form

Factor				*Factor Group*	*Major Aspect*
Effectiveness					
Reliability					
Simplicity				Performance	
Convenience					
Appearance					
Uniqueness					
Economy					
Timeliness					
Understandability				Salability	Item
Tradability					
Buyability					
Legal					
Newness					
Proprietary				Defensibility	
Experience					
Support Services					
Technical Service					
Market Coverage					
Entrenchment					
Dependency				Marketing	
Volume					
Penetration					
Management					
Design					
Engineering					
Materials					
Techniques				Technology	Company
Labor					
Facilities					
Purchasing					
Dependency					
Capacity				Production	
Location					
Management					

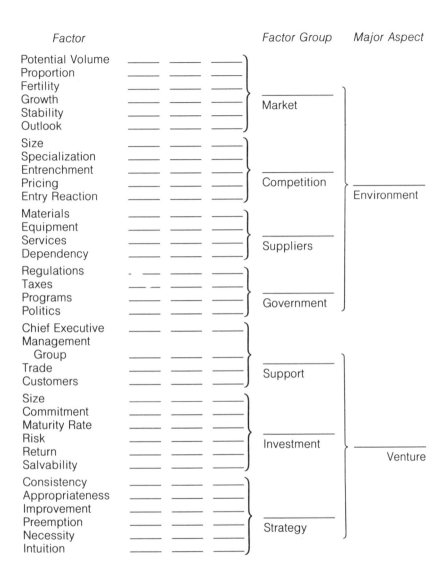

Factor	Factor Group	Major Aspect

Potential Volume
Proportion
Fertility
Growth — Market
Stability
Outlook

Size
Specialization
Entrenchment
Pricing — Competition
Entry Reaction

Environment

Materials
Equipment
Services
Dependency — Suppliers

Regulations
Taxes
Programs
Politics — Government

Chief Executive
Management
  Group
Trade
Customers — Support

Size
Commitment
Maturity Rate
Risk
Return — Investment
Salvability

Venture

Consistency
Appropriateness
Improvement
Preemption
Necessity
Intuition — Strategy

ADJUSTING THE SYSTEM FOR YOUR COMPANY

It is possible to handle all your factors (69 if you use this whole list) by weighting them equally. However, it is generally better to adjust the system to reflect the strategic assets of your corporation. This helps concepts that lean on the company's strengths. There are books written on this topic alone, but there are seven asset areas that you should consider.

Asset	Issues
Financial	*Financial resources of the company.* Does the company have sufficient funds to invest heavily and wait for a return, or is the company thinly financed thus requiring a quick return of its investment?
Marketing	*Degree and extent of marketing expertise.* Does the firm have a marketing orientation, or is marketing seen more as a selling function and somewhat less than a very important function?
Management	*Abilities and depth of management skills.* Is management aggressive and well established, or is management in a state of transition?
Manufacturing	*Type and competitive efficiency of manufacturing assets.* Is the firm manufacturing oriented and among the low-cost operators in the industry, or is the plant dated and a relatively high-cost facility?
Raw Materials	*Availability of necessary materials.* Is your company generally facile at obtaining new types of materials, or is purchasing oriented towards current businesses?
Organization	*Type and depth of administrative support system.* Does the firm have the internal support systems to make this venture successful, or, through rigidity or lack of departments/systems, are new ventures hampered?
R&D	*Skill and creativity in research and development.* Is the corporate culture conducive to successful R&D? Has the firm or personnel separately been successful at innovation, or is the firm more of a follower?

Once you have decided what the special strength or strengths of your company are, it is best to weight those factors more heavily. From my experience, a maximum multiplier of 3 should be used (and this only in the most extreme cases). Normally, a 1½- or 2-time multiplier will give sufficient weight to your company's special strength. (In other words, you *multiply the numerical value given to the factor by the multiplier value* in totaling up the points merited by the concept.) By weighting these areas of strength, you really are allowing those concepts or business propositions that rely heavily on your company's strengths to gain extra value in the evaluation. Discussing your company with your

colleagues should result in agreement as to the areas of special strength. Very often a company's areas of strength are
related to its growth cycle and the growth cycle of the industry. These can be different (for example, an embryonic
company in a mature industry) but are very often the same.
In any case, recognition of this area can assist you. As a rule
of thumb, the relationship between stage of life cycle and
areas of strength can be found in the following chart:

Stage	Assets Most Likely to Be Dominant
Embryonic	Management R&D
Early Growth	Finance Management Marketing
Early Maturity	Marketing Manufacturing, Raw Materials
Late Maturity	Manufacturing, Finance, Organization

THE USE OF THE DELPHI METHOD TO IMPROVE YOUR ANALYSES

Most likely in your screening process, you will not be working alone. It is always advisable to do this as part of a small
group of people who will be involved later in the implementation of the outcome. This allows not only for more
precise input in the screening process, but also helps other
members of the firm to feel part of the process. Traditionally, each member of the team rates the concepts, and the
leader then presents the group with the (average ratings)
results. (It is far superior, from a time efficiency standpoint,
to have the members rate the concepts individually than to
attempt to work as a group on each concept.) But modification of this process may offer some benefits.

Some years ago, the method of evaluating the outcome of
future events (in this case, business propositions) called the
Delphi Method was developed. Basically, the Delphi
method is based on several assumptions:

1. The people performing the evaluation are relatively expert in their field.

2.   They are known to one another so they are assured that mutually competent people are engaged in the same venture.

3.   Each evaluation is done twice. After the initial evaluation, each member has a chance to review the combined output of the group and resubmit a revised estimate. It is this second estimate that is then summarized, averaged if that's appropriate, and then used.

Regardless of what evaluation system you will use, you are most certain to satisfy conditions 1 and 2 automatically. You will be using experts. Most of them will be within the firm (members of the new product committee, department heads, management, etc.). Some of them may indeed be outside the firm and might involve your advertising agency, a new products consulting company, or some other group that could lend expertise to such a venture. You already have people who qualify as experts in some portion of your venture, and most qualify as knowledgeable in the remaining portion.

Therefore, to obtain the benefits of the Delphi system, you merely need to circulate the (combined) results of the first rating effort to all the participants and then ask them to consider each concept again and to rate it given any revised thinking they might have.

For every little extra time and effort, you will obtain dramatically better results. First, after having been given the chance to observe the combined opinions of their respective colleagues, many participants will revise their thinking on the second sweep. Further, having been part of this evaluation twice, the members seem to "buy in" to the worth of the concepts to a much greater extent. Since these are people whose support you will need as you go through the development process, this can be an invaluable addition.

A Few Last Thoughts

So far in this chapter, I have approached the topic of evaluating concepts as business propositions from a mechanical standpoint. There are three last thoughts that I need to discuss if you are to deal successfully with this type of business.

First, whatever system you select, it should be accepted by the other key members of your firm that will be affected by its output. They should be allowed to participate in the factor selection and in the decisions on factor weighting. They must also be allowed to participate in the evaluation of the concept/business proposition unless they are the top management of the corporation. If this is the case, an understanding of and agreement on the system is sufficient.

Second, don't reject subjectivity, but don't allow it to obviate the result of your systematic approach. There is ample opportunity for subjectivity in the selection of the factors and their weighting.

Third, don't be misled by the "good" idea that seems so important and so worthwhile that you stop the process and do not screen all your alternatives. Good ideas have a way of getting lost for any number of reasons—legal issues, lack of customer interest, technology problems, management decisions, etc. It is essential in this area that you work with as many propositions or new product concepts as you feel comfortable with, at least in the evaluation stage. Once they move beyond this stage and take on the form of a project, then the limitations of corporate resources will place some constraints on your behavior. Early on, however, look at as many potential opportunities as possible.

10

Simulated Test Marketing

Herbert P. Hupfer
Elrick and Lavidge, Inc.

The new product development process can generally be characterized as consisting of a number of stages or phases, such as:

- Idea generation.
- Idea screening.
- Concept evaluation.
- Product evaluation.
- Commercialization.

Clearly, not all successful new products follow this path. Some originate as by-products of a production process, while others are born out of advancing technology.

136

WHAT IS TEST MARKETING?

One option along the way to developing a new product is test marketing. As the name implies, test marketing involves marketing a product on a limited scale or "test" basis rather than distributing and promoting it regionally or nationally as a fully commercialized product.

BEFORE TEST MARKETING

To test market a new product, a firm must have the capability of producing a number of finished-looking units of the product. The units produced should closely resemble in appearance the types of goods buyers normally see for sale in the marketplace—they should not be prototypes. In addition to having sufficient quantities of the product itself, firms must have at least a reasonable fix as to how the product will be priced and the primary channel of distribution that will be utilized in disseminating it to potential buyers. Firms must also have in mind the message they intend to use in order to inspire sales.

Test marketing is not an indispensable phase of new product development. Given that the product can be produced, priced, promoted and distributed, there certainly is nothing to prevent an organization from "rolling out" the product in earnest in anticipation of success. Indeed, it would be misleading to think that all products go through (or should go through) this rigorous testing procedure.

REASONS FOR TEST MARKETING

While not all products are test marketed, there are some clear advantages for taking this step before commercialization. Although there are a number of reasons for test marketing, *the primary reason is to develop an estimate of sales for the new product.* In effect, the sales estimate provided by the test market becomes the final hurdle a product must negotiate before its market introduction. Generally speaking, most products that have come this far in the new product development process have at least some potential. Therefore, it's important to have some sales standards in mind before beginning the process.

Test marketing also has the advantage of providing an opportunity to test alternative marketing plans. For example, before a large-scale introduction of a product, a manufacturer may be interested in knowing the impact of alternative price levels on the sales of the product. In this type of situation, the test product might be marketed in several locations which have been matched on key marketing criteria, such as population size and level of competition. This enables the manufacturer to optimize the price charged for his product.

In addition to alternative price levels, different levels of advertising spending may be implemented in order to see their incremental effect on sales. Product design, packaging, and distribution alternatives also might be optimized as a result of a test market.

The use of a test market provides a final check for product defects. While many products undergo extensive testing before they reach the test market stage, products produced on a production-scale basis may differ in their ability to perform from those originally developed as test models. Moreover, mishandling of the product in the channel of distribution and misuse of the product on the part of the end-user also may contribute to a higher level of product failure than anticipated. It makes good sense to determine potential performance problems before they reach a mass scale.

WAYS TO TEST MARKET

There are several ways in which products can be test marketed. One way would be to produce a quantity of the product, then distribute and promote it within a limited set of markets or sales territories. This often is referred to as *field test marketing*.

Virtually any type of product or service can be field test marketed. Because the product is tested in the real world, field test marketing produces results that are difficult to criticize from the standpoint of realism.

On the other hand, field test markets frequently are expensive. The cost rises quickly when sufficient quantities of the product must be produced for distribution purposes. Costs also rise when media space has to be purchased or when sales personnel have to be familiarized with the new product.

Time may also prove to be a problem with field test marketing. Three to 12 months may pass before sufficient information has been collected to forecast sales.

Releasing products to the marketplace also may cause the developer of a new product to lose some control over the product itself. For certain items, particularly those of an industrial nature, the test product might be "bootlegged" from the test city to other areas. And, even if the product remains entirely within the test area, competitors frequently learn about the existence of the product, in addition to learning about how the product will be distributed, priced, and promoted.

A second approach to test marketing is to use what is called a *simulated test market (STM)*. Unlike field test markets, simulated test markets do not involve securing distribution for the product among wholesalers and retailers or promoting the product through any mass media. In simulated test markets, prospects for a new product go through a series of stages designed to provide them with the key pieces of information they need to know in order to judge whether they would buy the product.

Generally speaking, simulated test marketing involves the following steps:

- Recruiting participants for the test—either a general audience or a more specific group of respondents.
- Securing background information—usually awareness, usage, attitudinal, and demographic data.
- Exposing test participants to information regarding the

new product; attempting to create interest in the product by presenting its primary selling proposition.

- Exposing test participants to the test product (and others) via a store setup within an interviewing facility; further stimulating interest in the product via its packaging and pricing.
- Determining the reactions to the test product before use; assessing the deterrents, if any, to trial.
- Determining the reactions to the test product after use; assessing the deterrents, if any, to repurchase.

Advantages and Disadvantages of STMs

Simulated test markets offer several advantages over a field test market. They are much less expensive (starting around $40,000) and usually can be completed in 8 to 12 weeks, depending on the length of time participants are given to use the test product. Simulated test products also are less likely to be discovered by competitors. This helps keep the user's marketing plans confidential. In addition, it keeps competitors from disrupting the test.

STMs are not without their drawbacks, however. At this time, the biggest problem rests with the limited range of products that can be tested using a STM. For the most part, simulated test markets are used to evaluate low-cost, frequently purchased consumer products such as the following:

Food Products

Salad dressings	Package dinners
Seasonings	Sandwich spreads
Snack foods	Frozen dinners
Fruit drinks	Frozen vegetables
Spices	Juices
Alcoholic beverages	Coffee
Sauces/condiments	Margarine
Baked goods	Mayonnaise
Frozen baked goods	Coating products
Dessert products	Meat/Poultry
Yogurt	Dairy Products

Household Products

Cleaners
Cleaning aids
Floor care products
Bleaches/additives
Detergents
Fabric softeners

Soap pads
Paper towels
Tissues
Rug cleaners
Insect repellent

Personal Care Products

Deodorants/antiperspirants
Cold/cough remedies
Antacids/stomach remedies
Vitamins
Baby products
Dental care products
Hair care products
Children's vitamins

Skin care products
Skin cleansers
Skin moisturizers
Men's toiletries
Analgesics
Laxatives
Cosmetics/fragrances
Suntan products

Another limitation of simulated test markets is that they do not provide much information regarding the distribution of a product. For example, they do not provide information as to how difficult it will be to secure distribution and how much distribution ultimately will be achieved. Moreover, they do not aid the user who is interested in answering questions about dealer discounting and product breakage or spoilage.

Systems Available

There are a number of simulated test marketing systems from which to choose. Some of the more popular systems, listed in chronological order according to when they were developed, are as follows:

LTM (1965) Yankelovich, Skelly & White

COMP (1971) Elrick and Lavidge

Assessor (1974) Management Decision Systems

Simulator ESP (1975) National Purchase Diary

Bases (1979) Burke Marketing Research

As mentioned, all of these systems involve a series of phases through which potential buyers of a new product are led in order to measure their reactions to both the idea and the product itself. Although there are substantial similarities among the systems regarding their overall procedure, a number of issues that arise at each stage of the process require further examination.

RECRUITMENT OF TEST PARTICIPANTS

Simulated or laboratory test marketing systems recruit participants in a number of ways. Some systems recruit participants for the tests in shopping malls. Other systems recruit consumers by telephone or in grocery stores.

Regardless of the specific manner in which respondents are recruited, one of the key questions to consider when selecting respondents is the specific nature of the product to be tested. If the product to be tested falls within an existing product category or is likely to compete directly against one or more categories, participants in the test typically are consumers who buy products from the product category of interest. On the other hand, if the product to be tested appears to be unique enough to create a new product category, participants in the test tend to come from a more general consumer audience.

Regardless of how test participants are contacted, the purpose of the recruitment phase is to focus on those individuals who are most likely to have at least some interest in the new product. The idea of focusing on logical prospects for the product is based on the premise that few products, if any, are likely to appeal to everyone.

PRODUCT UNIQUENESS

The notion of uniqueness should be carefully examined. In developing new products, a strong argument can be advanced for developing products that occupy their own niche in the marketplace. It is important to remember, however, that total uniqueness is not a prerequisite for success. Indeed, some highly unique products may appeal to only a very limited audience or to no one at all.

As a correlate to the notion of developing entirely new markets, managers responsible for developing new products frequently feel their new product offering will expand the product category rather than play the traditional "zero-sum" game of trading market share with existing products. The idea of product category expansion becomes particularly enticing when the proportion of nonusers is large relative to the proportion of users.

When considering the possibility of product category expansion, it is important to take a careful look at the current state of development of a given product category. Emerging categories may well be expanded by new product offerings. However, other product categories, such as toothpaste, deodorants, and laundry detergents, are not likely to offer as much potential in the way of new product opportunities via the category expansion mode.

The entire discussion of market expansion rests substantially on how a given market is defined. For example, the sales of gel types of toothpaste offer expansion opportunities that appear to be much greater than the potential for expanding the total toothpaste market.

USE OF INCENTIVES

The available simulated test marketing systems utilize a variety of incentives designed to encourage the participation of consumers. Money, trading stamps, and special store coupons all have been used to one extent or another to enlist cooperation.

Systems that recruit test participants from consumer shopping malls frequently are required (by the field firm) to provide some sort of incentive. This is because the mall interviewing portion of a simulated test market frequently lasts between 20 and 30 minutes.

The best type of incentive to use is frequently debated by the providers of simulated test markets. Systems that use money (cash) are criticized by others who feel that respondents are being bribed and therefore may react positively to the test product out of indebtedness. Critics of coupons argue that the coupons pinpoint the test product for respondents and provide it with an unfair advantage compared to other competitive offerings. This unfair advantage is argued to overstimulate trial of the test product, thereby producing unrealistic results.

The use of an incentive frequently is tied in with other aspects of a specific system that may not appear immediately obvious. For example, if the theory of the system is to maximize the number of people who buy the test product in the simulated test store, coupons are frequently used. On the other hand, if the emphasis of the system is to maximize realism by having respondents use their own money, coupons will be avoided.

If cash is used as an incentive, generally speaking, the amount of the incentive is usually $1.50 to $2.00. The incentive typically is positioned as a "thank you" for participating in the study rather than as seed money.

BACKGROUND INFORMATION

At some time during the course of the simulated test marketing procedure, the different systems secure background information from participants in the test. A variety of subjects are covered when gathering the background data. Some of the topics covered include the following:

Unaided and aided awareness of brands within the product category of interest (assuming there is one).

Brand used most often. Other brands used. Brands aware of but not used.

Frequency of using and/or buying similar products or participating in activities related to product usage. Extent to which usage is shared.

Ratings of selected product benefits and attributes with respect to their importance when choosing a brand from the category.

Ratings of a number of brands within the category on selected product benefits and attributes.

Purchase intentions toward a number of brands within the category.

Household/respondent characteristics:

Age	Household size
Sex	Number of age of children
Income	Employment status
Education	Unemployed/part-time/full-time
	One or two incomes

The background information can be used for a variety of diagnostic purposes. Some of the questions that can be answered through the use of this information are as follows:

- What are the demographic characteristics of those persons who appear to be most interested in the products with respect to:
    Age
    Income
    Sex
    Stage in the family life cycle
    Marital status?

- To what extent are test participants aware of brands in a category on an
    Unaided basis
    Aided basis?

- Does the new product address an important consumer need?

- How is the new product perceived vis-à-vis other products in the category with respect to its ability to satisfy important consumer needs?

- In terms of purchase intentions, how do test participants feel about the test product vis-à-vis existing brands in a category?

- Who are the best prospects for the product with respect to
    Brands currently used
    Frequency of using any brand in the category?

The importance of collecting background information from test participants cannot be overstated. This information allows the researcher to carefully examine the marketplace in terms of how it has reacted to a new product offering. The ability to carefully examine the characteristics of consumers who have favorably and unfavorably reacted to a test product frequently is not present in a field test market.

EXPOSURE TO A COMMUNICATION REGARDING THE NEW PRODUCT

In order to determine consumers' reactions to the new product, respondents who participate in simulated test markets must be exposed to the new product idea. In almost all cases, an advertisement is used to provide the necessary information.

Most simulated test markets try to create a situation they refer to as 100 percent awareness; that is, everyone participating in the study sees a communication regarding the product, and therefore 100 percent of the test participants should be at least somewhat familiar with it. Researchers, of course, realize that creating a situation of 100 percent awareness in an actual marketplace is virtually impossible. To account for this discrepancy, the models factor down the sales prediction they generate by using awareness levels that are likely to be achieved in the marketplace.

MEDIA TO USE

Information about the new product is provided to participants using a variety of media. In the past, television, radio, and print all have been used. Television is the most common.

In deciding on what media to use when conducting a simulated test market, consideration should be given to the type of media that would be used if the product were to be introduced to the marketplace. Misleading results may be obtained if TV is used as a medium in the test and the product ultimately is advertised using print media.

NUMBER OF ADVERTISEMENTS SHOWN

The number of commercials to which respondents are exposed and the context in which they are shown vary from system to system. In some cases, the number of advertisements shown may be as few as one; in others, it may be as many as seven or eight. In most cases, three to five ads are used. In order to avoid calling undue attention to the advertisement for the test product, it probably is a good idea to use more than one ad. It is also advisable to rotate the order in which the ads are shown.

PLACEMENT OF ADS IN THE CONTEXT OF A PROGRAM

Sometimes the ads to which respondents are exposed are shown in the context of a television program (in case of print, the ads are placed in a magazine or newspaper). The theory behind this procedure is to create a more realistic environment for viewing the ads. The problem with showing the ads in the context of a program (or some other type of medium) is that it increases the length of the interview— an interview that is already fairly long because of the number of steps in the procedure.

DEGREE OF FINISH OF ADS

When exposing consumers to a number of advertisements, it is advisable that all of the advertisements be in the same degree of finish. That is, if the test product has a fully finished commercial, then the advertising for the competitive products also should be fully finished commercials. In order to avoid the expense of producing fully finished advertise-

ments for the test product, most simulated test markets using television as a medium use animatics (pictures, sometimes sketches, with a voiceover). If animatics are used for
the test product, they should also be used for the other ads.
This is frequently accomplished by videotaping commercials of the other products when they are aired and reducing
them to animatic form.

TYPE OF ADS USED

When participants in a simulated test market are exposed to
a number of ads, the type of ads they see varies from system
to system. In many cases, respondents are exposed to advertisements for competitive products. The notion here is to
create a situation of 100 percent awareness for a number of
the key brands in the product category. This not only provides camouflage but allows the researcher to see how respondents react to brands they do not use but which are
commercially successful. Reactions may provide interesting
diagnostic information as to why consumers refrain from
buying existing yet successful brands in the category.

   Some systems expose the survey respondents to a number
of ads, all of which are for products in different categories.
The idea here is to create a situation closely parallel to the
way in which consumers are exposed to advertisements
when viewing a given medium.

ADVERTISING RECALL

After participants in the survey have been exposed to the
advertisements, many systems require them to report what
they recall seeing in the ads. Frequently, this is done by
having respondents write down what they remember about
each of the ads. The purpose of asking respondents what
they recall from the ads is not to "test" the ads per se.
There are other, less expensive ways of doing this. Rather, it
is done to determine precisely what is coming through to
respondents in terms of the advertising message and to un-

cover any misconceptions they may have about the test product.

STORE SETUP IN SIMULATED TEST MARKETS

Once respondents have been exposed to the idea of the new product, the next step normally is to take them to a different area of the interviewing facility (usually a different room) in order to expose them to the new product itself. For the sake of realism, participants in the test are exposed to a shelf display containing a number of products (similar to displays seen in a grocery store or drugstore).

PRODUCTS TO BE DISPLAYED

If a simulated test market is being conducted on a new brand within an existing product class, the other products on the shelves generally consist of the major competitors within the category. Since the major competitors may differ from one geographical area to another, a shopping survey should be conducted about a week to 10 days before the test is started. To do this, interviewers in the area of the shopping center go to a number of stores to check what brands are available, the number of shelf facings, and the price of each of the brands. This information can be used to determine the specific brands to be placed on the shelves of the display. It also is useful in deciding how to price competitive products in the simulated store setup. If the new brand is to be competitively priced, the store check information also serves as input in determining the price of the test brand.

In addition to putting competitive brands on the shelves, it may be desirable to include brands from other product categories. This might be particularly beneficial from the standpoint of appearance when the brand being tested is in a category having only a limited number of brands. The additional products help fill out the display, making it appear more realistic.

In deciding whether to include other product categories on the store shelves, there may be a tradeoff between realism and cost. In many cases, having a number of product categories on the shelves is likely to improve the appearance of the display. However, the cost of these additional products may be substantial in some situations. The cost of additional products is likely to become particularly important when the work is being conducted in a number of locations.

When the product to be tested does not fall into an existing product category, there is more flexibility in terms of the other products to be included on the store shelves. Some vendors of simulated test markets suggest that products likely to compete for the same dollars as the test product should be placed on the store shelves. Others feel that, within reason, the other products on the shelves do not make much difference as long as they do not differ considerably from store to store.

Regardless of whether the new product fits within an existing product category, in situations where the testing is conducted in more than one location, an effort should be made to keep the physical store setup consistent from one store to another. Naturally, strong regional or local brands may prevent the stores from being identical.

NUMBER OF FACINGS

The number of facings in a simulated store does not have to exactly replicate the "real world." One reason for this is that the number of facings in food and/or drugstores often varies from one store to another, thereby making it impossible to duplicate the "typical" store setup.

In setting up the store shelves, it should be kept in mind that one of the key objectives of the setup is to expose consumers to the package and pricing of the new product. In order to do this, the new product should be given an adequate number of facings. Generally speaking, the test product and the major brands in the category (assuming there is a category) should be given approximately the same number of facings.

For display purposes, the test product should be placed somewhere on a middle shelf, preferably toward the center of the display. Placing the test product on a middle shelf eliminates the need for people to reach up or bend down in order to pick up the test product. While it is unlikely that the test product always will be ideally located on store shelves, nothing is gained by making it difficult for participants to see or buy the product in the test.

Purchase Opportunity

Once respondents have been exposed to the store setup, they are informed that they may purchase any of the products they see on the shelves. They are also told they will be charged the prices marked on each of the products.

Most systems insist that respondents be brought into the store shelf area one at a time. This avoids any interaction among the test participants—interaction not likely to take place in a normal store setting.

If a respondent chooses to purchase something and removes it from the shelf, it is important that there be an adequate supply of backup product to immediately replace the unit that was removed. In this manner, *each* respondent sees *exactly* the same store setup, minimizing the chance for the physical display to influence consumers' reactions to the products.

Even though all of the respondents are aware of the test product and have an opportunity to purchase it, not everyone does so. In fact, the proportion of test participants who actually buy the test product in the simulated store tends to range from 5 percent to 50 percent, depending on the product category, the price of the product, and other factors.

Some of the reasons consumers do not make purchases in the test center have little to do with how they feel about the test product. The most frequently cited reasons include the following:

- They already have a sufficient quantity of the product on hand at home.
- The product is perishable (e.g., frozen) and consumers do not wish to carry it around with them.

- Consumers are bargain hunters—they think they can get the product cheaper someplace else.
- Some people are reluctant to try new products until they have more information about them.

POST SHOPPING EXPERIENCE EVALUATION OF TEST PRODUCT

After respondents have completed the shopping phase portion of the procedure, some of the simulated test markets have test participants rate the new product (and some other products they are familiar with). Ratings are given for a number of key product benefits and attributes and for purchase intent. The purpose of this step is to measure consumers' reactions to the test product after they have had the opportunity to learn about its key selling proposition, its packaging, and its pricing—all of which are key elements in stimulating trial.

The importance of this phase of the simulated test market procedure cannot be overstated. One of the key problems in the development of successful new products manifests itself when a new product attempts to generate trial. Since respondents at this phase of the STM procedure are reacting to the marketing program for a new product rather than the product itself, it is possible to identify aspects of the marketing program that are likely to be deterrents to trial. This can be done by comparing reactions to the test product of those consumers who are likely to buy it with those who exhibit negative purchase intentions.

USE OF THE TEST PRODUCT

In order to make sales predictions for the types of products tested using simulated test markets (i.e., low-cost, frequently purchased items), it is necessary to determine whether consumers who try the product would repurchase it—frequently referred to as the "repeat purchase rate." To estimate a repeat rate, the extent to which consumers are satisfied with the performance of the test product must be measured. The purpose of the usage portion of STMs is to provide test participants with enough experience with the test product to properly evaluate it.

Theoretically, consumers' reactions to the test product can be secured in several ways. One way is to have them try it right at the test center. There are several positive aspects of measuring consumer reactions to the test product in the test center. First of all, it saves time because respondents can give an immediate reaction to the product, rather than waiting for some usage period to elapse. Secondly, it is efficient because reactions to the product can be secured from every participant in the test, rather than from only a portion of them as is the case when respondents are recontacted after usage.

For many of the test marketing systems, the store experience serves as a means of getting the test product into the hands of consumers. Those who do not buy the test product in the test center frequently are given a sample of it as an additional "thank you" for participating in the test. Respondents who buy the test product also are given a "thank you"—a product not related to the test product but similar in value. Using this procedure, one way or another, every participant in the test walks away with the test product.

There are several points in favor of having respondents take the product home in order to evaluate it. One is that many products are used at home in conjunction with other products, thereby making proper testing at the facility impossible. Another is that some products, because of their nature, are impossible to test in an on-site facility (e.g., shampoos, medicinal products, floor wax, etc.). As a rule, having respondents use the test product at home produces more reliable results. For this reason, virtually all simulated test markets involve an in-home use test of the product.

LENGTH OF USAGE PERIOD

When an in-home use test is involved, one of the decisions that must be made is how much time to give respondents to use a product before they are recontacted. Generally, the usage period depends on the nature of the product being tested. Food products, for example, may involve a relatively short usage period (a week to 10 days) because they are likely to be consumed in a relatively short time. Other items, however, such as medicinal products, may require a much longer usage period—possibly four to six weeks— because the problem addressed by the product may occur on an infrequent basis.

When deciding on the length of time to give respondents to use a given product, consideration should be given to the notion that test participants may already have an inventory of similar products on hand at home. A respondent is not likely to open a new bottle of vitamins, for example, until they have consumed the vitamins they are currently using. This being the case, it may be several months before respondents even have an opportunity to use the test product. If this situation is encountered, there are ways to accelerate trial of the new product. One way to do this is to enclose a note and possibly an additional financial incentive along with the test product given to respondents at the test center. The note informs them that some of the participants in the mall portion of the interviewing will be called back to get their reactions to the product they were given. The note essentially asks respondents to use the test product in case they are one of the persons recontacted.

In addition to gathering information regarding how consumers feel about a product after use, the follow-up interview can be used to secure other types of information including:

- To what extent, if at all, will use of the new product be exclusive, or will the new product be shared with other products?

- With what other products, if any, did consumers use the new product?

- What other products, if any, will be replaced by the new product?

- How frequently will the new product be used?

- Are the instructions, if any, easy to read and understand?

- What problems, if any, do consumers have in using the test product?

METHODS OF SECURING AFTER-USE INFORMATION

A number of techniques are employed to secure information from test participants after they have had the opportunity to use the new product. The most common is telephone interviewing. Telephone interviews are advantageous because they can be done quickly, thereby minimizing the time it takes to measure consumers' reactions to the test product.

Personal interviewing is also used as a means of gathering after-use information. Personal interviews allow the researcher to use self-administered forms to collect after-use data. This is important because much of the information secured by STMs in the mall intercept (before-use) portion of the procedure is also gathered using self-administered forms. By using the same interviewing technique, differences between before-use and after-use data can be read with much greater sensitivity. Thus, the issue of how the data are collected is not to be taken lightly.

SALES WAVES

Some simulated test markets offer what they refer to as "sales waves." Sales waves, which usually are considered to be an option by those organizations offering them, are interviews conducted with STM test participants after they have had additional time (beyond the initial usage period) to use the test product. Some systems offer as many as four additional waves of interviewing.

As the name sales waves implies, test participants are given the opportunity to make additional product purchases—usually from among a set of the products that they saw in the store portion of the test. In addition, test participants generally are asked a number of other questions designed to measure their attitudes toward and usage of the test product. If a person does not buy the test product at the time of the first or second wave, they are frequently dropped from future interviews.

Compared with purchase intentions, sales waves provide actual sales data for calculating first repeat. They are particularly useful in situations where consumers may tire of using a product (sometimes called "wear out") and where the consumer needs to use a product several times in order to properly evaluate it.

ACCURACY OF STMs

STMs report being reasonably accurate: within one to two share points of actual market share or within 10 percent of actual sales volume. Like any other forecasting tool, however, sometimes the predictions generated by STMs are not within these limits, although erroneous predictions tend to be rare.

On average, simulated test markets probably produce sales estimates that are just as accurate as those produced with field test markets. When the results of an STM vary dramatically from the actual sales generated in the marketplace, one or more of the following scenarios usually helps explain away the difference:

- The marketing program for the product was changed between the time the product was tested using an STM and the time it was introduced to the marketplace. If the product, the way it is promoted, or its price is changed, one has to expect actual sales results to be different from what is predicted.

- The product received a substantial amount of publicity, either positive or negative, which influenced sales. It is difficult to predict how much publicity a product will get and whether the publicity will be positive or negative. Moreover, it is difficult to model the impact of publicity in an experimental setting.

- The environment in which a test product competes changes. Substantial changes in the price of competitive products or the amount they spend for promotion may create a hostile environment for the test product. Changes in price and promotion may be the result of defensive reactions on the part of competitors to the introduction of the test product. Predicting competitive reactions, however, is not easy in a simulated test market.

- One or more of the assumptions on which the STMs forecast is based proves to be false. Most STMs postulate likely levels of awareness and distribution for the new product. Sometimes the new product simply fails to reach the levels that were anticipated.

In any case, effective use of simulated test markets can enhance the likelihood of successful commercialization of new products.

11

Product Optimization
Designing and Developing the Best Product Features

James C. Adamek
Conway/Milliken & Associates

INTRODUCTION

Moving a good idea from a concept to a successful new product is a long journey. Developing successful products requires success in all of the following components.

1. Product ideas and concepts that are based on accurately assessing consumer needs, wants, and expectations. Generating good ideas is a major focus of many new product development programs. Scores of systems are available for generating, screening, and refining product ideas and concepts.

2. The product itself; its physical components, ingredients, and characteristics. Determining the formula of the physical product is a research and development and production function.

3. Early stage product performance evaluation. Consumers are asked to try and evaluate product prototypes. A "winning" product formula is chosen.

4. Marketing execution. At this final step, product name, packaging, and media plans are formalized. Test marketing of the final branded, priced, advertised product is usually the final step in the product evaluation process.

Consumer marketing research has been active in generating product ideas, building and screening product concepts, evaluating product performance through central location or in-home use testing, evaluating names, package designs, and advertising effectiveness. All of the above activities utilize a sample of *consumer* evaluations to judge success or failure, with one notable exception—point 2, participation in product construction. Physical product components, or what the product is made of, has been considered to be "more properly" a laboratory research and development function. As a result, marketers have needlessly neglected applying their consumer research expertise to product formulation.

Consumer marketing researchers who work with product buying behavior, attitudes, needs, and expectations may tend to de-emphasize the importance of physical product components and emphasize "good ideas."

Generating good ideas is the major focus of many new product development programs. Ideas are generated and screened and the surviving idea is refined through concept testing. The expanded concept is made stronger by adding brand name, product name, packaging, and positioning strategies. The actual physical product takes a backseat to concept development and execution.

However, it must be remembered that the success of a new product ultimately depends on the performance of the physical product. This "product-first" emphasis is based on two related observations:

1. A good product can survive weak concept development, faulty positioning, poor brand image, and a limited media campaign.

2. A mediocre product cannot be saved by concept rewrites, positioning changes, brand image, or large media budgets.

Product Testing

Product evaluation at central locations or through in-home use tests has been a frequent task for marketing researchers. Product tests usually concern relatively few products which are subjected to a complex consumer evaluation process. Such product screening/evaluation studies have been successful in picking winners and losers as well as quantifying components of consumer responses to specific products.

A good system for identifying a winner or loser is *not* necessarily the best system for building the best product. This discrepancy is most clear when we consider the process of a traditional product test.

In traditional product testing, consumers are asked to evaluate products on a variety of scales and measures. Product performance is profiled on dimensions such as taste, texture, color, brightness, fragrance, shape, size, weight, flavor, strength, sweetness, naturalness, quality, value for the money, buying intention, or a product that fits my needs. Open-ended diagnostic questions probe for what was most liked about the product and what was most disliked.

Other open-ended questions attempt to probe the purchase decision process: "Why would you definitely/probably buy (or not buy) this product?"

Following consumer tests of a product, data is analyzed, conclusions are drawn, and a judgment made whether the product is a winner or loser. Even if judged a winner, several important questions remain unanswered. First, have we made the best possible product? Even though we have a winner, could we have made a product consumers would have liked even more than our winner?

The second unanswered question applies to both winners and losers. Can consumer evaluations from traditional product testing help in proving precise direction for product changes and improvements? For example, consumers tell us they would like a diet soft drink more if it were less bitter, a little sweeter, and more carbonated; a cheese product more if it had a smoother mouth feel; a shampoo if it were a bit more sudsy. In order to improve these products, *amounts* of physical ingredients must change (amounts and ratios of aspartame and saccharin in a diet soft drink, water content and type of machine processing in a cheese product, detergent level in a shampoo).

What has been missing in product testing is the *direct link* between *physical ingredients*, product *characteristics*, and consumer *acceptance* of products. Little attention has been given to the problem of predicting consumer preference as a function of variations in physical ingredients or product characteristics. As a result, direction and recommendations for product development have been communicated in terms of consumer sensory evaluations. Marketing research has contributed little in terms of specifying levels of physical ingredients and product characteristics that will produce positive consumer evaluations.

Without precise direction for modifying amounts of product ingredients to match consumer preference, new product development can become a costly and time-consuming trial-and-error method: i.e., product formulation, consumer test, product reformulation (based on "best-guess" ingredient modifications), consumer retest, etc.

PRODUCT OPTIMIZATION

Product optimization systems have been developed to predict *consumer* product acceptance as a function of variations in *physical ingredients* or product characteristics.

Theoretically, the behavior of any product system (physical ingredients and characteristics) is governed by quantifiable laws. By applying these laws, it is possible to determine "optimum conditions." Most chemical reactions have been studied using this approach. An unknown response (yield from a chemical reaction) is studied as an unknown *function* of physical ingredients. By determining this unknown function, levels of physical ingredients can be manipulated to produce an optimum condition (maximum yield from a chemical reaction). In the field of chemistry and chemical engineering, methods have been developed for modeling response surfaces and locating optimum conditions (Box, 1951, 1954, 1955, 1957).

A powerful set of *experimental designs* and *methods of analysis* known as *response surface methodology* have been developed to describe response surfaces as a function of physical variables (Bradley, 1958; Graybill, 1976; Hunter, 1958, 1977). Response surface methodologies have been applied to a wide range of problems including education and psychology (Hill & Hunter, 1966). In marketing research applications, the "response surface" is represented by consumer evaluations of test products.

Product optimization establishes a direct link between physical product components and consumer acceptance of the product. In order to establish this link, consumers are asked to evaluate a number of products that have been systematically varied in amounts of physical ingredients and components. These test products represent ingredient levels ranging from not enough to almost right to too much. By

---

FIGURE 1

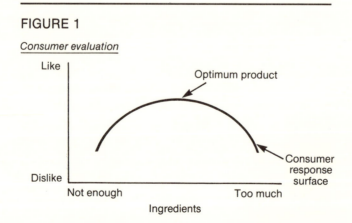

finding out how consumer preference changes as a function of ingredient levels, we can fine tune the exact amounts of ingredients that will produce the maximum consumer acceptance—the best possible product.

Figure 1 shows consumer "liking" increasing, reaching a maximum, then decreasing with further increases in ingredient amounts. This curve illustrates a basic tenet of optimization modeling. A range of ingredient variations, including test products consumers like less because of too much or too little of an ingredient, enables us to find the optimum ingredient formulation.

Product optimization covers the following areas.

1. Test product design. How many formulas are needed? How many products do we need to test, and what are their ingredients?

2. Consumer evaluations. Who and what do we ask consumers to do? What kinds of questions do we ask? What sample size is needed?

3. Analysis. What precise ingredient amounts result in the best product?

Test Product Design

In order to build the best possible product, consumers evaluate a representative sample of all possible product variations.

Products may consist of tens or even hundreds of ingredients or product characteristics. It is not necessary to test variations in *all* product ingredients. Some ingredients are not expected to influence consumer product evaluations (for example, some preservatives or inert ingredients). Other ingredients may not be varied due to medical or legal considerations. For example, *one* size of fish cakes may be dictated by packaging considerations. One amount of an active antacid may be required by medical or legal considerations.

However, there are many ingredients and components in which variations are known to affect product preference: aspartame in soft drinks, amounts of orange and pineapple juices in a fruit punch, pork and beef ratios in a canned

meat, machine processes producing differing cheese tex-
tures. The *precise* relationships between ingredient variations and end effect on consumer acceptance need not be
known—only trends and directions. The product optimization system quantifies the precise relationship between ingredient variation and consumer reaction to the products.

Sampling Product Versions

Specifying product formulations to be evaluated by consumers is essentially a problem of sampling product space.
Combinations of ingredients could possibly yield an unmanageable number of possible products. The number of possible products (P) increases with both the number of functional physical ingredients or product characteristics (I),
and the levels of variations in each ingredient or physical
characteristic (L). The number of possible product variations
increases exponentially as a function of the number of ingredients $P = L^I$. For example, five ingredients each having
five levels or variations can result in $5^5 = 3,125$ possible test
products.

Central Composite Designs

Product optimization usually involves the use of "second-
order" empirical models. That is, the consumer "response
surface" has a curved shape.

In order to adequately sample a product space, efficient
study designs must be developed to estimate all linear or
main effects as well as the interaction effects among ingredients. A sufficient number of test products must be evaluated
to adequately measure the effects of functional ingredients
on consumer response. For example, in the case of *two*
functional ingredients (A, B) the following effects must be
estimated by the study design: two first-order main effects
(A, B); two second-order quadratic effects (A^2, B^2); and one
interaction (A × B) effect. Central composite experimental
designs have many desirable properties, including the ability to obtain sufficient estimates of these ingredient effects
using the smallest number of products.

FIGURE 2

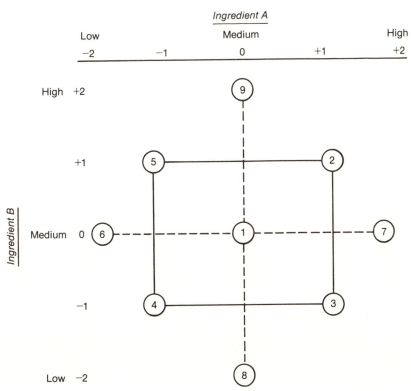

Figure 2 illustrates the construction principle of central composite designs.

Essentially, the construction of central composite designs entails extensions around a center or starting point ①. The ingredient levels defining the center point may come from an existing product formulation, a competitive product formulation, or a best estimate based on product experience or previous research.

Number of test products as well as *amount* of ingredients for each test product are determined by sampling product space around the center point. In the above example, if each of the two ingredients were varied at five levels, a total of 25 products would be possible. Using a central composite design, nine test products would efficiently sample the 25 product variations.

Central composite, rotatable designs have a number of desirable characteristics. Since we may not know in which *direction* from the center the optimum consumer response surface will be, it is important to use a design that gathers information with the same intensity in all directions. A rotatable design exhibits constant sensitivity regardless of direction.

Consumer Evaluations

As mentioned earlier, traditional product testing asks consumers a large battery of questions about a few products. Product optimization asks questions about a larger number of product variations, but the questioning procedure is short, simple, and straightforward.

A representative sample of consumers are asked to evaluate a representative sample of test products. Since consumers are the ultimate judge of product success or failure, as in traditional product testing, consumers are asked to evaluate the test products rather than expert, trained raters or in-house employee panels.

Product optimization modeling does not require large samples of consumers. Typically, 120 evaluations of each test product are sufficient. As with most research designs, repeated measurement (i.e., one consumer evaluates all test products) is preferred since it tends to reduce within-subject error variance. In a fully repeated measurement design, a total sample of 120 consumers would evaluate all test products.

Consumers need not evaluate all test products in a single session. The study design may be divided into subsets conducted over several days or weeks if necessary. It is well known that bias may occur through such factors as testing at different times (Hunter, 1977). However, these bias effects can be reduced by dividing the design into subsets or blocks. Blocks are fractions of the total number of products evaluated by a consumer in a single session. For example, a total of eight test products may be blocked into two groups of four products. At each session, a consumer would evaluate four test products. The three sessions could be separated in time by hours or days. Fortunately, designs can be chosen so that time interval has a minimum bias in measuring the effects of physical ingredients on consumer response. Such designs are termed *orthogonally blocked.*

In cases where fully repeated measurement designs are not practical (such as alcoholic beverages and medicinal products), subject blocking may also be used. That is, *one* consumer evaluates *only* a subset of the total number of test products. For example, one consumer may evaluate only four of the eight test products. In this example, a total of 240 respondents would be required to obtain 120 evaluations per test product.

Overall Rating

The stated objective of product optimization is to develop a product formulation that produces the maximum positive consumer response or highest level of consumer acceptance. How is positive consumer response measured?

Consumers are very good at telling how much they like or dislike a product. They are *not* as good at rationalizing or explaining the reasons for their preference decision. In many cases, consumers form strong product likes or dislikes but are unable to clearly verbalize the *reasons* for product preference.

Product optimization testing does *not* require the consumer to rationalize a product preference decision or to be an expert rater, nor does it require any special training or sensitivity. Consumers are *not* asked to make complicated connections between product preference and sensory evaluations. Consumers are *not* asked if they would like a product more if it were sweeter, or chewier, or sudsier, or more fragrant.

Optimization testing only requires consumers to make the same straightforward product evaluations they constantly make in everyday life: that is, "Do I like or dislike this product, and how much do I like or dislike it?"

The criterion for maximum consumer acceptance is an *overall* rating. That is, "all things considered how much do you like or dislike the product you have tried?" Overall rating is not necessarily synonymous with a like-dislike dimension. Depending on the particular product, other dimensions (such as effectiveness for medicinal products) may be used. However, what does not change is the basic criterion of an *overall*, all things considered, consumer response to test products.

Perceptual Profiles

In addition to an overall rating, consumer evaluations of other sensory characteristics (e.g., saltiness, sweetness, flavor strength) and product characteristics (color, shape, texture, brightness) are important diagnostic sources of information.

However, ratings of color, sweetness, and so on are *not* used as input to the optimization model. Certainly these sensory dimensions influence product evaluations; however, the most important measure is the end-product influence of these sensory components. That is, "All things considered, how much do I like or dislike this product?" It is not necessary for *consumers* to analyze, rationalize, or dissect their holistic product preference decisions. Product optimization places the burden of expertise and precision where it belongs—on the marketers, *not* on the consumer.

Scales of Measurement

Product optimization systems are not scale bound. That is, response surface methodologies can be utilized with most scaling techniques that generate at least interval scale data.

Early studies in psychophysics have shown the greater reliability of comparative over absolute judgments (Nunnally, 1967). People are not accustomed to making absolute judgments in daily life. A high degree of confidence can be obtained in responses obtained using a comparative frame of reference.

Line Scales.   Verbally anchored line scales combine the advantages of a *comparative* measurement technique with a measure of *magnitude* of response. Overall "liking" using line scales is obtained in the following manner. A respondent sees a line scale anchored at each end: "Dislike very much" and "Like very much." A person indicates how much they like/dislike a product by marking the line between the verbal anchors. All product ratings are made on the *same* continuum. One respondent's overall ratings of products A, B, C can be illustrated as shown in Figure 3.

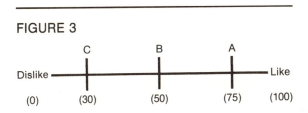

FIGURE 3

Responses on the line scale are coded using a 100-point scale. In Figure 3, product C received a "like" rating of 30; B, 50; and A, 75. In terms of psychometric theory, the reliability of individual rating scales is a monotonically increasing function of the number of scale points (Garner, 1960; Guilford, 1954). The 100-point line scale provides sufficient discrimination among relatively large product sets evaluated in a single testing session.

Analysis Example

Figure 4 shows an example of product optimization modeling using two ingredients: If each of the two ingredients were varied at five levels, a total of 25 products would be possible. Using a central composite design, nine test products would efficiently sample the 25 product variations.

The test formulations needed are shown in Table 1. The center point ① product contains 3 milligrams of ingredient A and 3 percent of ingredient B.

Products were evaluated in two sessions and were therefore blocked to minimize time bias between sessions. Products in Block I (2, 3, 4, 5) were evaluated in one session.

FIGURE 4

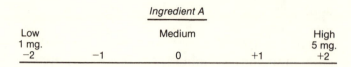

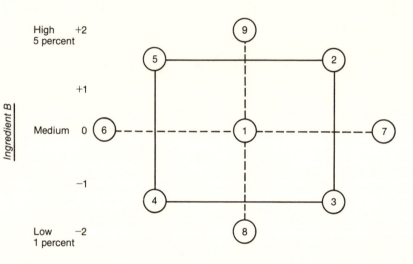

TABLE 1

Test Product	Ingredient Levels*		Ingredients		Block
	A	B	A (mg)	B (pct)	
1	0	0	3	3	I, II
2	+1	+1	4	4 ⎤	
3	+1	−1	4	2 ⎥	I
4	−1	−1	2	2 ⎥	
5	−1	+1	2	4 ⎦	
6	−2	0	1	3 ⎤	
7	+2	0	5	3 ⎥	II
8	0	−2	3	1 ⎥	
9	0	+2	3	5 ⎦	

Note: mg = Milligram; pct = Percent.
*0 = Center point.
 − = Below center point.
 + = Above center point.

Products in Block II (6, 7, 8, 9) were evaluated in the remaining session. Test product ①, the center point of the design, was evaluated in both blocks.

The first analytic step in the product optimization system is developing a predictive model to explain the observed consumer "liking" as a function of variations in physical ingredients. Using the previous example as an illustration, respondents rated the nine test products using an overall like/dislike rating. Additionally, consumers rated the test products on other sensory dimensions (color, sweetness, aftertaste, natural taste, refreshing taste). Product ① was a current product. Table 2 shows the average overall "liking" ratings obtained for the nine test products.

TABLE 2*

| | Ingredients | | Overall Average Rating* |
Test Product	A (mg)	B (pct)	
1 Current	3	3	53
2	4	4	38
3	4	2	⑤⑧
4	2	2	38
5	2	4	40
6	1	3	33
7	5	3	43
8	3	1	[28]
9	3	5	33

○ = Highest overall rating.
□ = Lowest overall rating.
 * = 100 point scale.

In traditional product testing, this first phase may have been the end goal of consumer testing. A winning and losing product have been identified. Test product ③ scored significantly higher (overall rating = 58) than all other products including the current product (①, overall liking = 53). Product optimization testing asks a further question: "Can we make a product that consumers will like *even more* than test product ③?"

Multiple Regression

The first step in the analysis procedure is the fitting of a least squares regression model to the observed consumer evaluations of the test products. The following diagram shows the average overall ratings in parentheses for each of the 9 test products.

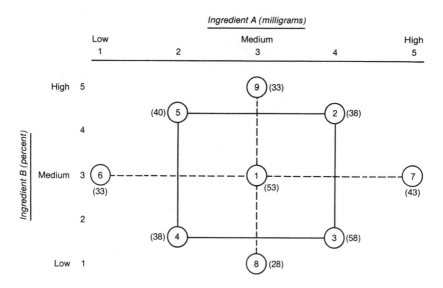

Inspecting these results, it is apparent that the optimum product formulation lies in the *direction* of product ③ . That is, starting from the center (53), higher overall ratings are associated with increasing amounts of A (greater than 3 milligrams) and decreasing amounts of B (less than 3 percent). However, the highest amounts of A (5 milligrams) and lowest amounts of B (1 percent) result in reduced overall rating— ⑦ (43), ⑧ (28).

Regression analysis was used to predict overall rating. Average like rating is the dependent variable, and the variations in ingredients A and B are the independent or predictor variables.

Several quantities are of interest in the multiple regression output: (1) the final multiple regression coefficient, R and (2) regression coefficients.

In this example, the final multiple R (.97) was high. Squaring this quantity (R^2 = 94%) shows that 94 percent of the variability in consumers overall liking rating is being accounted for by variations in the physical ingredients of the test products. This high degree of fit among ingredient variations and overall rating enables confident prediction of overall rating as a function of physical ingredient variations.

The table below shows the standardized regression coefficients (betas) associated with each ingredient effect.

Ingredient Effect	(Beta) Regression Coefficients	t-value
A	b_1 = 5.32	3.23
B	b_2 = 6.25	3.80
A × B	b_{12} = −2.89	2.30
A_2	b_{11} = −4.35	3.50
B^2	b_{22} = −2.98	1.96

Predicted liking can be thought of as a *weighted* function of the ingredient variables A and B. The regression coefficients are weights assigned to ingredients in order to predict liking. In the above example, all coefficients were significantly greater than 0 (*t* values greater than 1.96). Not only do linear and quadratic components contribute significantly to the variation in overall rating, but also the interaction between the ingredients (A × B) is needed to adequately predict consumer acceptance. Overall rating can be expressed as a function of ingredient variations according to the following model:

Overall rating = b_0 + Ab_1 + Bb_2 + ABb_{12} + A^2b_{11} + B^2b_{22}

where b_0 equals an intercept constant.

Screening Ingredient Effects.   The above regression results can be used to illustrate several principles of product optimization modeling. As mentioned previously, the nine test product formulations were chosen so that both too much and too little of an ingredient *lowered* consumer acceptance of the product. The chosen range of ingredients therefore produces a curved response surface.

A central composite design "senses" the presence of a curved surface. If the response surface is curved (bowl or hill-shaped), the difference between the overall rating at the center of the design (53) and the average rating of the eight remaining test products (39) will be greater than zero. In the above example, the estimate of the curvature effect is 53 − 39 = 14.

In terms of regression results, a curved surface will be indicated by nonzero interaction (b_{12}) and/or quadratic (b_{11}, b_{22}) regression coefficients.

Nonsignificant regression coefficients for ingredient *main* effects (b_1, b_2) may occur for several reasons. (1) Ingredient variations have no effect on consumer acceptance of the product (low impact ingredient). (2) Ingredient effects are highly correlated. For example, if variations in levels of ingredient B produce the *same* overall rating as similar variations in ingredient A, ingredient B will be redundant. That is, variations in B give no new source of information not already provided by ingredient A. Therefore, the weight (regression coefficient) of B in explaining overall rating will be small. (3) The ingredient intervals were varied over too *narrow* a range to produce significant effects on consumer response to the product.

Small-scale, ingredient screening studies may be necessary *before* final product modeling in order to define *adequate ranges* of *high-impact ingredients*. Given these ranges of high-impact ingredients, product optimization modeling fine tunes the best possible ingredient amounts.

Optimization Model

Once the multiple regression model has explained *observed* consumer liking as a function of *test product ingredient* variations, the task now becomes one of finding the *amounts* of ingredients that will produce the maximum consumer liking.

This process can be thought of as a *reverse regression* procedure. Input to the optimization model are the regression coefficients, which express the weights or amount of contribution of these ingredients in explaining overall liking. Essentially, the optimization model involves the solution to a set of simultaneous equations. These equations define that point on the response contour where consumer liking is at a maximum.

Using this generated optimum product formulation, the multiple regression model is used to predict overall liking. Shown below are results of the model's optimum product contrasted with the current ① and highest-rated test product ③.

Product	Ingredients		Overall Rating
	A (mg.)	B (percent)	
Optimum	3.75	2.58	64
① Current	3.0	3.0	53
③ Test	4.0	2.0	58

The optimum product would contain 3.75 milligrams of A and 2.58 percent of B. This optimum combination of ingredients resulted in a predicted overall rating of 64, significantly higher than the current product (53) and the highest-rated test product (product ③, overall rating, 58).

Sensitivity Analysis/constraints

Once the optimum product formulation has been obtained, the further question becomes, "How sensitive is consumer acceptance to deviations from the optimum formula?" Sensitivity analysis is the process of determining changes in the optimum formulation that will produce a significant reduction in the predicted overall liking score.

Sensitivity analysis uses the ingredient model developed through regression analysis. This model enables us to predict overall rating for any amounts of ingredients A and B. In the above example, a decrease of 4 from the predicted optimum of 64 was considered a significant decrease (1.96 × standard error of estimate = 4). By holding one ingredient at the optimum level (e.g., B at 2.58 percent), the regression equation is solved for amounts of A that would lower predicted overall rating to 60. The procedure is reversed to find optimum *ranges* of ingredient B.

The following shows maximum ingredient variations that will *not* significantly lower predicted overall rating. Variations exceeding these maximums are expected to result in a significant decrease in overall rating.

Sensitivity Analysis

1. A Optimum = 3.73 mg.
    B Maximum variation = 2.1 to 3.2%
2. B Optimum = 2.58 pct.
    A Maximum variation = 2.9 mg. to 4.5 mg.

Sensitivity analysis may have some additional practical applications. For example, the cost of ingredients may be an issue. If, in the above example, B is an expensive ingredient, the goal of sensitivity analysis is to determine the *least* amount of ingredient B that can be used in the optimum formulation without significant decrease in positive consumer response (2.1 percent)

Perceptual Profiles

Consumer evaluations of products on other sensory dimensions and product attributes are important sources of diagnostic information. How consumers respond to color or brightness, or texture, or sweetness of a product enables a more complete description of overall rating in terms of other sensory components and product attributes.

As part of the total product optimization technique, respondents are asked to evaluate test products on attribute dimensions appropriate to that product. Each test product then has a perceptual profile consisting of average ratings on product characteristics.

Correlating overall rating with other product attribute ratings has several uses. First, the size of the correlations (r) indicates the magnitude of relationship between overall rating and specific sensory characteristics. Second, once these correlations have been determined, a perceptual profile can

TABLE 3

Attribute	r Overall Rating	Current Product	Optimum Product*
Color	.784†	20	46‡
Spiciness	.072	49	51
Saltiness	.182	50	47
Sweetness	.713†	29	59‡
Aftertaste	.630†	34	38

*Predicted rating.
†Significant r.
‡Significantly higher than current product.

be predicted for the optimum product. Table 3 shows an example of perceptual profile results.

The size of the correlation coefficients (r) shows that consumer evaluations of color, sweetness, and aftertaste are highly related to overall rating. That is, when consumers like a product overall, they also tend to like the color, sweetness, and aftertaste. Similarly, low correlations indicate little relation between overall liking and perceptions of spiciness and saltiness.

Comparing the perceptual profiles of the current product and the predicted profile of the optimum product highlights product differences and similarities. In the above example, consumers would be expected to like the color and sweetness of the optimum product *more* than the color and sweetness of the current product. In contrast, the current and optimum products would be seen as similar on the dimensions of spiciness, saltiness, and aftertaste.

SUMMARY

Product optimization modeling brings consumers into the product development process at an earlier time—a time when prototype products are being developed. Consumers are the final judges of a product's success or failure. As such, these consumer judgments are available in providing direction for product development. These consumer judges are not asked to be expert trained raters, nor does product evaluation require any special discrimination abilities. Consumers need only be able to provide the straightforward product decisions they are familiar with, "All things considered, how much do I like or dislike this product?"

Product optimization modeling asks consumers to evaluate a wide range of product alternatives that have been systematically varied in amounts of physical ingredients or product characteristics. These product alternatives contain ingredient amounts from too little, to just about right, to too much. Study designs are available (e.g., central composite designs), which adequately sample a large number of possible products. Such designs specify both the number of test products and the formulas for each test product. Consumers are asked to evaluate test products in a controlled setting designed to measure overall consumer product acceptance as a function of systematic product variations.

In order to build the best possible product, optimization modeling provides a preference-ingredient link. A mathematical model is fitted to observed consumer evaluations of a range of test products. By knowing how amounts of physical ingredients affect consumer product acceptance, a product formula is designed to produce the maximum possible consumer acceptance.

Product optimization modeling integrates consumer testing with the design and analytic techniques of response surface methodologies. Such an approach can be more time and cost efficient than developing products by successive approximation. In the approximation approach, consumers evaluate finished products. If their reactions indicate that the product needs improvement, no precise preference-ingredient link is available to guide product reformulation in terms of amounts of ingredients and/or physical product characteristics. Hence, a costly, time-consuming development cycle begins: product formulation, consumer test, product reformulation, consumer retest, and so on. But obtaining consumer reaction to a range of alternatives and determining the best product (optimum formula) in a single step can result in substantial product development savings.

BIBLIOGRAPHY

Box, G. E. P. "The Exploration and Exploitation of Response Surfaces." *Biometrics* 10 (1954).

Box, G. E. P., and J. S. Hunter, "Multi-Factor Experimental Designs for Exploring Response Surfaces." *Ann. Math. Stat.* 28 (1957).

Box, G. E. P., and K. P. Wilson, "On the Experimental Attainment of Optimum Conditions," *JRSS Serv.* B 13, (1951).

Box, G. E. P., and P. V. Youle, "The Exploration and Exploitation of Response Surfaces: An Example of the Link between Fitted Surface and the Basic Mechanism of the System." *Biometrics* 11 (1955).

Bradley, R. A. "Determination of Optimum Operating Conditions by Experimental Methods, Part I—Mathematics and Statistics Fundamental to the Fitting of Response Surfaces." *Industrial Quality Control* 15 (1958).

Garner, W. R. "Rating Scales, Discriminability, and Information Transmission." *Pychol. Rev.* 67 (1960).

Guilford, J. P. *Psychometric Methods.* New York: McGraw-Hill, 1954.

Graybill, F. A. *Theory and Application of the Linear Model.* Belmont, Calif.: Duxbury Press, 1976.

Hill, W. J., and W. G. Hunter. "A Review of Response Surface Methodology: A Literature Survey." *Techonometrics* 8, (1966).

Hunter, J. S. *Response Surface Methodology.* Lexington: University of Kentucky, 1977.

Hunter, J. S. "Determination of Optimum Operating Conditions by Experimental Methods, Part II—Models and Methods." *Industrial Quality Control* 15 (1958) and 16 (1959).

Nunnally, J. C. *Psychometric Theory.* New York: McGraw-Hill: 1967.

12

Consumer versus Industrial Product Introductions

Debra J. Rosenfield
Pfizer Inc.

Introducing a product to a consumer audience involves a marketing strategy selection process that is similar to the process of introducing products to industrial audiences. Furthermore, it may be hypothesized that the purchase decision process involves similar steps whether the audience is a consumer or industrial purchaser. However, there are subtle differences in the tactical application of the strategy selected and in the evaluative criteria as determined through analysis of environment, competitor, markets, and resources that distinguish consumer and industrial product introductions. To the astute marketer it will become clear that there are intersections between the two areas which can provide methods of problem-solving that transcend the boundaries between consumer and industrial product launches.

The purpose of this chapter is to describe the distinctions and similarities between consumer and industrial product introductions through discussion of the four types of strategic analysis and to discuss key implications for managing the tactical application.

ENVIRONMENTAL ANALYSIS

The term *environmental analysis* often conjures up images of a triangle wherein the government, industry, and consumers are all seen taking corners. This is particularly apt to occur in response to those instances involving a new product or ingredient that may have displayed unpalatable characteristics in premarket testing or when a new product is claimed to have characteristics similar to a product that has already been scrutinized by government, industry, or consumer-interest groups. Each side of the triangle has a vested interest in seeking "due diligence" on the safety, effectiveness, and costs associated with the product. These interests arise from environmental factors such as economic pressures (e.g., declining growth rates in an industry), demographic changes (e.g., the aging population), changing social values (e.g., the increasing concern with physical fitness), and innumerable other factors.

Distinctions.   The major differences in environmental analysis for the purpose of consumer and industrial introductions appear to be in: (a) the priorities given by the marketer to issues of *safety, effectiveness,* and *cost* of the new product and (b) whether the product has a model by which potential emotional response to the product may be judged. For example, a new rear-engine automobile to be marketed directly to the consumer would evoke reactions from the consumer based on safety data, past media coverage of the product, and personal comparisons with similar prior products. On the other hand, evaluation of a similar vehicle to be marketed to a fleet manager would probably entail analysis on cost effectiveness first, followed by analysis of safety data and personal opinions. Of course, the size of the purchase dictates the length of, and time devoted to, the analysis.

This divergence in ordering of priorities may also be exemplified by a recent event affecting manufacturers and consumers. With the rash of over-the-counter medical product tamperings several years ago, consumers were less inclined to purchase a new supply of medication due to considerations for personal safety—an emotional response to an environmental factor. Industry responded by analyzing the impact on sales and then investing large sums of capital to design machinery that would produce tamper-evident packaging. Thus industry placed cost first and safety second.

Similarities.   The interrelated maze of environmental issues concerning the three interest groups must be carefully balanced within the marketing plan so that *similar messages* regarding so-called hard data (i.e., facts on safety, effectiveness, or cost) are given to all interested parties. The intent is to provide a common ground to market to, satisfying the needs of individual interest groups but circumventing the interest group's need to insert personal perceptions that could potentially destroy chances for a successful launch.

Marketing Implications.   Before launching a product to the consumer, a thoughtful environmental analysis will often reveal gaps in the consumer's understanding of a given set of circumstances. For example, the 20 year-old consumer today probably has a shaded recollection of events that occurred as recently as 10 years ago. However, through use of electronic data retrieval systems, the media can easily and quickly recall such events, therefore potentially coloring the retrospective glance afforded the consumer and thus perhaps inadvertently and improperly focusing the public's attention before adequate information-laden public relations programs can be implemented. Conversely, a huge market exists, based on the proportion of baby-boomers vis-à-vis the rest of the U.S. population, that allows marketers of consumer products the opportunity to release products aimed at evoking a favorable response to a familiar product.

On the industrial side, social values and emotional response will play a second-hand role to political and economic issues surrounding the new product.

COMPETITIVE ANALYSIS

Competitive analysis, for purposes of establishing cost leadership, product differentiation, and targeting within a market, offers no significant differences in the *process* of creating the analysis from information sources. The *implementation* of each step in the process yields some key distinctions in the data collection/interpretation and thus in the results of the analysis.

A useful analysis of the competition, whether in industry or consumer markets, will allow the manufacturer to determine (1) important product attributes as perceived by the end-user and (2) key deficiencies in competing products, both real and perceived. Furthermore, new markets for the product may be brought to light during careful collection of competitive intelligence.

Collection of information to be used in the competitive analysis of consumer goods may be quite different than that for industrial products for several reasons.

1. Bulk Nature of Industrial Products.   Industrial products tend to be sold and recorded as bulk units. Thus there are less total units to track. Tracking of these units may be more difficult, however, because analysis can involve translating units of finished goods sold, back into bulk units of product. Furthermore, the bulk product may be sold into several industries at different rates (e.g., commodity-type products such as sugar or liquid sterilizers for machinery cleanouts may be sold to various industrial users), thus complicating the task of competitive data collection.

Total unit sales of a consumer product may be greater than total unit sales of an industrial product, but generally more organized and accessible sources of data are available. Examples of these sources include: secondary sources such as published market research studies (IMS, SRI, etc.), primary data gathering methods such as tracking studies, surveys, focus panels, or collection of information from the field sales force.

2. Packaging.   Industrial products, commonly an ingredient or part of a future finished good, often are sold in bulk. Attractiveness of the packaging may be an unimportant variable in industrial competition. In consumer products, appearance is a key variable in securing shelf space and thus increasing the potential for sales.

3. Alternate Uses for Products.   The determination of alternate uses for products delineates a third distinction between introducing products to consumers and industry. The consumer adds value to the product by applying its use in more than one circumstance. The exchange of ideas between consumers encounters few barriers, in part due to the social mobility of the consumer and in part due to the rapid growth of electronic communications. These secondary uses are readily tracked through private or publicly available market research studies and via the clues yielded through sales to new types of distributors.

Alternate uses of industrial products often must be conceived by the product's marketer for a variety of reasons including fragmented distribution systems, government restrictions, and patent restrictions. Moreover, until recently, dialogue between industries that would encourage cross-pollination of ideas was sparse. The advent of formal forums for industrial information exchange (e.g., Health Industry Manufacturers Association) and sophisticated systems for collection of competitive intelligence has broadened the life cycle for many products through alternate product uses. For example, the business development manager of a new hydrophilic polymer formulation originally developed solely for medical applications could turn to any or all of the industries listed in Table 1 as potential licensees of the product. Close examination of a competitor's tar-

TABLE 1: Sample of Potential
Applications for a New Hydrophilic
Polymer Material

Industry	Potential Application
Medical	Artificial cartilage/implants
	Contact lenses
	Dilators
	Grounding pads
	Transdermal drug delivery
	Wound dressing
Toys	Stretchable dolls
Consumers	Diapers, absorbant pads
	Plant watering spikes
	Kitchen towels
Electronics	Coatings for wires
	Grounding pads

get audiences will often reveal alternate uses of the product. Ultimately, however, the burden of determining new products rests with the marketer.

CONSUMER/MARKET ANALYSIS

A consumer market analysis should lay the foundation for the written marketing plan. All prior analyses must be considered when constructing a theory dedicated to the purchasing motivations of the buyer, whether consumer or industrial. The process is standard regardless of the customer, but the logic of the hypothesis and tactics for execution of the marketing plan will vary by type of product and target audience.

One of the most useful models for rationalizing the hypothetical purchase decision process is adapted from a model of the standardized industrial consumer behavior model. (Engel, et al.) The model, shown in Figure 1, supports the premise that all end-users should be analyzed and marketed to in a similar fashion since the iterations involved in the actual process do not change by virtue of the product being

FIGURE 1: Simplified Model of the End-User Purchase Decision-Making Process

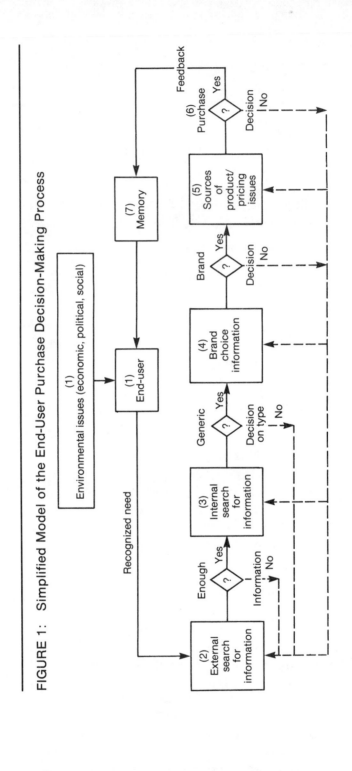

sold. The second benefit attributable to careful use of this model is the ability to visualize valid market segmentations.

Description of the Purchase Decision-Making Model

1. The consumer is constrained in rational decision making by influences exerted through social, political, and economic parameters developed and instilled as part of one's life experience and as an effect of environmental concerns with safety, effectiveness, and cost.

2. With these omnipresent factors and a *recognized need* for a product, the consumer begins an external search for information regarding types of competing products, benefits, deficiencies, etc. This generic information may be gathered through journals, word-of-mouth, and so on.

3. When enough information has been accumulated, the data is assimilated through cognitive processes into a rational decision regarding the type of product needed to satisfy the recognized need.

4. The brand choices, as made available through media, personal contacts, economic demands, etc., are narrowed into a decision to purchase a specific (branded) product.

5. Available sources for the product are investigated, and pricing takes place.

6. The final purchase decision is made.

7. Once the purchase has been consummated and tested (i.e., the product has been tried), feedback on safety, effectiveness, and cost are rationalized into a judgment regarding the fit of the product with the recognized need. This feedback is retained in memory for recall when the need for product is once again recognized.

Similarities.   There is a uniqueness to this model that transcends the line between consumer and industrial product introductions summarily imposed by marketers. The model aspires to ensure sustainable repeat purchases by highlighting key pre-purchase decision points. Clearly, the need for reinforcement of the buyer's intent, specifically at these key decision points, provides justification for longer-term marketing strategies in support of a new product. Additionally, the need to measure the buyer's perceptions of a product vis-à-vis his real needs must necessarily precede a product's positioning.

In developing target audiences from the model's process, it is possible to determine those users most predisposed to the product due to prior use of a similar product, as opposed to those who have had no experience with this kind of product before. Intuitively, it is easier (and generally less costly) to persuade a purchaser to switch to a new product with which he or she is already familiar than to win a sizable audience that has no logical basis for comparison.

Distinctions.   There are three major distinctions evident between consumer and industrial market analyses.

1. Target Audiences.   Upon close examination of the model presented in Figure 1, several inferences regarding target audience selection may be drawn, most notably the presence of three distinct targets that are functions of the timing of the process:

- Targets whose purchases require a longer length of time between each decision point.
- Targets whose purchases require a longer length of time between actual purchases.
- Targets whose purchases are based on a greater need for information than other purchasers.

Table 2 displays the differences between industrial and consumer purchasers relative to the lengths of time spent with these decisions and those practical variables on which effectiveness of the model appears to be dependent. The dependent variables in each situation require special attention from marketing management. They combine to form the basis of a tactical plan designed to guide the purchaser through the predesignated process with as few external and unforeseen disturbances as possible. This is not to say that purchasers may be led through the maze of steps without error simply through use of the model. Deviations from the charted marketing course, however, will provide much-

TABLE 2:   Relative Differences between Industrial and
Consumer Purchasing Decisions for New Products

Targets May Be Segmented on:	*Relative Timing and Dependent Variables For:*	
	Industrial Users	*Consumer*
Time between each decision point	Longer. Variables dependent on: • Corporate pressures (e.g., costs) • Need for adequate documentation of decision • Need for hierarchical consensus on decision • Information searches can take longer (due to a real need for the product)	Shorter. Variables dependent on: • Greater accessibility to information • Impulse buying (due to perceived need or want for the product)
Time between purchases	Longer. Variables dependent on • Production cycles • Storage capacity • Time required for collection of finished goods usage data • Time required for assimilation of usage data and feedback to memory • Time needed to disseminate information through corporate hierarchy • Distribution system (i.e., filling the pipeline versus getting the end-product used)	Shorter. Variables dependent on: • Size (cost) of purchase • Usage patterns • Assimilation of feedback
Depth of information searches	More depth Variables dependent on: • Need for compliance with good manufacturing practices (GMP) • Need for competitive bidding, other company policies • Past experience with similar products	Generally not as deep. Variables dependent on: • Size (cost) of purchase • Urgency of need • Effectiveness of advertising and promotional "reach" • Past experience with similar products

needed insight into competitive and environmental activity that should be acted on as new variables (thus providing new potential targets) with the objective of regaining control of the process and the sale.

2. *Sources and Levels of Information.* For a variety of reasons, some of which were made clear in the preceding description of the differences in target audiences and some of which are due to the traditional sales orientation of marketing management, sources and levels of information disseminated to the two types of purchasers being compared exhibit real differences.

Students of marketing have learned that advertising copy should be geared toward pre-high school reading levels and that, at some frequency of message repetition, retention will occur. The quantity and quality of useful consumer information has thus suffered at the hands of lessons learned years ago. The recent trend of increased consumer awareness coupled with the greater ease of electronic communications has caused a movement toward dispensing higher levels of information to interested consumers. Moreover, new consumer products resulting from advances in technology typically relegated to industrial products has spurred the need to focus consumer attention on product use (e.g., microwave ovens, home pregnancy tests). In specific industries, easing of government restrictions has allowed heretofore "professional" products to move into the over-the-counter world of mass marketing. For example, a number of prescription cough and cold remedies recently received approval to be marketed over-the-counter (i.e., without a prescription). This move triggered a need for greater consumer awareness regarding proper use of such medication as well as a need for adequate information concerning the indications and contraindications of such usage. Formerly this task was the responsibility of the physician and/or pharmacist. Of course, continued physician/pharmacist endorsement was welcomed, but the burden of convincing consumers shifted with the new marketing strategy.

Environmental, competitor, market, and resource analyses must therefore seek conclusions that determine the most effective methods of communicating product information to the purchaser, who is now compelled to make more decisions. The level of information should not be so great as to confuse the purchaser but simply enough to satisfy the information search and facilitate comparisons.

In direct contrast to the seeming *urgency* of consumer information, industrial purchasers are often primed for new product introductions months or years ahead of the anticipated launch through publication of reports to government agencies (e.g., results of clinical trials), press releases, trade journals, and so on. Manufacturers with publicly traded equity will advise Wall Street analysts of product "breakthroughs" that will affect future industrial purchasing patterns. Industrial purchasers are directly supplied with monographs, corporate position papers, competitors' reports, etc., until convinced to try the product or not.

An example of this disparity in sources and levels of information lies in the brilliant marketing strategy utilized by the manufacturer of a new sugar substitute. The product was marketed to industry with a preplanned pull-through from the consumer. Industrial purchasers in several industries were privy to information released to trade journals and made public through filings with government agencies—all on a pre-launch basis. Safety issues were the primary focus of the campaign. The consuming public was the target of a media *blitz*, post-launch, that utilized print and direct mail to offer free samples of candy containing the sweetener. This focused attention on taste. This comprehensive strategy, extending the marketing chain from raw material to finished good to consumer, addressed all links in the chain, effectively employing a tactic rarely used in industrial marketing due to its exorbitant cost. However, the strategy echoed the very traditional approach to marketing: force the consumer's impulse (taste) but appeal to the industrial purchaser's need for so-called hard data (safety).

3. Timing of the Reinforcements. The timing of promotions and advertising, as reinforcement at key decision points in the model, becomes a pivot point that either ensures repeat purchases or unwittingly encourages product

switching. When confronted with choices on the shelf, a
consumer planning to purchase something as commonplace
as toothpaste may involve the entire model in fractions of a
minute, effectively arriving at the decision to purchase a
specific brand due to recall of advertising or satisfaction
with a prior purchase. Thus, in launching a new product,
the advertising message must be clear, concise, and rein-
forced at the point of purchase by some easily recognizable
factor. The value of coupons, unique packaging or another
identifying factor, especially for the new product, is readily
apparent.

The industrial purchaser more often has the luxury of
having sales literature in hand while formulating the rationale for a purchase decision. The message in the sales literature also must be clear but may reiterate many more product
attributes/competitive deficiencies than typical consumer
advertising. Furthermore, in light of the greater length of
time between purchases and the smaller average number of
total purchases per year, information regarding such factors
as product availability, pricing and promotional terms must
be tightly controlled in order to take advantage of the time
"windows" presented to the new product manufacturer by
the industrial product purchaser. These windows become
more important as concerns with production margins inten-
sify the movement toward annual buying contracts with
prime vendors.

RESOURCE ALLOCATION ANALYSIS

When introducing a new product, allocation of scarce resources, such as advertising/marketing/promotional dollars
and production and warehousing facilities, becomes a variable important to the implementation of a successful
launch. This parameter will constrain both consumer and
industrial product introductions, but, again, the tactics applied will vary due to industry "givens" such as channels of
distribution, media acceptable by the trade and/or target audience, seasonality of product usage, pricing pressures, and
promotions.

Levels of Distribution. Every product has an associated marketing chain through which product flows from manufacturer to end-user. In the most simplistic model of a marketing chain (see Figure 2), the manufacturer of the indus-

FIGURE 2: Simplified Model of Industrial and Consumer Distribution Chain

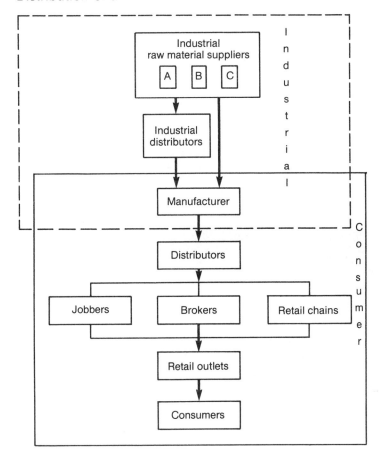

trial raw material has two methods of getting the product sold: through direct access to the purchaser and through distributors who have direct access to the purchaser (Hlavacek & McCuiston, 1983). In the former method, a one-level selling effort can yield a substantial sale of the product. Careful selection and use of distributors can also deliver a large sale of the product with but one additional step in the process.

The consumer product marketer is faced with the multi-level challenge of having to address each link in the marketing chain (which can include distributors, jobbers, brokers, retail chains, mass merchandisers) to reach a single consumer in a selected target audience. The additional burden of having to monitor the advertising message, sales promotion continuity, and timing at each link activates the need for in-depth pre-launch planning and for the provision for rapid turnaround of feedback on the new product. In addition, collection and assimilation of competitors' movements within each distribution link is vital to the successful consumer product introduction.

The effectiveness of the launch depends on complete and effective marketing to the preceding link. In a recent packaged goods product launch, with four steps from manufacturer to end-user, the manufacturer addressed each link of the chain with a separate array of merchandising tools, although each succeeding distribution link received the collateral pieces given to the one below (see Figure 3). Note that the distributor sales force merchandising kit had 21 items and the dealer kit contained only 16.

Advertising/Marketing and Promotional Expenditures. For reasons discussed earlier, distinct differences exist between consumer and industrial product launches. The hype often associated with the traditional consumer "blitz" tangibly differentiates consumer product launches from the smooth but lengthy industrial product introduction. This practice persists due to traditional marketing thinking and is encouraged by customary distribution systems. Yet the tactics being used are beginning to converge. As more grass-roots public relations programs are endorsed for consumer product launches (especially in technology-driven industries such as medical devices, electronics, and automotives) and more industrial marketers begin to accept the benefits of

FIGURE 3:   Addressing the Links in the Marketing Chain: A Recent Packaged Goods Product Launch

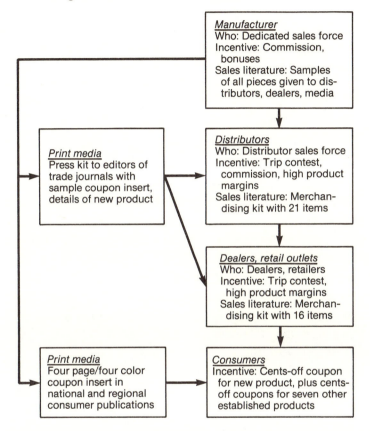

branding commodity-type products as well as using the consumer pull-through approach, the two disciplines will potentially see synergies in areas of marketing previously unexplored.

CONCLUSION

Real differences exist in launching products to consumers versus industry. That such biases exist today may be attributable to the slow evolution of marketing management's thinking away from its traditional and often fragmented orientation in sales, technology, and operations and its stereotypical consumer-based background. Conceptual emphasis on environmental, competitive, market, and resources analyses, as drafted into the marketing strategy, will forge the convergence of approaches to the task of launching industrial and consumer products. Specific trends currently driving this melding of marketing disciplines are founded on the premise that the common denominator is in the process. These trends include:

- Increased number and strength of consumer interest groups are catalyzing the need to disseminate better information at all levels in the marketing chain.
- Mobility of management between industrial and consumer product manufacturers is offering some cross-pollination of tactics to each side.
- Advances in technology will be more readily transferred from the industrial sector to consumers.
- The need to simplify consumer distribution channels will cause marketers to evaluate industrial marketing chains for possible use as models.
- Advertising agencies are evolving into marketing services organizations geared to support all phases of strategic marketing planning and spanning all types of products.
- Greater use and acceptance of formal forums for dialogue between consumer and industrial product management will allow for more widespread exchange of ideas.
- The role of the corporate planner will be broadened, adding the additional responsibility of creating interdivisional dialogue among divisions previously given full autonomy.

Thus acceleration of the convergence will be driven by standardization of process while acknowledging that real differences exist in product development/usage and in the tactical manipulation of the purchasers.

REFERENCES

Engel, J. F., R. D. Blackwell, and D. T. Kollat, eds. *Consumer Behavior*, 3d ed. Hinsdale, Ill.: Dryden Press, 1978, p. 32. Adapted from Jaeger's model.

Hlavacek, J. D., and T. J. McCuiston. "Industrial Distributors—When, Who, and How?" *Harvard Business Review*, March-April 1983, pp. 96–101.

13

Ensuring New Product Success

The Applications of Innovative Eye Tracking Service

Elliot Young
Perception Research Services, Inc.

The success or failure of a new product is determined by the behavior of the shopper as he or she makes a purchase decision. Advertising, point-of-sale displays, and promotions are designed to work in harmony as stimuli for product selection. Yet, in reality, one word—*curiosity*—is the key to new product success. The marketer who can whet the consumer's appetite, while conveying uniqueness and good value, is the marketer whose new product has a chance to succeed.

In addition to traditional verbal questioning, we have pioneered the use of *eye tracking shopper behavior* to uncover those new product concepts likely to be successful and, conversely, those proposed new introductions likely to fail.

It's often difficult for marketers to accept that the vast majority of new products will fail. Yet, year in and year out, the statistics vary little; thus, the need to improve the comprehensiveness of pretesting research and the appropriateness of eye tracking to observe the shopper as he or she ponders a new entry.

When evaluating new products, we work under the assumption, *unseen is unsold.* A new product must break through clutter, it must get attention, it must generate an opportunity to sell. Of equal importance, a new product must convey uniqueness, it must convey good value, it must convey a point of difference.

Eye tracking documents the ability of a new product to break through clutter. Eye tracking can be used to watch shopper behavior, i.e., to uncover those concepts that stimulate attention, involvement, readership, and consideration. By observing behavior, eye tracking uncovers items that tend to be quickly bypassed or totally ignored. Experience has shown that new products which fail to generate curiosity are new products which will ultimately fail.

A number of rules should be followed meticulously to ensure success:

Rule No. 1—Do Your Homework, Tightly Define the Target Audience. All too often marketers tend to be general in their definition of potential buyers. The tendency has been to utilize such broad definitions as "women, 18 to 24," or "males, 35 years of age or older, who are regular users of specified brands."

New products should be targeted to more specific segments of the population. Demographics are not enough. Lifestyles, areas of business responsibility, and educational background are all critical pieces to be utilized in developing the buyer profile.

Rule No. 2—Pretest Your New Product with Target Consumers. The rush to introduce a new product often leads to "shortcutting" of the research function. Strange as it may seem, after all the work is done to define the target consumer, initial pretesting of advertising or packaging is implemented in a general, rather than a specific, manner. Too often marketers are obsessed with testing to beat "normative levels," while forgetting that most normative data is generated from a general audience, rather than the tightly defined target. Logic dictates that, if a new product and its advertising are being designed to reach a tightly defined target, the pretesting research *must* be conducted with this target. New product scores obtained with general audiences often lead to an erroneous sense of security.

Rule No. 3—Always Pretest Using the Consumer's Frame of Reference.   The objective of pretesting is not simply to confirm that the product will be successful but, rather, to uncover any potential pitfalls at an early stage. With this in mind, it is essential that the new product be presented in a competitive framework. The marketer must have information that will confirm the ability of the packaging or the advertising to break through clutter and to generate an opportunity to sell.

When pretesting advertising, eye tracking can be used to determine if the shopper will get into the ad, i.e., if the ad has an ability to stimulate that magical curiosity leading to sale.

The eye tracker records the shopper's discriminating process. It pinpoints what they see, what they read, what they get into and, of course, what they quickly bypass.

Work with eye tracking goes back to the late 1800s, and work continues on an ongoing basis all over the world and in outer space. The 1983 Skylab research experiments included a number of eye movement studies.

The first serious application of eye tracking in the communications research industry began in the late 1950s. Perception Research Services nurtured this experimental work and, in 1972, established an ongoing network of testing facilities to observe consumer behavior and reactions to new product advertising, packaging, display material, and outdoor boards.

Eye trackers instantaneously record viewer behavior onto magnetic tape at a rate of 30 readings per second. They are accurate to within one half of one degree. They display, on video monitors, the actual "seeing" experience—where a person is looking superimposed directly onto the item he or she is observing. Therefore, an advertiser can see, in the form of a white "bouncing dot," what people are drawn into, what they read, what they study, what grabs their attention.

In order to improve the odds that a new product will be successful, pretesting research must be comprehensive, it must evaluate the proposed product on the dimensions of stopping power, imagery, price perception, interest in trial, and uniqueness. The research should address each of the pitfalls that might lead to failure.

It is generally agreed that a strong advertising execution can "carry" a poor or average new product. However, it is also agreed that a strong new product can be ruined by advertising that lacks the ability to interest the reader or shopper. With this in mind, pretesting evaluates an advertising agency's "best efforts" to bring the new product to life. The agency develops prototype magazine advertising. Consumers are exposed to a series of ads with one new product prototype ad included in the grouping. The eye tracker records the involvement generated by the new product's advertising.

The use of eye tracking, along with comprehensive verbal questioning, provides the marketer with both evaluative and diagnostic insights. It enables him to understand if the new product and its advertising convey desired marketing strategy, if they stimulate curiosity, if they appropriately position the product. Thus, the function of pretest research is to determine if an advertising execution effectively conveys the marketing strategy.

A second function of pretest research is to uncover areas of deficiency and to provide diagnostic help to fine tune advertising and promotional executions. New product research should be both evaluative and diagnostic. It must serve as an input to ensure effective communication and greater return on advertising investment.

Rule No. 4—Don't Overlook the Importance of Packaging. The success or failure of a new product is often directly affected by packaging. Most marketers now concur that, in many instances, "the package is the product." The package must serve as the final vehicle to close the sale. The package must break through clutter. The package must justify price/value to the consumer.

For many years, marketers and their advertising agencies worked on the assumption that the package was incidental and that appropriate advertising and media weight would be the ultimate factors for determining a new product's success. The emphasis is changing; marketers now realize that the package is the single common denominator. The package is in every store; the package is in every TV commercial; the package is in every print ad; the package is the product. A study published by POPAI/DuPont documents that almost two thirds of all purchases in the supermarket are not planned. This figure highlights the fact that consumers are flexible in their purchase behavior and that a strong new product package, with prominent shelf positioning, can determine new product success.

Eye tracking of packaging is a viable input in determining and ensuring marketing success. Eye tracking can be used to document stopping power in the cluttered on-shelf environment. A marketer should understand how a shopper scans the category. This leads to development of shelf planograms, which eliminate the possibility of a new product being "lost" in clutter.

Eye tracking is also used to see how shoppers read package labeling. The eye tracker shows designers how elements on the labeling are working and, most importantly, which elements tend to be ignored. A designer uses various tacks to reach the shopper. Eye tracking research uncovers which ones work and, at the same time, provides insights for improving packaging prior to its reaching the supermarket shelf.

New product research should also uncover consumers' feelings about the product and its packaging. Does the package convey efficacy, good taste, functionality? Is it aesthetically pleasing? Does it justify the price? In sum, does it help close the sale?

A marketer buys space in a store; he does not have 30 seconds of TV time. He must have a package with stopping power because the shopper can pass a category without ever seeing his product. Eye tracking has documented that:

- About one in three of the packages on a shelf are generally ignored as a shopper makes a purchase decision.
- Ideal shelf positioning can result in a 76 percent increase in brand visibility.
- Upper shelf location receives 35 percent greater attention than positioning of a brand on a lower shelf.
- Additional facings can result in greater consideration. A doubling in facings (from two to four) has resulted in a 34 percent increase in a new product's attention on the shelf.

The linking of new product packaging and advertising research has shown that a new product's package not only can affect shelf visibility in the store, but will also significantly influence the stopping power of advertising. Often the package becomes the focal point in a new product ad. A poor package reduces ad involvement and, accordingly, advertising effectiveness.

Packaging is equity. A primary example is Chivas Regal. Here, the package is the product, and the package justifies a premium retail price. When one considers the multimillion-dollar investment that will be made to package a new product, packaging research becomes a wise investment.

Rule No. 5—Avoid the Common Trap; What People Say and What They Will Do Are Often Quite Different. The common cause for the high rate of new product failure is often thought to be poor research design. In actuality, researchers readily admit their quest for magical, predictive, questioning procedures is frustrating. If verbal questioning were predictive, the rate of 8 in 10 new product failures would not persist. Yet the tendency exists for respondents to try to "please" interviewers, i.e., to provide the answers they think the interviewer is searching for. In reality, the most difficult task of any marketer is to motivate a shopper to switch brands. The shopper who has built a long-term relationship with a product is generally satisfied with that product. Their likelihood of switching or trying something new is directly influenced by the packaging of the new product, its appeal in the in-store environment, and the effectiveness and attention-getting ability of advertising and promotion for the new entry.

Market researchers tend to evaluate new products and new product packaging alternatives by placing them side by side in front of the shopper and administering a wide variety of preference questions. Experience indicates that, while this approach may "force" a winner, in reality the marketer often ends up uncovering the strongest of two potentially weak alternatives. A more insightful indication of consumer curiosity and interest in a new product is to position the product alongside potential competition. Thus, shoppers are considering the product alongside those brands they might currently be using. The new product that piques curiosity and has stopping power on the shelf is the new product entry worthy of serious consideration.

Rule No. 6—Don't Get Discouraged.   A successful new product is hard to come by, and many of those that carve their niche in the marketplace were researched and fine tuned again and again before the magic formula for success was achieved. Eye tracking research has been a part of the marketing effort for these and many more new product entries:

- Captain Morgan Spiced Rum
- Land O'Lakes 4-Quart Cheese
- RC 100 Cola
- Creme de Grand Marnier
- Eagle Snacks
- Dow Tough Act
- Spartus Vitamins
- L&M Superior Cigarettes
- Kellogg's Nutri-Grain
- GrandMa's Cookies

Many of the products the shopper sees on the shelf today are a result of extensive new product advertising, packaging, point-of-sale display, shelf configuration, and taste test research.

Research evaluated each new product against predetermined marketing objectives. The research utilized question and answer and eye tracking of target consumers' behavior to help lead to success at the cash register.

New product introductions are expensive. They represent a significant corporate risk. Many marketers have found that eye tracking can improve the odds for new product success.

The added dimension of observing shoppers as they discriminate within categories and between brands (eye tracking) uncovers potential failures at an early stage. Eye tracking pinpoints products likely to be ignored, and after all—unseen is unsold.

Part IV

Marketing Issues

14

Innovative Ways to Unorganize for New Product Success

Lynn Gilbert
Gilbert Tweed Associates
Jeffrey Fox
Fox & Company, Inc.

If it is true that "words are cheap, and deeds are dear" then most companies do not want new products. At the very least they haven't got the heart or stomach to go through the agony and tedium of conceptualizing and introducing new products. Companies talk new products and new markets, but they work the old ones. Companies say that 35 or 40 percent of their sales in five years will come from new products. Yet they devote less than 5 percent of their people budget to new product development.

The halls of companies are littered with the bones of one-time new product managers. The company culture and "idea killers" crush the life out of the new product process.

Company resistance to new product risk-taking can be obvious and vocal: "Manufacturing can't make it." "The return on investment is too low." "We can't divert precious selling time for an unproven idea." "The trade won't stock it at that price." And so on. Or the resistance can be insidious and invisible. The silent killer is the toughest barrier for the new product manager to hurdle. This is the company structure and its committees, hierarchy, politics, rituals, inertia, and analysis paralysis. If the silent, risk-adverse, anti-innovation infrastructure doesn't deter new product development, it definitely prolongs the process and takes the fun out of it.

CEOs and boards of directors understand this dilemma. They know the problems, but the solutions are unconventional and don't follow what are apparently good management rules. Senior executives are not willing to do the things necessary to foster in-company creativity and to counterbalance the no-change mentality of most companies. So CEOs resort to tried and untrue solutions. They create "New Product" or "Commercial Development" departments. They hand out a couple of "Director of New Products" titles. Sometimes they create a "Corporate New Products Group" (which usually fails). They allocate a little bit of money, give the person a pep talk about how important new products are, proclaim undying support, close the door, go back to managing the business, and let the gossamer threads of company inertia strangle the new products director.

The answer is to unorganize.

UNORGANIZATION IDEAS FOR NEW PRODUCT DEVELOPMENT

1. Get rid of the "new product review committees" or whatever euphemism is being used. In many corporations "review" often means dilute, compromise, and defeat, and permanent committees are where things go to die.

2. Junk the organization chart's neat little boxes and lines and have the new product people report directly to the

division or company president. Do this regardless of company size, seniority, salary levels, titles, etc.

3. Ditch all the regular reports and controls and other innovation dampeners that companies employ.

4. Forget about overly rigid annual business plans, budget and variance reviews, return on investment criteria. Provide sufficient legroom; fine tuning can be accomplished later.

5. Send a memo from the CEO to all employees emphasizing the importance of the new product effort and giving total support and clout of the president's office to the new product person. The new product manager writes the letter.

6. Have the board of directors establish a new product performance standard for the CEO and use it to determine his annual compensation.

7. Disregard the corporation's compensation system (grade levels, parity pay for top and average performers) and pay the new product manager ample money. Be sure that new product success is rewarded with big bonuses—say two, three, or more times the base salary. Treat your successful new product person the way the marketplace economy treats a successful entrepreneur.

8. Start a "Genesis Group" open to anyone in the corporation. People join as volunteers. They can work on pet ideas, new products, or new business, and these projects can be on or off the company charter. The Genesis Group gets its own place—a special office, lab, or unused meeting room. The locks are changed, and only members of the Genesis Group and the CEO get keys. The new product person runs the Genesis Group. The group does not write monthly reports, trip reports, or any of the other corporate standards.

9. Hire the "unorganization man" (or woman) to do the job of developing new, novel, and numerous products and businesses. Successful new product individuals are not going to be like the rest of the organization. They are anti-organization, anti-systems and procedures, and anti-

controls—and they are anti-losing. They are the corporation's love-hate focus. They are probably a company's
most important potential contributors and the most
likely candidates to leave.

The shrewd CEO knows how to recognize this unusual
management species, fully knowing how to seek them out,
free them from the chains of the enterprise, motivate them,
and keep them working for the company.

CHARACTERISTICS OF THE SUCCESSFUL NEW PRODUCT PERSON

1. *General management skills.* Often mislabled and mis-
   perceived as specialists, new product people are actually penultimate corporate generalists. They have to
   touch and manage every piece of the corporate machinery to make a new product happen. Their creative skill
   is very special, but they are general managers.

2. *Green thumbs.* They are gardeners, growers, and nur-
   turers who make little seeds grow into big trees.

3. *Blank page vision.* It is much easier to run a business
   than to start one. It is easier to manage a brand than to
   create one. It is easier to manage the marketing than to
   start with a blank page.

4. *One man bands.* They can play all the instruments,
   and they have to. They can run, pass, kick, line the
   fields, and collect the tickets. They know about manufacturing, finance, research, sales, personnel, legalities,
   advertising, and budgets.

5. *"Miss-a-meal" pains.* They are hungry. They are not
   sated. They are nourished by creating something.

6. *Christopher Columbus syndrome.* They are explorers
   and discoverers. They cannot sit in port. They are always looking for solutions to problems, recognizing
   good answers, seeing new ways. They are interested in
   newness.

7. *Night sight.* They can see in the dark. They see light at the end of the tunnel. Often the darker it gets, the more lucid their vision becomes.

8. *Lead from the middle.* To change, to create, requires reorienting the organization. The winning new products people have to be "sell guys" not "tell guys." They must lead the organization from within, working in the bowels of the structure, effecting gradual acceptance of the concept. This marshaling ability convinces R&D that it can be formulated, manufacturing that it can be made, sales management that it can be sold, and so on.

9. *Velvet hammer.* They keep hitting, but they don't hurt or inflict lasting damage.

10. *Stamina.* Developing new products is a tedious, tiring, draining endeavor. Success requires enormous physical and mental stamina. High energy levels are required constantly.

11. *White liar.* Often the organization needs to be tricked into going forward. A little white lie here and there about how successful the new product will be generates company confidence. New product managers know that success breeds success and that confidence is critical to winning. If they can get the organization to believe in their ideas, the chances of success increases.

12. *Veterinarians.* They must hear the unsaid, the unarticulated. Just as a vet derives solutions from mute patients, so too the new product person hears the clues, needs, desires, and wishes of the marketplace . . . even when the marketplace says nothing.

13. *Ideaphile.* New product people love ideas. They collect ideas. They talk about ideas and write them down. They keep idea notebooks. Ideas stay on their mental shelf—in inventory—until they find a use for them. New product people accept and appreciate ideas regardless of the source. "Ideophiles" don't care if the idea is original to them. They can't be bothered with

all the unproductive discussion about idea ownership. Their interest is making the idea a reality.

14. *Biblical.* When Moses said, "Let my people go!" new product creators heard him. They let their people do their job, and they do not interfere. They do not put the pencil to every suggestion. They encourage the attempt. They praise the little victories. They never criticize failures or goof-ups.

15. *Audacious.* Big success comes from big thinking. The ideas are often simple, but audacious big ideas are the well-spring. New product winners think boldly, execute enthusiastically, and go for the gold.

16. *Tinker, tailor, try.* New products are rarely perfect the first time. They usually require tinkering and tailoring. Concepts are tried and tried. New products people tinker, doodle, try, reinvest, figure, scheme, make some changes. They fail often but on their own turf—in test—not in the marketplace.

17. *Execution overkill.* The new product idea does not have to be perfect before market introduction. It just has to be better than what's on the market. Even though the concept is not perfect at the outset, the marketing execution will be. Successful new products are a product of relentless, meticulous execution. New product managers overkill on execution. When Pampers disposable diapers were first introduced they didn't have plastic closure strips. But they had other consumer advantages, and Procter & Gamble overkilled the introduction execution to get the job done.

18. *Manners matter.* The new product winner says thank-you and please 50 times a day. He knows that other people are needed to succeed, and he appreciates their support. He knows that the other people in the organization are busy with their own jobs and, reflective of the realities of a company, they are subconsciously against the fear and pain and cost and risk associated with birthing new products. The sensitive new product manager understands the human issue and always deals sincerely and politely with all.

As in many aspects of business and industry, the solution to a problem is often obvious and simple—that's why it is usually overlooked or discarded. This method of managing—by *unorganizing*—is so contrary to modern B school dogma, that it is hardly ever found in today's corporate world and is antithetical to all management principles. But whether we look at the development of the wheel or the IBM PC, we see that new products were developed by individuals who were able to tap all available resources without the constraints of corporate hierarchies or organizations that stifle innovative and productive contributors.

Let these individuals be part of the *unorganization*, and you will have a breeding ground for tomorrow's CEOs and presidents. This is where generalists grow, learn, and prosper. Free them up, and you will create a new resource within your own organization that will be more fertile, more productive, and create more profit than ever expected!

15

Naming the Product

David R. Wood
Interbrand Corporation

INTRODUCTION

For centuries producers of goods have marked or branded their products. The reasons for this are probably twofold. First, branding was a means of identification within the marketplace. It identified a product's source and helped consumers choose between similar products. Second, in the early days of craftsmanship, prior to mass production, workers undoubtedly had a strong sense of pride in the creation of a product. Hence the craftsman, or manufacturer, "signed" his product much as a painter or sculptor did. It is interesting to note that this type of personal identification, which was the forerunner of today's trademark or brand name, is beginning to reappear in our mass-production environment. For example, every Rolls Royce grill is signed by the craftsman who made it, and every McIntosh computer carries the signatures of the entire team that developed and created the product.

Over the decades and centuries, the role of the trademark or brand name has remained virtually unchanged throughout the world—it is the ultimate identifier of source and the ultimate means of distinguishing between similar products. It provides a unique way for consumers to exercise freedom of choice in their selections of goods and services. There are, however, three principal ways in which this system has been further developed.

First, legal systems throughout the world have recognized the inherent value and importance of brand names to both manufacturers and consumers. Hence, a rigorous system of registration has evolved for all forms of intellectual property. Trademarks, patents, copyrights, and so on confer real ownership of intellectual property and make the rights of owners defensible against trespass and similar infringements.

Second, the concept of branding has been extended to services and other nontangible goods. Today the providers of financial, insurance, or retail services enjoy the same protection as providers of tangible products.

Third, and perhaps most important, we have learned that branding is intimately involved in the overall development of product personality. We no longer seek to identify only according to product, size, shape, and price. Today branding must appeal to a much more complex range of subliminal consumer desires and requirements. Consequently, we try to imbue our brand names with a series of hidden messages and signals. In this way, we develop a series of nontangible, nonpractical, nontactile qualities that will manifest themselves in marketplace advantages.

Modern, sophisticated branding increasingly addresses itself to the "product gestalt," not simply to the product's practical qualities and applications. If this approach is successful, a brand will eventually attain a mystical mix of values, both tangible and intangible, which are appropriate to consumers on both a conscious and subconscious level.

In the final analysis, these nonpractical factors residing in the brand name can make the difference between a market leader and an also-ran.

BRANDING STRATEGY

In the early days of branding, the key objective was quite simply *identfication of source*. Hence, a great percentage of the early brands simply used the names of people or companies (e.g., Ford, Gillette).

A short step from that form of rudimentary branding was the *collective brand name*. Often used when the company was started by several people or when it was involved in many products or industries, this approach led to such names as General Motors, General Electric, and International Business Machines—no magic, no marketing, simply straightforward, unemotional statements of fact.

Branding came of age in the late 19th and early 20th centuries. In these years, major product segments became competitive, and manufacturers began to realize that they could gain competitive advantage by branding their products in other than a generic or purely descriptive fashion.

In 1880, for example, Harley Procter realized that White Soap was nice but it could be copied, it was not protectable as a trademark, and it appealed only to the practical, commodity instincts of the buyer. So in that year, he renamed his soap Ivory, and the rest is history.

During the late 1800s and early 1900s, some of the great, classic, enduring products were developed and introduced—along with brand names that took a giant step away from their generic, commodity orientation toward the era of marketing, positioning, and hidden persuasion. Many brands introduced during those years not only survive but continue as market leaders to this day. They include:

- Kleenex (1924)
- Oreo (1921)

- Coca-Cola (1890)
- Budweiser (1880's)
- Zippo (1932)
- Camel (1913)
- Ivory (1882)
- Maxwell House (1892)
- Kodak (1900)

For the first time manufacturers applied the principals of marketing to the business of branding.

In a sense manufacturers began to realize that branding had evolved from a brief statement of fact about the product or its origins (Ford) or its scope (General Electric) into a much more subtle mix of information, persuasion, distinctiveness, and protectability.

BRANDING TODAY

We've come a long way from the relatively simple, unsophisticated, inexpensive days of the early 1900s. Today we are faced with ever-increasing difficulties, costs, and assaults in a product-oriented marketplace.

In a market as complex and huge as the United States, product development and launch costs are awesome. New product failure rates are terrifying and show no signs of falling below 70 to 80 percent. Market share is critical because it provides the funding for new products.

To launch a new cigarette on a national scale today costs in excess of $100 million; single share points in the breakfast food or beer segments are worth tens of millions. We need to pay extensive and precise attention to every single aspect of the final product.

And key among all these aspects is the brand name. An overwhelming proportion of all of the physical qualities, performance attributes, and advertising and promotional messages reside in the brand name. We buy our products by reference to brand name, which comes to represent, in our minds, a summary of the key qualities of the product.

It is for these reasons that branding has become an increasingly critical element in the development, launch and life cycle of almost all new products today. The brand synthesizes the product's physical, aesthetic, practical, rational, and emotional qualities. In so doing, the brand must be both appropriate to the segment and the consumer and sufficiently differentiated from its competition as to be both unique and protectable.

In the 1970s, companies began to examine the ways in which brand names were developed. It quickly became clear that existing methods (which were, for the most part, highly subjective, nonprofessional, inefficient, and inward-looking) would not be able to meet the requirements of an increasingly sophisticated and competitive environment. At this time, branding emerged as a separate and discrete area requiring professional attention, much as advertising (and later, packaging and graphic design) had years earlier.

Hence the 1970s saw the emergence of specialist companies that used the tools of modern marketing, research, and design to develop brand names and overall brand personalities.

The law was a key factor in this new service area. Because trademarks represent legally registrable and protectable property and because the volume of registered trademarks had grown greatly during the 1950s and 60s, the role of the legal expert, the trademark attorney, became increasingly important.

As a result of this development, professional marketing services got involved in naming products. It is interesting that this took so long since brand naming is a daunting process that, if not handled properly, can result in serious delays in launch or costs in litigation, relaunching, repackaging, and so on.

Today, through the use of a series of stages and tools, brand names are built to meet an established set of marketing criteria, rather than left to the whim of the new product manager, the chairman of the board, or the marketing director's aupair girl!

STAGE 1—STRATEGY DEVELOPMENT

In the strategy development stage, a series of objectives are established for the brand name. These objectives may include such things as length, beginning letter, languages in which the name must function, meaning and pronunciation, and type of brand name preferred (e.g., suggestive, descriptive, etc.). Other elements to be considered may include competitive environment, how the product will be promoted and purchased, the importance of the graphic impact, the requirement for trademark registration, possible future uses of the brand name on other similar products or a line of products, how a corporate or umbrella/line name may be used with the new brand name, and what type, if any, product descriptor will be used.

Because all of these elements can affect the final brand name, they must be factored into the branding strategy.

STAGE 2—BRAND NAME DEVELOPMENT

Once the strategy is developed and we have a series of objectives, the business of brand name development begins. We at Interbrand make extensive use of consumer groups at this stage. Since the brand name must speak longest and loudest to the market segment it is addressing, we feel that early consumer involvement assists greatly in ensuring that the final result will have complete consumer acceptance.

Also used for brand name development are sophisticated computer programs, and a massive computerized Name-Bank. Similar steps are taken in foreign markets when a brand name is being developed for international use.

Throughout this process, the trademark attorney plays a key role. The legal realities of trademark registration differ from country to country and within different classifications of goods and services. The trademark attorney keeps the process on target and prevents it from becoming a purely creative exercise with little chance of producing a practical, usable, and registrable result.

STAGE 3—SCREENING

The next step involves screening the creative production. Screening should be done to ensure that the final list of names meets all the objectives that have been set for the project. Names should be screened against the branding objectives, for legal availability, and for international use involving both meaning and pronunciation in the specified languages.

STAGE 4—TESTING

The resulting short list of brand names is tested with target market consumers in any one of a number of ways. Such testing can be important to ensure consumer acceptance, to ensure the names have no negative associations, and to aid in making the final decision. Again, name testing of this nature can be done on an international basis.

The result of this type of organized, step-by-step approach to what was previously regarded only as a highly subjective and creative area is the development of a series of brand names to do specific jobs and to meet specific criteria.

In the final analysis, however, we are always talking about branding that creates a level of distinctiveness—in a consumer relevant fashion, and via an entity to which we can lay exclusive claim.

Once we have that, we have the nucleus of a valid and valuable brand name commodity. Apply to it the power of graphics, packaging, advertising, and promotion (and add a lot of skill and luck), and we can find a handful of letters that imparts a bewildering amount of practical information, rational messages, pictures, subliminal triggers, and more.

16

New Product Brand Considerations

Naseem Javed
ABC Dial Inc.

A name is only one element of a new product, but it is perhaps the single most important factor in a successful new product launch and continued market acceptance. This chapter is about names and the process of naming products.

A product name must do more than merely designate—otherwise all products could simply be numbered. In the crowded, competitive, fluid world of the late 1980s, a product name must function as a total message. This message deserves clear thought, and it must be structured as cleanly as possible. That name, as a message, will compete with hundreds of other messages, other signals. It is imperative, therefore, that the message get through and that it stand out from the rest. The name must be easy to remember, it must be subject to minimum distortion, and must be salient to the targeted receivers. The name must have power.

While you read this paragraph, hundreds of names will be registered, accepted, or rejected in North America. With millions of uses of various names for products and businesses, duplication and confusion are very common problems. Thanks to computerization, we now have data bases that can quickly produce lists of alphabetically or phonetically similar names. Some sophisticated data bases can even translate names and look for similar meanings in other applications or languages. Statistics regarding the most frequently used name elements have also been compiled. In the early part of 1984 there were 185,020 companies in the United States that used the word International as part of their name, 11,600 using Micro, 17,530 using Software, and 17,740 using Tech. Is it any wonder that the consumer becomes confused and that laws regarding registrability are starting to get tougher for the protection of companies already in existence? The large number of new products and companies, and the new and advanced methods and trends in searching names, have set precedents over and above the conventional procedures of name development and searching that have been carried on by corporations and their respective lawyers in the past. The legalities of name protection itself are complex. Of the approximately 400,000 lawyers in the United States and Canada, only a few are fully conversant with the problem and with the rapid technological changes in name search and availability procedures. Conventionally, corporations would ask their lawyers to take a list of names and search for conflicts. Lawyers would write to each state and have clerks check against some file card or semiautomated system. They would then come back with an OK or Not OK opinion. This was the only basis a lawyer had to give a registrability decision before the product was launched. Law journals are filled with cases where names came into conflict after the launch—but that's an area for the legal profession to pursue. In this section, I would like to focus on the following aspects: creation, availability, and protection.

STRATEGY OR LUCK?

When you look at the pages of history and pick out success-ful products, it may appear that the names were created ca-sually or that they were based on some simple solution. That may have been true, but today things have changed completely. As more and more products are introduced, their creators choose to forsake the more obvious kinds of names in favor of ones whose origins are less apparent. From S.O., for Standard Oil, was coined the term Esso. A general-purpose vehicle, G.P., became Jeep. Polyte-trafluoroethylene yielded the name Teflon. There are many different sources and inspirations for names. Some of the most common inspirations will be discussed here.

Surname.   A preliminary look at a list of Fortune 500 com-panies reveals that a large number use either the founder's surname as a name or combine the names of people who had a major part in the creation of the firm or the product that made the firm successful. The desire to immortalize oneself by naming a company or product is very strong. Of course, since the earliest times people have striven to bring glory and honor to the family name. Once a family had achieved a desirable reputation and goodwill within the community, no effort or expense would be spared in keep-ing the name untainted and beyond reproach. If possible, they would zealously guard the name to keep others from duplicating it and thus taking away the business their good-will had established. Today millions of dollars are spent on advertising a good name, in bringing it to the attention of the buying public, and making it signify "leadership" among its competitors in the marketplace. Carl Franz Bally, Tomas Bata, Marcel Bich (Bic pens), and Laszlo Biro all had interesting surnames that have made history and become famous as successful international products. Boeing, Kraft, Cinzano, Colgate, and Porsche are all surnames.

Surnames with slight modifications have been used for product names as well. Konishiroku produces cameras called Konica. Sir Joseph Lister's formula for antiseptics was used in the product called Listerine. John Rawlings invented a plug called the Rawlplug. Charles Revson's company adapted his surname to become Revlon and also used his given name in a line of products called Charlie. Surnames have always been used (with varying degrees of success) in naming products and companies, and they probably always will.

Classics.   The classics have also provided the basis for many product names over the years. This lends a double-barreled effect, giving an exotic and impressive-sounding name for those who are not aware of the story behind it and an extra level of meaning for those who are. Ajax is the name of a cleanser, but not all of its users are aware that Ajax was a participant in the Trojan War, a Greek soldier who was renowned for his strength and bravery. Mazda is the Persian god of light, and the name, which was originally applied to a brand of light bulb, has now become familiar as the name of a car. Vulcan, the Roman blacksmith god, has provided the name for metal products as well as a specifically processed rubber. There is a whirlpool bath called Adonis, named after the beautiful Greek youth, and tripods called Hercules, named after the mythical Greek hero renowned for his great strength.

Place Names.   People have also used place names with some success, like the Japanese coastal city of Hitachi, West Germany's Hoechst, and Shibaura, a region in Japan where the Tokyo Shibaura Electric Company operates (hence Toshiba). Many people automatically associate the word Corning with Corningware and are not aware that this is the name of the city where the factory and offices of the Corning Glass Works are located. Similarly, Pontiac, Michigan, yields a name for cars, although the name Pontiac itself has much more ancient roots. Hershey Bars get their name from the town of Hershey in Pennsylvania. Oneida for the stainless steel products comes from Oneida, New York. Obviously place names can have histories of their own, but when the location becomes the birthplace of a new product that subsequently bears that name, the product is considered to be named for the place rather than for whatever person or event the place itself received the name.

Dictionary Words.   Another approach to name creation is to use already familiar dictionary words that have little or no relation to the product being named. Carnation has been used for both cigars and milk. Apple, although not associated in any natural way with computers, is fast becoming identified with them. The names of constellations, zodiac symbols, gemstones, flowers, animals, and everyday items have all been used to name products and companies. If the association is too remote, however, it may be difficult for the buyer to relate the name to the product or to remember it when it comes time to make a selection. Many detergents, for example, are given simple, natural names that make the buyer think of rushing water—like Tide, Surf, or Cascade. This reinforces the idea of washing in the mind of the consumer. Some products are named for human qualities and emotions, like Cheer and Joy or Pledge and Promise. To connote purity, wholesomeness, and honesty, Henry D. Seymour chose the image of the Quaker for his oatmeal cereal, Quaker Oats—and it worked. As indicated before, the name is one of the single most important factors in a product launch, so it stands to reason that a product should not be named carelessly or arbitrarily.

Simplicity.   Simplicity can be attributed to names like Celanese, Cellophane, and Celluloid, which not only convey the message of cellulose but also leave a strong imprint when the consumer is confronted with the product and with its meaningful and suitable name. The mind quickly recognizes the key components and features of the product. The Italian scooter by Piaggio called Vespa, meaning wasp, was appropriately named because of the total design of the scooter, which appeared like a wasp, humming through the busy streets. The company continued on to produce a three-wheeled car called Ape, the Italian word for bee, and an outboard motor named Moscone, meaning blue-bottle, a common water insect. Not only were the names appropriate for each of their respective products, but the company was able to associate the products with each other in the minds of consumers. In America there is a similar association in the naming of cars using the images of wild animals, such as Mustang, Jaguar, Cougar, and Lynx.

When you think of words like apple, carnation, rose or shell, you quickly recognize or see a flash of an image: a computer, milk, tea, and gasoline. This quick recall is the direct result of the strong message, a combination of the word itself and a product, that has been conveyed through advertising over a period of time. Names may have other justifications. Aquascutum, for example, has the advantage of having been in use since 1853 and being the Latin for water-shield, a very appropriate choice for a line of rain-wear. Despite its pronunciation problems, it can be justified as a product name. This is only possible, however, if the name gets a unique, distinct, visual formation, a recognizable sound, and an identity.

Many names have been coined from different sources. Such names are unique and easier to protect from a legal perspective, but extensive advertising campaigns may be required to familiarize the public with them. Esso and Teflon have already been mentioned. Coca-Cola was named after two ingredients of the beverage, the coca leaves and the cola nut. Brylcreem comes from brilliantine (a hair dressing preparation) and a stylized spelling of cream. There are endless examples of names that have been coined in this way, some far more appropriate and successful than others. Because these words are not familiar to the consumer, great effort on the part of the NPD team must be undertaken, and that great effort usually entails great expense. Most small companies do not have the resources to achieve the kind of status that Exxon, for example, has come to have. Product launches depend on effective advertising, which can clearly carry the suggestive, effective, emotional messages for the quick response of the consumer.

Foreign Languages.   In a similar manner to coined words, words from foreign languages are also not immediately understood by consumers. Sometimes used to provide a more "sophisticated" impression, the romance languages, particularly French and Italian, have furnished names like Chauffeur, Riunite, Capezio, and Fleur de Lys. A more exotic feeling is evoked by names like Kon Tiki, Hai Karate, and Liebfraumilch. Names like Bambino and Cafe are easily accepted by the buying public.

Latin has also provided a source for some names. The Latin word for tree, arbor, yielded the name Arborite. As mentioned before, Aquascutum is Latin for water shield. Nivea, from the word niveus, meaning snowy, is a good name for a cool, white skin cream.

Alpha-Numerics.   Yet another trend in naming is alpha-numeric names. The most famous example would be the corporate name change of the Minnesota Mining and Manufacturing Company—to 3M. Would they have been better advised to use an acronym or some other coined word based on the old name, like MinMin? Hardly. Numbers used in combination with letters or words are often used to name products. Some examples of this would be A-1 Steak Sauce, 2nd Debut, 7-Up, 9 Lives Catfood, Rub A-535, and for those who sleep six hours or less, the 18-hour bras. Numbers alone have also been used for product names, like 4711 cologne from Germany or 1878 Rye. But imagine the confusion in the marketplace if all products were simply numbered. There are legal ramifications as well. How can you protect a number from use by others? You can't. A number provides no identification with goods or services in the public's mind; instead, it is likely to cultivate feelings of mystery, mistrust, and Orwellian depersonalization. In dealing with long strings of numbers, there is an acute problem with human memory. Words have meanings, and even nonsense words take on meaning by association (Exxon, for example), whereas numbers do not have that quality.

Variations.   Another simple naming device is to alter the spelling slightly by omitting a syllable or changing a letter. Using this method, new can be spelled nu and quality becomes kwalitee. These strangely spelled words can be strung together to give different effects. The deviant spellings are eye-catching, if annoying to language purists, and can help to distinguish similarly named products in the marketplace. Some of these deviations can be based on regional pronunciations. For example, in New York City and other places in the eastern United States, names like Nevalose, Wonda-cloth, and Kleer Wite may be found. Other variations in pronunciation produce names like Bit O Honey, Faskota, Thun Thoot, and Gli-door. Another common method substitutes letters or numbers for words. This is at work in names like X̲-PERT, E̲-Z̲ FLO, CANT-B̲-LOST, U̲-C̲-LITE, FITZ-M̲-ALL, and probably the most famous of all, BAR-B̲-Q̲. Numbers are used to replace the words to (2) and for (4).

Other names rely on a simplified spelling, omitting "unnecessary" letters to get the idea across in a faster, more unique way: SNO SHOO, DUAEZY, TUF-GRIP, GOURMAY, STA-TRU, D'ZERT, DED-N-DUN. Words can be made to look different by substituting vowel graphemes (as in EVU̲R READY, HYGE̲E̲N, NE̲E̲T) or consonantals (as in MAJ̲IC, K̲LEAN, FOLDZ̲TITE, RUF̲F̲ & TUF̲F̲). Names can use literary devices like puns to get the attention of the consumer. Seizer for a clamp plays on Caesar. Names like Clothes Encounters, The Saucerer's Apprentice, Sir Plus, The Brick Shirt House, and Hard Wear (this last for a break-dancing outfit) cleverly play on familiar words and expressions. But no matter how names are created and selected, either through an extensive process of rearrangement, twisting sounds, adding letters, dropping syllables or through the miniaturization of lengthy concepts using acronyms and prefixes, or any other devices, the fact remains: the art is not creating names but matching ideas with a few letters of a symbol that may convey the story to the consumer appropriately.

Name Development Must Be Justified, Otherwise Names Are but Noise

Of all the purposes of a name, the key use is to get the purchaser to buy the product. Even then, names are conceived for corporate identification, for suppliers, financial backers, shareholders, the general public, media, and so on. So then, what is a good name? We could answer by acknowledging that a name must be *memorable, distinct, protectable,* should not convey any wrong connotation in this complex social structure of ours, and so forth. If the main purpose of the name is to attain purchaser's acceptance, then let's carry this aim into the fine disciplines of psychology, buyer's behavior, and response to products. Products are to fulfill our needs, our emotional needs.

Product launch depends on effective advertising, which could carry the suggestive, effective, emotional messages for the quick response of the recipient. In summary, a name must sell: it must sell the product, the concept, the application, and, particularly, the fulfillment of the special emotional need for which the product was initially designed.

Persuasion, An Art

A product has a function—something that it does or achieves that perhaps no other product can match. For example, Aqua Velva strongly suggests water, and the soft touch on a scrubby shave will feel like velvet. Bug Off suggests bugs dropping dead all over the place. Broil-a-matic suggests automatic broiling, without a lot of hard work on the part of the cook. Close-Up toothpaste will let you do that, Cross-Your-Heart bras do. Human nature craves emotional comforts and seeks out suggestions of that comfort constantly.

"And Man, born to do little or nothing . . . "

A short walk in a shopping center may conclude that man certainly was born to do little or nothing. The art of selling products that promise to achieve things without the buyer having to raise a finger is very much in evidence in our culture. Products bear names like Easy On, Easy Off, Hassle Free, Lestoil, Touch-and-go, Once Only, One Wipe. The sense of least possible physical exertion and consumption of human energy has made a lot of North American products become symbolic of "effortless consumption behavior." Other examples that cater to this tendency to want things done as easily as possible include Nice N' Easy, Easy Flo, Easy Lock, and Easy Fill.

The Jet Set Society: "O Time, let me count you seconds apart . . . "

Lately if things are not "Insta", they appear thick and sluggish. Things must be Quick Flow, Quick Start, Drip Dry, Snip Snap, Jet Set, Jiffy, Zoom Broom, Instant Serve, or Wisk. Well, let's face it, life is on the go.

Upstairs & Downstairs Syndrome

No society can do without class distinction. There are the lords and ladies, the saints, the kings and queens, the rich, the diamonds, the jewels and gold, the seals of approval, the protocol, the richness of thought, the exclusivities, the limited editions, the restrictions—they have all successfully conveyed and uplifted the powers of the product. There is an air of distinction about names like Saint Michael, Lady-bird, Knight, Castle, Silver Chalice, and Prince Matchabelli. There is a seal of approval implicit in names like First Class, Crest, Cordon Bleu, and Edition Limitee. People trust the endorsement of professional associations. They enjoy buying products that seem to promise the finer things of life, products named for flowers and their essences, the stars, the galaxies, the zodiac signs, the kings and queens of mythology, and virtually anything that sounds royal or regal. Included in this category would be products named after literary figures and famous historical persons, like Tolstoy Vodka or Napoleon Brandy.

On the other side of the coin, there is "Downstairs"—the mass of people, those affected by the sagging economy, the unemployed, people on welfare, and those who enjoy searching for bargains and getting their money's worth. For them, there are names like Budget, Janitor-in-a-Drum, Mister

Save, Mister Economy, Crazy Joe, Joe T.V., Cobra Beer, Thrifty, Econo Pac, and Ever Save. There are names that evoke the popular belief that the Scottish are a clean and thrifty race: Scotch Tape, McDonald's, McIntosh.

"And those things never wear out!"

Before the tidal wave of Japanese quality control systems hit North America, the general conception was that of the throwaway society. Accuracy, dependability, and reliability were a big question. Names that reflect the new concern with precision and quality are Accugraph, Accumeasure, Accumatic, Accuprint, Accuraflo, Built-rite, Champion, Duragraphic, Durapoint, Durashine, Duralight, and so on. People tend to trust the advice of physicians, so names that seem to reflect the endorsement of doctors are popular: Doctor Ballard's, Dr. Pepper, Medico, Crest, Doctor Oh, Doctor Fowler's. Yet there are still some vestiges of the throwaway generation left: Dis-pak, Dispose-a-glove, Dispovac. Still other names refer to the product's ability to deal with obsolescence, for example, Adjust-a-grip, Adjust-a-size, Multi-clone, Multi-form, Multi-pac, and Multi-scan. Our emotions and senses need comforting, and sweet, simple, narrow messages, as illustrated here, quickly conveyed by the sound of a name, may help identify those special needs within our hearts and souls.

An Affair to Remember: Memory, the Key Factor

Many names, without their appropriate, magic products, may sound funny, meaningless, and, at times, ridiculous. Can you imagine a hula-hoop or a janitor in a drum?

If the single most important object of the name is to convey a strong message to the first purchaser, then it must be clearly understood that no name can survive its memorability cycle without having a clear, distinct, strong, and manipulative association with the product itself. A name must have this strong association with its product, and the more association, the better. To properly assess the value of this aspect, simply write on a sheet of paper 10 to 15 names that come instantly to your mind. You have to be fair about this. Either you remember these names because you have used the product in the recent past, or you can see them around your office. To do this correctly, you must close your eyes and list 10 to 15 names. Try it. And as you carry out this process, you will be amazed how the associations come to your mind before the names themselves. That's why naming a product is the art of matching a simple, cute name to a brilliant idea. When a new name is matched with its proper symbology, a definition of colors, and a multimedia manipulation strategy, all of a sudden it leaves a strong image and eventually becomes part of our daily lives.

So a name is like a picture, worth many thousands of words. And what makes a name tell its own story, although it may appear to be a question of luck, depends purely on strategy; a strategy whereby the key features of the product, along with its persuasive appeal, promise to fulfill an emotional need of the consumer.

Confusion, by Accident

There are many famous marketing situations that hinged on inappropriate name selection, particularly those involving products marketed internationally. Poor research and well-meant but misguided decisions resulted in low sales, and in some cases led to expensive lawsuits. The story is often told about Coca-Cola's first attempt to market their soft drink in China. Wanting the name to retain its English pronunciation, the company had a translator find Chinese characters that would be pronounced in a roughly equivalent way. It was only after they had gone through the expense of bottling and distributing the drink that they discovered the actual translation was urging the Chinese consumer to "bite the wax tadpole."

The Egyptian private airline Misair overlooked the fact that their name when pronounced means misery in French. The makers of Irish Mist whiskey learned that translation is important when they tried to market their product in Germany under that name. They soon discovered that mist is

German for manure. If adequate search techniques are not utilized, a company could find that their much-prized name selection is already being used in one of the jurisdictions in which they operate. The name Big Foot was the choice of the Goodyear Tire and Rubber Company of Akron, Ohio, for a new line of tire. But after spending $6.5 million on development and promotion, it turned out that another company operating in Ohio was already using the name for *their* tires. "Back to the drawing board" was a costly walk in this case. The name Adam for a computer was disputed by two companies, Coleco Industries and Logical Business Machines Corp.; this issue had to be settled in court. Budweiser couldn't be called King of Beers in Canada because a similar trade name was held by a Canadian brewer. There is a tendency among companies to simply "shelve" products that run into name problems in an attempt to avoid additional cost.

THE PROBLEM

There are approximately 60 states and provinces, each providing name search facilities of some kind to the legal profession and the general public in North America. The guidelines for approving and rejecting proposed names vary drastically. Over decades, departments in charge of commerce would maintain a brief, calligraphed record of a business name. The systems of name approval never became standardized because each jurisdiction made its own name availability policies based on geopolitical relationships and the rate of commercial growth. Today in each office of the secretary of state, each name checking section maintains some kind of a manual, semiautomated, partially computerized, or fully computerized data base system, which is used by the name checking clerks. Traditionally, name checking clerks do not enjoy their work for one major reason: each name submitted requires a decision, whether qualified or arbitrary.

There are 400,000 lawyers in the United States and Canada, most of whom specialize in some field. Traditionally and by law, each lawyer can act as a trademark agent, and, apart from trademark registration, they can also call or write to specific states to obtain names for proposed corporations or new products. There are very competent corporate lawyers (although good ones are rare), but they specialize more in other corporate matters rather than in the logistics of computerized name data bases and the daily routines of name searching. Name searching has become a significant problem due to a sharp rise in the number of small businesses and the new entrepreneurial trends (information-type businesses and the explosion in new products). Telecommunication and software companies are setting up names and operations overnight in 20 or 30 states at a time, and so are the franchise operations. Excessive jurisdictional expansion makes the name data bases in each state extremely large and complex, and they can become unmanageable if kept on manual or semiautomated systems.

In summary, name searches are really being done by junior civil servants who have no concept of the overall view, and these searches for the most part are requested by lawyers who are also unexposed to all the matters of name search and record-keeping procedures. Consequently, this trend has taken too long, and it is often a nightmare to the new product development manager of a large corporation launching a new product. It is equally difficult for those setting up new corporations who are faced with a major advertising campaign and other issues. Therefore the proper search for a name for a new product or business activity must always identify these key questions:

> What method of searching is used, under what guidelines, on what size file of names?
>
> Will the name be protectable?
>
> Will the name be available and protectable in each state and in other countries, and over what period of time?
>
> Are the end-users aware of the loopholes in the system?
>
> Is there a name protection plan?
>
> Is there a long-term naming policy?

Now that the problems with name searching and protection have been discussed, we can examine the usual methods companies use to obtain names—the methods currently being used—and make some recommendations for improvement. To clarify the process, the various steps have been listed in point form. There is, of course, the old-fashioned way (that is, "Leave it to the lawyers"), and then there is the "Nu-Way" (employing marketing and computerized systems with a name search specialist).

In any event, the following checklist will help identify certain areas that may add more power to your name development unit.

THE OLD SYSTEM

1. *Name Development Team identifies a list of names.*
   a. The list may vary from a few names to hundreds.
   b. A purely creative form, this does not accommodate any registrability rules.
   c. Names may be in order of priority, but there may not be an alternate strategy to make names available.
2. *Names are submitted to lawyers for clearance.*
   a. Lawyers may or may not know the marketing objectives at this stage.
   b. The lawyer writes, or in an urgent situation attempts to call, certain or all states asking for approval.
3. *A clerk in the secretary of state office checks the name.*
   a. Clerical attitudes and performance prevails.
   b. Proposed names are checked for identical names.
   c. Total lack of background information prohibits any keen observation on not-identical but qualifiedly similar names.
   d. Decisions are based on a certain bias, reflecting local state guidelines.
   e. Response may vary from days to weeks. Final response may be an OK or Not OK opinion.
   f. Reluctance exists to make qualified decisions.
4. *Lawyer receives response.*
   a. The number of records in each state, procedures, and guidelines vary.
   b. Response varies.

    c. Lawyer accepts OK or Not OK opinions and formulates a decision.

    d. Lawyer may formulate a name availability strategy at this point.

    e. Lawyers are inclined not to argue availability guidelines.

5. *Lawyer reports results to Name Development Team.*

    a. If results are not satisfactory, the entire process starts again.

    b. On the second or third time around, the lawyer may acquire insight into the marketing objectives of the total case.

    c. A final name may be selected over a long period of time. If the name is rejected, only a short time remains for a final selection.

6. *Lawyer gives the go-ahead on a name.*

    a. The lawyer may then start to formulate a protection plan.

Summary. Sometimes this exercise takes forever, thus leaving no time for selecting a good name toward the end. Lawyers may have to deal with civil service state by state, and often the lawyers themselves are not conversant with the intrastate guidelines and the marketing objectives.

1. If the name is not suitable from a marketing standpoint, the lawyer may not know it and may not care about it.
2. If the name is not protectable in the long run, lawyers may thrive on the ensuing litigation and big court cases.
3. If the name is fully protectable, the lawyer will be asked to formulate a protection plan and then to police the marketplace to make sure no one else is using it.

Recommendations

Name development, name searching, and finding an available name must be done by a professional. Lawyers should be specifically instructed to only verify reports of availability and, once they are satisfied with the results, to institute a protection plan and give the company a final go-ahead. The name protection plan is the only function for which a lawyer should be called. Naming is purely a marketing strategy, and searching for availability is no longer a legal function—it is a highly specialized electronic function.

The following outline reflects the recommendations above. In the "new" or "proposed" system, the job of name creation is shared between the NPD team and a name specialist, and this specialist undertakes the searching process previously performed by lawyers. The firm's lawyer will still be called on to formulate a protection plan for the final name, a function more in line with his expertise and experience.

THE NEW WAY

1. *Name Development Team and a name specialist identify a list of proposed names.*
   a. Several groups consisting of a few names are proposed.
   b. Each group is identified with a specific objective.
   c. Name specialist eliminates a large number of proposed names that are not suitable by bringing in availability input and registrability rules.

2. *Names are submitted to name specialist to arrange for clearance.*
   a. Data bases are utilized to assess availability of the proposed name.
   b. Preliminary results are often available on a same-day basis.

3. *Key secretaries of state and jurisdictions are contacted.*
   a. Alternate names and prior knowledge of rules and regulations are available.
   b. All responses are discussed and questioned by the specialist with the department.
   c. Unavailable names are quickly modified under a predetermined policy.

4. *Name specialist prepares a report.*
    a. Extensive reports are produced indicating the avail-
        ability of the name and potential problems associ-
        ated with it.
    b. No reports are prepared for unavailable names.
5. *Name Development Team seeks approval of the lawyer.*
    a. Lawyer's approval is based on a solid, extensive re-
        port.
    b. Lawyer, based on justification, gives the go-ahead
        and institutes a name protection plan.

Summary.   In most cases, this exercise takes no longer than
a week; it therefore leaves excellent testing time for reas-
sessing available names, allowing the team to stay ahead of
schedule. Although name search specialists may deal with
the same system of civil service and record-keeping, the
centralized knowledge of all rules governing each state, and
the extensive manipulation of electronic data bases with
complete understanding of marketing objectives, design,
symbology, etc., produces effective results. To a name specialist, the suitability of the name is everything. The specialist will not act as a lawyer and will not provide a legal
opinion. Rather, the specialist will set the quality standards
of search procedures and bring quick results during the
highly creative process with full understanding of registrability. Once the name is finalized, the specialist will
strongly recommend that an organized name protection plan
be put in place and executed only by an experienced
lawyer.

FUTURE OF NAME SEARCHING

How and when you should create an idea for a proposed
business activity is a difficult question. But once you have
clearly understood an idea in the form of a product, service,
or business, then the naming of the concept becomes a crucial exercise that demands speed. Why? Because somehow,
in our minds, one single identifiable name is the storyboard
of the entire concept. The sooner the idea can be associated

with a final name, the quicker peace of mind can be achieved and brains can be readied for the next concept.

Imagine that sitting on your desk there is a terminal able to search a name and show you instantly how the name is being used, state by state, province by province, country by country. Imagine that by pushing a single key you could find out the complete story of the name in use, the type and size of the product, its entire history, and more. A terminal of this kind is not too far away. By the end of 1986 there will be a few such systems in North America. At present there are some on-line systems with partial capability to provide instant information on proposed names and on names already in use.

In 1978, the federal government of Canada decided to stop providing name search approval or rejection to the legal profession or the general public directly. They appointed certain companies who would directly access government files and generate a name approval or rejection report required for all registrations. The government made that decision for two reasons. First, each name search required a decision, and it was realized that a private organization could offer varied service and a flexible fee structure to accommodate different levels of searching, thus providing better service to the marketplace. The second reason was that the searches were often being provided at no charge; therefore, the department was costing the taxpayers millions of dollars. Following the federal government's decision, various provinces in Canada adopted a similar policy. This trend of privatizing the name search sections, and of various jurisdictions letting the specialists provide highly customized service, is on the rise. It is expected that by 1990 most states will adopt this policy based on the excellent results of the Canadian experience.

17

The Role of Package Design within the New Product Development/Marketing Process

John Stevenson Blyth
Peterson Blyth Cato Associates, Inc.

From the designer's initial perspective, the new product exists in terms of its purely physical attributes. It has a form that must be contained. It may be a liquid, granulation, or solid. It may be a beverage, sugar, a medicated gel, or an appliance. However, before the precise means of containment can be considered and the specific identity developed, the uniqueness of the product must be determined. This uniqueness may emanate (1) from its mode of manufacture, permitting the production of a product never before accessible, (2) from the opening of a new market with products evolving in its wake, or, (3) in a few cases, from the perfection of new packaging forms to broaden product dimension.

Some products by definition determine their potential. A sugar-free carbonated beverage, a tampon, and a hair dryer are examples of how the uniqueness of each product can have an acute effect on audience choice. A sugar-free beverage with nutritive advantages, a tampon that can be made at a fraction of the cost of others, and a hair dryer run on solar power all stand to place their marketers at distinct advantage, both in terms of their product categories and their potential consumer universe.

It would be hard to overstate the importance of product uniqueness. The lack of a meaningful, expressible difference is one of the chief reasons for new product failure in the marketplace. Another prevalent reason is that the marketer overstates or overpromises or—inversely—fails to communicate the product in readily understandable terms. In a harsh, busy marketplace that grows more crowded each year, these faults can be ignored only at the marketer's extreme peril.

A measure of the force of competition is the fact that, over the last two decades, about 20 percent of the total brands on store shelves can be defined as new. More vividly, one United States toiletries manufacturer derives fully 40 percent of its income from products debuted within a given five-year period. Given the stability of the marketing conglomerates (whose strength is measured in share of market in product categories where they sell multiple brands) and the kinds of shelf space and advertising support these conglomerates can demand, the undefined, undifferentiated new product faces the hardest task of all: simple survival.

In this atmosphere, the canny marketer examines all available options during the new product's development. Of these, one of the most important is forming the organization that will develop the packaging and marketing program and setting up a realistic, workable timetable for the production, distribution, and introduction of the product.

THE PACKAGE, THE CONSUMER, AND THE MARKETER

No element in the entire new product marketing program must fill as many roles as the package. Like a kaleidoscope, it is perceived differently by all who view it.

It is to the marketer's advantage to understand that the most acute packaging perspective is that of the consumer. Very often, to even the discriminating, well-educated consumer, the package is viewed as the product. It is certainly the consumer's primary source of information about the product. It discloses the contents, the quantity, the convenience or protective features, the value, the use instructions and, most definitively, the points of difference from other products. To the consumer, a package is to a product what a book is to words. One simply doesn't exist without the other.

In the most basic terms, the package does the job of keeping the product manageable from the place of manufacture to the point of use and of clearly explaining its function and protecting the contents until they are consumed. If the package is inadequate to its job, if it is ambiguous or misleading, the product will not be bought a second time.

For the marketer, the package assumes additional identities. It is the most economical, efficient, and durable vehicle to move the product to the point of consumption, preserving the product as nearly as possible in its condition at the moment of production. The optimal package must at the same time dispense product while protecting it from destructive influences. Where necessary, it must comply with governmental regulations. It must not interact with the product in a negative manner. Also it must adapt itself to every environment in which it is placed, even extreme conditions.

In the absence of all other external influence, it must support or enhance the quality of the product, stimulating the desire to purchase.

Given these two sets of criteria, other factors must be considered. The first are historical. They involve the long-term trend to personal selection by the shopper. An outgrowth of increasing labor costs at the retail level and the growth of larger-scale marketing outlets to sell higher volume, self-service led almost directly to the consumerist movement and its demands for greater safety, honesty, and integrity in the marketing of products.

Interestingly, even the consumerist movement has not dampened the traditional American attitudes of acceptance and willingness to try new ideas and their marketplace embodiments, new products. The problem is one of reconciling the requirements of the marketer with those of the consumer.

Into this role moves the package designer—the individual who has grown up during the era of marketing upheaval and has repeatedly shown the ability to comprehend and manage the forces at work and their social, economic, and sometimes philosophical implications. Through an independence of position and perspective, the package designer serves as a bridge across which information flows from both marketer and consumer, tempered by a deep and thorough knowledge of the workings of the marketplace.

Because of this unique perspective, the package designer lives in what to the new product marketer is the *no-man's land* of development and introduction. From the beginning, the marketer is treading water. This water is deep, mysterious, and fraught with potential dangers. While there is excitement about a new product, there is also an underlying fear that the whole idea is too costly or that there will be no market for it. If the package designer is chosen judiciously, the new product's market becomes familiar territory, one in which the designer's insights can shed the light that banishes these fears.

This is so because the independent designer is just that—independent. Not dedicated to a single marketing company's philosophy or perspective, the designer is often sought for the objectivity of viewpoint not always accessible to company marketing executives.

In addition, the designer lives in the marketplace on a day-to-day basis. The intense observation of consumer likes and dislikes and responses to the smallest change in packages and their graphic elements as well as to other conditions imposed by the marketer all go into the shaping of the design perspective.

Knowing the history and current configuration of a market makes the designer a unique guide to the introduction of the new product.

THE ROLE OF PACKAGING DESIGN

Marketing executives are becoming increasingly convinced that packaging is a key ingredient in the new product program. The reason is the impact of brand imagery, a primary function of design. There was a time not too long ago when the designer tended to be a missionary in the marketing wilderness, endeavoring to communicate the value of the package in the overall introductory program. This isn't the case anymore. Too much documented evidence establishes the role of packaging as one of marketing's most potent weapons. In our own Peterson Blyth Cato Reports, for example, interviews with 500 marketing executives indicate that executives believe packaging to be the single most important factor in the purchase decision of the consumer. This finding is confirmed by studies of independent researchers. As tellingly, a separately published report states that more than 90 percent of the leading packaged goods marketers in the United States use design consultants.

Now, with a proliferation of product categories, it is acknowledged by marketers and designers that the function of the package is to target specific consumer groups with products that offer minute advantages or differences.

This idea carries further. The brand imagery established by the package transcends its physical origin. Beyond a certain point, the consumer doesn't think simply of the package, but rather of the image originating with the package and conveyed through a multitude of other promotional media.

This imagery, an outgrowth of what advertising agencies call the "unique selling proposition," becomes the perception of the product in the consumer's mind and the single most important motivator of purchase. Thus, for all marketing purposes, the brand imagery conveyed by the package becomes the product until the purchase is made and the consumer opens the package. At that point, the value of both depend on the consumer's satisfaction—which in turn can be enhanced by the package and its design.

The brand imagery launched by the physical package is expressed in real terms that generate specific reactions by the consumer. This is a function of the three Cs of design: configuration, color, and copy. Through the meticulous development of brand imagery with these tools, the designer engenders precisely the visual qualities associated with the uniqueness of the product. For a premium-level food, these characteristics can include appetite appeal, elegance, exclusivity, convenience, and other qualities. With pharmaceuticals, brand imagery can emphasize efficiency, reliability, and purity. These strengths of brand imagery not only help to select the consumer, they also function to build the consumer's faith—a critical element for new products.

Where the new product is precursor to an entire line or series, care in developing the optimal brand imagery is an absolute necessity. The future of the line depends on it.

From the moment the first package is exposed to the first consumer in a retail situation, the process of equity building begins. One of the vaguest terms in the marketing vocabulary, equity is nonetheless one of the most potent. It is a function of time, of consumer experience with the product, and of advertising. Because of the power of contemporary communication, it can be built in months rather than in the years required many years ago during the adolescence of marketing techniques.

Equity, in the marketing sense, doesn't appear in most dictionaries. It is simply the value that accrues to a product beyond the monetary worth of its development and production. It is a blend of goodwill and other perceived values that accumulate during the product's lifespan. It results from uniqueness and perceived performance, both factors considerably influenced by brand imagery. It follows then that the brand imagery which most effectively conveys the product concept to its audiences is the one most capable of helping to build the strongest and most durable equity for the marketer—and the one that places the new product at its greatest competitive advantage.

The concept of projecting uniqueness is based on a presupposition: that each product category has its own "look." Generally, this is so. Traditionally, for example, wine bottles have been configured to indicate a specific type. More recently, vintners have been developing unique custom glass molds as well as adopting alternative materials and structures in their search for new markets and new consumers. Some examples are the metal "soft drink" can with easy-open pull tab and the plastic bag in a corregated paper box for larger-quantity sales.

This desire for the unique package is well-founded. A unique configuration is memorable. There are other advantages, too. The package with a new kind of dispensing feature provides an additional reason for the consumer to purchase the product. A unique configuration that brings a new type of product to the market is the visual justification for the product and simplifies the product's acceptance in the consumer's mind.

A unique configuration or creative graphic concept provides the new product marketer with one advantage that only now is beginning to be appreciated. This is the power of a package so different and so obviously superior that its introduction makes all of the competitive packaging seem dated or inferior. This package, usually but not always the result of a technological advance, represents the highest order of brand imagery. It is known as the preemptive package, and its arrival at the marketplace generally leads to a scurrying by the competition for "improvements" and other changes aimed at restoring their own shares of market. These changes can range from frank imitation to a search for alternatives with the patina of newness. Meanwhile, the preemptive package builds its own share of market, while the imitators never quite reach its level of acceptance.

Other factors, of course, help to determine the unusual package's growth. The polyethylene bottle for motor oil is a case in point. Much cleaner and more convenient to use than the traditional metal-end composite can, the bottle is also competitive from a price viewpoint. Its share of market grows annually. But this growth could have been hastened by an early, firm program of support by the oil companies marketing them, and by powerful, distinctive brand imagery that developed an emotional advantage over canned oil.

Historically, design has been given little significance as an instrument of establishing not only the new product, but others that may flow from it at a future time. One reason is that the marketer, viewing only the short-term factors in bringing the product to the consumer, may have no idea, first, how consumer acceptance can develop because of the package and, second, whether the new product has potential in other forms. Because of the sophistication of packaging as a marketing instrument, careful development of the modes of packaging can bring to the marketer's doorstep a larger consumer universe than was originally anticipated. This is a much more common phenomenon to the marketer who plots strategies in terms of decades, rather than seasons. Even the company planning a single package for the new product has, in itself, the potential to explore submarkets that can be even more profitable than that originally entered. This segmentation is a technique that package designers have understood for many years. Very often, their developmental programs are keyed to just such eventualities as parts of master plans they help develop for their clients. Examples abound. A product introduced in one form is adapted to another. The mode of dispensing is varied to broaden use. Even the addition of sizes may require modification beyond simple adaptation. Often the effort is justified. The life cycle of a product can be extended considerably by just such activities.

Consistency is a marketing virtue. From the time the product imagery is refined until the final package is to be placed on the store shelf, the adaptation and translation of that imagery in various promotional and advertising applications become part of the marketing program. It is the job of brand management, working with the designer, to make certain that the imagery is in no way diluted or subverted. Much of the work the marketer and designer accomplish is directed at the development of a unified, understandable imagery refined to have the most positive and durable impact on the consumer. If the imagery is dissipated or obscured at this point, even toward the goal of short-term gain, the entire future of the program may be jeopardized.

Meticulous attention to detail, on the other hand, can yield a strong promotional and advertising program because the original vision of marketer and designer is preserved intact. Almost every designer who has worked on a major new product introduction, and many marketers, can vouch for the truth of this statement.

Packages that achieve specific marketing goals aren't hard to find. Indeed, their longevity is testimony to their effectiveness. A product introduction combining elements of novelty and longevity is Jergens Aloe & Lanolin skin lotion,

with package design by my firm. Developed by the Andrew Jergens Company to enter the therapeutic segment of the market—and avoid intruding on its traditional lotion's share of the cosmetic segment—the package is a slim polyethylene dispenser for consumer convenience. Directed at a broad-spectrum market, the product provides two ingredients now popular in skincare use.

Use of the Jergens logotype as the first element in the graphic design is a quality confirmation and an effort to build the company's equity into the new product, while the product descriptive is a focusing on the two ingredients. The final typographic element—a statement incorporating the representations of an aloe leaf and a droplet representing the lanolin—reinforces the descriptive name. The green and blue color coordination within the typographic format, while not apparent here, brings a feeling of excitement and therapeutic value to the design system.

Unique physical packaging can offer a potent stimulus to sales in offering intriguing special brand identification for the product—along with utilitarian characteristics.

Spoonery Cheese™ natural cooking cheese is a new product from Land O'Lakes. This unique new product has been

introduced by Land O'Lakes of Arden Hills, Minnesota, and its unusual packaging designed by us. This project was a total packaging project from jar and custom overcap design to label graphics. Both the overcap and the descriptive statement, appearing in a banner across the front panel of the container, color coordinate with the variety of cheese—either mild, sharp, or extra sharp. The speckled crock-like jar combined with the custom overcap and the simple yet natural looking illustration of a wooden cooking spoon with a healthy dollop of cheese on it creates an appealing picture.

Excitement is also a function of balance. Nowhere is this more apparent than in a design system developed by May Bender Industrial Design for Conair Incorporated. For a line of more than 30 beauty accessories, MBID employs the folding carton, one of the most common vehicles of packaging, in a new manner. Distinctive silver imprinting and embossing, used in combination with meticulously photographed products and balanced typography, develop a format that carries tastefully from one product to another to impart a family appearance. The system works as though each package were acting to confirm the quality of the other—with the total effect magnetic even when displayed alongside Conair's higher-priced competitors.

Another extremely effective design concept is developed by Charles Biondo Design Associates for Venture Foods' introduction of Riche, a French-style, low-fat yogurt. Entering one of the most intensely competitive dairy food markets, the premium product is packaged in a six-ounce thermo-formed plastic cup that competes successfully with the more standard eight-ounce size in a price-driven market. Going against these larger sizes, the Riche container gives an

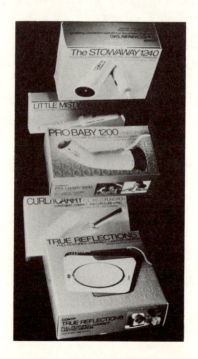

excellent size impression, its wide mouth facilitating product use. The design system, centering on a unique, easy-to-
read and highly appealing trademark or brand, derives visual
excitement from the depiction of a single illustration of
fruit, while the flavor designation and product descriptive
work together to bring unity to a display panel with six distinct elements. The system also contains the potential to
give Venture Foods a ready-made context for any additions
to the product line.

All four of these design systems have several common
denominators. All bring a high degree of pleasureable excitement to their product categories. All are highly visible,
tending to draw the consumer's attention not only to the
marketer's products but away from those of the competition.
All appear simple in the choices of elements: the consumer
learns quickly and concisely what the products are and
what they do. And all are original to the product categories
in which they are entered, standing as unique, precise solutions to their marketers' problems of product introduction.

SELECTING A DESIGN CONSULTANT

Ideally, the design consultant is brought into the new product process as early in its development as possible. There's
ample reason for this. Marketers have learned from recent

experience the effectiveness of packaging in underwriting a product's success. Further, the company's new product team may often tend to develop tunnel vision regarding the specific merchandising approach to the program: as an antidote, the early introduction of an educated, external perspective maintains the health of the program.

The important question is how to choose a consultant. There are several sources of package design. One is the advertising agency. Several agencies do provide package design as part of their overall staff services. There are some problems with this. Most significant is the possible subordination of the package development program to the instrumentalities of the advertising plan. The goal of a new product program should be a balanced presentation in which all elements coordinate and work together to achieve the precise aims of the marketer. Further, the package is a marketing tool developed specifically to have its greatest impact at point of sale, where the relationship is one-to-one. Its intimacy and its capability to have a direct effect on the purchase decision of the consumer are enhanced in the various advertising media only when the shelf package is its most potent. Too often, the design services provided by advertising services fail to appreciate the merchandisability of packages. A well-designed package can often trigger concepts that can be employed effectively in advertising and promotion; the inverse is rarely true.

A second source of design is the manufacturer of the package components. In recent years, many manufacturers have been providing design capability as part of their service. One flaw in this arrangement is that the design service is often committed to the specific container provided by the employer, with alternatives actively discouraged. The intent of a new product program should be to develop the package that does the best job of selling the product, regardless of its source. Drawing limitations on the range of choices at the outset seriously undermines this capability.

It must be admitted that packaging suppliers' design departments can prove helpful in maintaining essential quality control in the packages their companies produce. But their lack of marketing perspective and commitment to the employers' products remains a serious shortcoming.

The independent package design firm is the source of choice for many of the nation's most successful marketing companies. By definition, the independent designer has only two loyalties: first, to the marketer in developing the package that will sell the product most effectively and, second, to the successes that contribute so greatly to the satisfactions of the profession.

The backgrounds, sizes and capabilities of independent design firms are as varied as the marketing universe they serve. Ranging from the one-designer studio, which obtains mechanical, statistical and other supports externally, to the multioffice design organization with full in-house capacity to provide all supports, the independent design firm is accounting for a steadily increasing volume of design systems for product and service companies. In terms of product packaging alone, some estimates place this penetration at about 55 percent of all products marketed in all types of retail outlets. For perspective, this figure was less than 10 percent at the end of the World War II.

In selecting a design firm, the marketing organization should base its choice on criteria that most reputable sources will be happy to meet. These criteria can be measured through the responses to a small group of requests. First, meet with the principals of several firms. Request examples of their work, brochures or other literature. Ask for their client list. Seek permission to speak directly with their clients. Frankly discuss consultation fees, though this is a matter that usually arises when the initial design proposal is made.

The marketer should also expect the designer to have an understanding of design that sells product and a working knowledge of packaging technology, economics, and research.

When the marketer, after reviewing the alternatives, narrows the choices, the designers selected submit proposals that provide confirmation of the marketing/packaging objectives of the company, outline a method of approach and what will be accomplished at the end of each phase, and provide an estimate of costs for each phase and the time schedule to completion.

The primary source of companies seeking design firms is

the Package Designers Council (based in New York City), the nationwide professional organization of package designers who accept design assignments. Industry publications in many product and service categories can sometimes be consulted for designer listings and references.

THE FIRST MEETING

Whatever the source, individuals within the marketing company must be selected to work with the designer, enabling the program to move forward efficiently and economically. The company president or a key executive in the marketing hierarchy should be included at the outset. (If this officer is neglected until package development is nearly complete, a disagreement on approach can cost the company dearly in time and dollars.) The product manager, of course, is basic to the development team, as is the director of production. Working in conjunction with these three individuals—and through marketing with the advertising director—the designer can proceed toward development of the optimal package for the new product. The process goes smoothly if only those individuals necessary to establish parameters of the program are taking part.

A great advantage of this approach is the time savings. In terms of getting a product into the marketplace, time is the single most important factor. Lead times in the evolution of the designs, in preparation of the package components and production, when compounded with the distribution of the completed package, and in introduction and full marketing can be shortened by clear articulation of concepts and frank, realistic attitudes toward planning—all functions of that first meeting.

All available data relating to the new product and it market are brought out at the meeting. Questions that might be asked include:

What is the product name, if any?

What is the product description?

What is unique about the product?

Who are the competitors?

What are the specific demographics?

How will the product be sold? In what kind of retail setting?

What will the product price be in relation to competition?

Will it have endorsement by the company or other source?

Must the product be shown in use?

Is quality level a factor?

What specific copy must be included in the packaging?

Are there specific, unique legal requirements that must be met?

Are there specific instructional requirements to fulfill?

What is the general mood the package must impart?

A final topic of the initial meeting is the selection of an individual within the marketer's organization who will serve as liaison with the design firm. This individual will attend all subsequent meetings until completion of the program.

BRAND NAMES AND TRADEMARK

From the design/marketing perspective, the development of the best possible brand name and trademark is pivotal to the program. A memorable identity system is worth every moment and every effort that goes into it. Its creation challenges the imagination; its effectiveness can go a long way toward assuring the success of the product.

Brand names and trademarks come from several possible sources. The first is the product itself. If it is a product unlike any other, the uniqueness can suggest the identity.

Another possible source is location. Geographical names and symbols have been a wellspring of inspiration.

Still another is the specific performance characteristic of the product.

For the new company introducing its first product, the

firm's name can serve, especially since it is a source of future equity. There was a time when only a few people knew what IT&T, IBM, and Xerox connote.

Because of the huge number of names and marks already registered by the U.S. Patent and Trademark Office, developing an original, effective name and mark becomes more difficult each year. An existing, disused mark that has no current connotations can be purchased from its owner—especially if it is an obvious improvement over any that can be devised.

If an original name and mark are developed, it is critical that a thorough search be conducted to make certain they don't approximate the name and trademark of another company. This can be done when the specific logotype and supportive graphics are developed and can save the marketer from major legal problems after the product is marketed.

Generally, the tradename is kept short. It is believed that this approach is preferable because a short name is easier for the customer to remember. However, there are important exceptions. In a product category distinguished for its short, catchy names, a tradename that breaks the rule is likely to be more memorable than those of the competition. An example, developed by my company for Jergens, is "Gee, Your Hair Smells Terrific." It identifies a shampoo.

Supportive copy for the trade style, as a rule, should also be kept to the point and be as simple as possible. It should be interesting and informative. It should avoid exaggeration.

The initial design proposals deal with the specifics of the container choice and carry through to the secondary packaging—that is, the packaging that will protect and display the product containers on the way to and in the retail environment.

Much of the developmental work involves the unique primary container—the package dispensing the product. Secondaries, generally made with stock components, sell the primary container when placed in the retail setting. They range from the extended-panel folding carton, permitting hang-tag or shelf merchandising, to the "riser" card enabling selling out of the shipping container—itself a secondary package—to the uniquely designed floor stand; which can become an aisle-end selling environment.

Much is made of the unique primary package. However, for certain categories where product characteristics limit the range of development and choice, stock primary containers can serve the purpose well and may even accommodate the product's introduction because they are familiar to the consumer. They become a comforting framework for the presentation of a product.

Once the components are decided on, the graphic elements, including the tradename and mark and supporting copy, are developed as they may appear on the final package. These mockups are known as comprehensives, and their narrowing down to the few finalists that best express the marketing concepts is one of the most exciting periods in the entire program.

NOW, RESEARCH

It is at this point in the program that package research becomes a viable tool for the marketer and designer. The reason is the financial structure of the program. When we consider the budgets necessary to develop packaging, distribution and advertising, and promotional support, it makes sense to begin gauging the effectiveness of packaging alternatives before a final decision is reached.

The answers to be sought through research relate to all elements of the package. For example, consider the structure. If the product is in a single-use package, the unit price is higher. Most consumers realize that a single-use package delivers fresher product and no waste. This and the convenience may mean that consumers are willing to pay a higher

price than they would for the same product packaged in larger containers. The cost may well compensate for the value added. But this cost may materially reduce the profitability of the sale.

Color is another element to consider. The addition of a single color with attendant price increase can materially affect the way the consumer perceives the product and can be justified on this basis. But until the comprehensives undergo their first external research, this factor remains an unknown.

There is a third element in which premarket research can be vital. This is in the psychological gratification of the packages. In some product categories, choice of product is often determined by the consumer's self-image and position in society. In this situation, brand imagery is as significant as product efficacy, and price will probably be equated with quality.

One of the most significant factors to be tested is the trade device. A hundred names and trademarks can be developed for a single brand. When typed as part of a long list and sketched as figures, their only value is the appropriateness of the aural or graphic uniqueness. Until the devices are actually placed into a packaging context, they cannot be realistically evaluated.

The comprehensives themselves must always be measured against one another and (when narrowed down to two or three) against "live" competition in a retail-like setting. In the latter situation, the final package will be marketed, so impact measurements should be made as early as possible. This is critical because of the influence of competitive packages. Your design may seem powerful by itself but may lose its impact when placed in a group display under various lighting conditions.

There are several standard test modes. One is the focus group, in which small groups of consumers who fit the demographic profile set for the product meet separately to evaluate the final designs.

There are surveys conducted in malls and other shopper-frequented areas where consumers matching the established demographics are exposed to and queried about designs.

There are mechanical devices that track eye movement and measure different types of perception. Combined with additional testing techniques, they give some idea of the potential consumer's response.

All of these tools can help the marketer and designer eliminate or modify certain features that have made their way to the final selections. Their importance, however, is in an inverse ratio to the quality and range of information that went into the new product program at its inception. They cannot make up for a lack; they will only confirm it.

Premarket research and other testing techniques should never, therefore, become a marketing crutch. One fact of marketing life that remains unchanged is that judgmental analysis is still paramount.

To help make this analysis, the marketer is well guided by a checklist to determine which of the final designs best meets the original criteria for the packaging.

This new product checklist can include the following:

Does it stand out among competitors?

Does it stimulate interest or curiosity?

Can you tell immediately the nature and benefits of the product?

Is it unique and memorable?

Does it look reliable?

Does it seem worth the price?

Does it sell itself?

Does it convey the correct emotional appeal, such as appetite, efficacy, or purity?

Does it have the right degree of appeal in terms of gender, sophistication, warmth, informality, or other qualities?

Does it show the product adequately?

Is the descriptive statement easily understood?

Can you read the brand name and other vital product information easily and well?

Does it convey any negative connotations?

Does it at all exaggerate or overpromise in describing the product?

Is it in any sense condescending or patronizing to the consumer?

THE FINAL DESIGN

When management has evaluated all of the finalists based on the checklist, it is in position to select a design system to represent its product on the market.

At this point, the marketer's production director and the designer begin to schedule the delivery of components to the marketer's facility and the quantities and implementation of production line procedures. Where unique configurations and materials are involved, the designer can work with the production director to make certain the component specifications are met. Certainly where container decoration is involved, the designer will make certain all color standards and other physical criteria are adhered to by the suppliers.

A product distribution timetable is the central factor to the introductory period. Advertising programs are linked to it intimately, as is preselling to the retailers who will carry the product. The implications of faulty coordination are clear. If product arrives at retail too late, advertising is squandered by a company unable to meet demand. If product arrives too early, retailers believe they will be stuck with unsalable merchandise (unless the point-of-sale impact is so great that the package sells itself or its popularity grows through word-of-mouth). There are documented cases of this experience. Indeed, for many new product marketers, the package is the only advertising the product will ever receive. It's chances and growth in this kind of situation depend on such factors as the responses of competitors, the general need fulfilled by the product and the package's ability to communicate the satisfaction of that need, the degree of curiosity the package arouses in the consumer, and the product's relative value, price, and timing.

For the advertised new product, however, measurement of initial consumer response in limited or test markets can provide useful information. Such factors as dealer satisfaction with prepacks, seasonal modifications, and meeting new merchandising conditions can now be attended to by the marketer.

FOLLOWING THROUGH

As the product moves into full marketing, the work of the designer can enter a new phase. If product acceptance grows as anticipated and competition retaliates with imitative brands, steps can be taken to strengthen the marketer's position. These moves can range from graphic refinements to preserve and enhance the uniqueness of the package to secondary packaging opening the possibility of additional facings on the shelf or new display areas, such as aisle-end floor space.

Over the longer term, the designer can conduct periodic audits. These help to determine changes in the market that affect product, reasons for sales slippages, changes in outlets that sell the product, and, most importantly, the potential for future products (such as line extensions) to improve market share.

The success enjoyed by marketing companies is the direct result of careful planning. Where the entrepreneur is concerned, the new product package is given its best chances for success when that planning is founded on the elements of visual excitement: originality, freshness in appearance, the ability to carry the impression of newness—of having come into existence very recently—and greater concern with brand identity and positioning than with traditions and reputation.

NEW PACKAGING'S ROLE

One of the more certain roads to success is the discovery or implementation of new physical packages that make giant strides for various product categories.

Conceiving a package construction that improves on performance or provides a desirable alternative to those now in use isn't the difficulty. Implementation is. Some of the packages with greatest current potential have required years of effort and millions of dollars in investment.

One structure with this potential is the aseptic package. A coated paperboard container that poses a strong marketing

threat to traditional metal cans and glass bottles for beverages, the aseptic package, which requires no refrigeration, has been pioneered in the United States by a client, Ocean Spray Cranberries, Inc., for its line of juices. Along with a growing market acceptance by consumers, the aseptic packages provide the company with potential production economies that can help improve its competitive position in its markets.

Another such innovation is the retortable pouch. Combining plastics and foil laminates in structures that allow high-temperature, short-time food processing, the pouches are said to yield better-tasting products and, like the aseptic packages, require no refrigeration.

Acceptance of these two structures has broad, dramatic implications for the supermarket of the future. First could be the decline of refrigerator space; next, disappearance of frozen-food cases (both tremendous energy consumers for the supermarket operator).

On another level are packages innovated to open the range of product performance or provide novelty without necessarily displacing structures currently marketed. Such a container is the all-aluminum "bottle" for carbonated soft drinks. Aimed at ½-liter and larger container use, this bottle is said to offer quicker chilling and improved reclosability. Whether it will replace the large plastic bottles—themselves successors to the glass bottles that once dominated the market—will be a function of consumer satisfaction and demand.

In the truest sense, these new developments carry the potential to earn a legitimate role in the marketplace. For the new product marketer, however, uniqueness has many dimensions. Packaging design is the primary source and sole extradimensional expression of all of them.

18

How to Develop a New Product Sales Plan

Edwin E. Bobrow
Bobrow Consulting Group, Inc.

Marketing and sales people now have many more strategies to choose from in the selling of new products. Strategies such as personal selling, telemarketing, direct response, direct to user, to distributors, through retailers, and other "high-tech" as well as the more traditional "high-touch" approaches are available in developing the new product sales plan. Selecting the right combinations of strategies that will accomplish the sales goals, however, is not always easy. Using the company's traditional and established distribution patterns and sales force for the new product can sometimes prove inappropriate and ultimately disastrous. That is why each new product needs to be considered in its own light.

New product criteria should cover the issue of new products that require sales and distribution methods different from what the company now employs or is prepared to employ. Sometimes, in analyzing the selling strategies for a new product, management might decide that they do not want or are not capable of properly selling the new product because it does not fit current sales and distribution patterns. It is best to make this decision early in the development of the new product. Too often, all the planning, engineering, and even some of the marketing is completed only to find it too costly to set up a separate or new sales distribution network for the product. On the other hand, a company might decide early on that if they develop an acceptable new product, they will invest the dollars and people to sell and distribute the product even if new methods are required.

By establishing sales and distribution parameters, you will not be put in a position of force-fitting the new product to your sales and marketing system. Instead, you will be able to build the optimum sales distribution system that every new product should have.

If the new product meets the criteria and a sales plan is to be created, the first thing that must be clearly spelled out is the goals—and not just the sales goals because they cannot be developed unless the company goals and the marketing goals are known. Sometimes it is difficult for the sales executives who are responsible for the sales plan to obtain clear company goals. For some reason, the communication is not there or the company just doesn't spell out or share corporate goals. Nevertheless, it is incumbent on the sales executives to press for a clear understanding of where the company is going, even if it isn't formalized into a succinct set of goals or a mission statement. Plumbing management's wishes sometimes requires the sales executive to develop a set of goals that will provoke guidelines. In other cases, the marketing department will set forth explicit goals and clear sales objectives. In some companies, happily, interaction among sales, marketing, and other departments will be employed in order to develop goals. In all cases, outside-in information, from customers and the trade, will help immensely in the goal-setting process. There is little question that the setting of sales objectives cries for marketplace feedback. It is essential to proper goal-setting. Goal-setting can look like this:

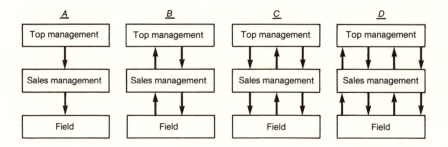

System A—Top management sets goals and communicates them down.

System B—Field and sales management provide input to top management; then top management decides and communicates them down.

System C—Top management sends proposed goals down, and the field and sales management respond with their ideas; then top management firms them up and communicates them down.

System D—Input goes up to top management, goals are proposed, reworked by field and sales management, and sent back up; then top management finalizes and communicates.

The authoritarian system, A, works poorly in most situations because it is difficult to set solid goals for a company without information being processed from the field into the company. Totalitarian orders issued from top management are born solely from management's perspective with no input or consideration of what field and sales management needs or perceives. System B is certainly a better method because feedback is considered before handing down the goals. System C is an even more enlightened approach than B because it starts with management sending down its ideas. But what often comes back up to top management is tainted as the field and sales management send back what they think top management wants to hear. If what is sent back is untainted, then the system works. Top management processes the untainted information from the field and sales management, and the goals then handed down generally will reflect the realities of the marketplace. System D gives the best possible flow of information. Everyone on every level is involved in contributing to the goals. They "own" what is developed because there is input up, down, and back up and down again. This method of goal-setting is highly motivational and usually comes nearest to producing goals that are the most realistic for that management team. The important thing is to employ some system in goal-setting—even the poorest system is better than not having goals that are clearly communicated within the company.

Once goals are clear, the strategies that will make up the sales plan need to be considered. One of the major strategic considerations is whether to use your established sales force and distribution network or whether to build one specifically for the new product or product line. It will help in making this decision if you ask yourself the following questions:

1. Who is the consumer or end-user?
2. How do they want to buy?
3. Where do they want to buy?
4. When do they want to buy?
5. What is the most economical way of reaching them?
6. What are current trade practices?
7. Is there a trend toward new or different trade practices?
8. Do we have a high or low level of familiarity and knowledge of the preferred distribution channels?
9. Are there various market segments that have to be addressed?
10. Which segment is most important, second in importance, etc.?
11. Do we need different sales and distribution approaches to each segment?

12. How do the sales and distribution needs match our capabilities and abilities?

13. What is the relationship to our goals?

14. Have we the right people to do the job or the ability to hire and manage them?

15. Does the item itself dictate a certain distribution system because it is highly technical, hard to handle, high priced, or needs servicing, or does it have other characteristics that dictate long or short distribution channels?

Other questions will arise that are unique to your situation. The important thing is to question realistically what the sales and distribution needs of the new product are and match them to the system you have in place. If you have no sales and distribution network, then you are totally unencumbered in your choice. You can decide if it is best to use a company-owned sales force or an independent sales agency sales force. You can choose to sell direct to the retailer or end-user or go through distributors. You may want to go with selected distribution or follow a strategy of saturated distribution. You might enter all possible segments at once or take on one market segment at a time. Much depends on product availability, competition, and, of course, your goals. All avenues are open to you, but select carefully because the product's success or failure may depend on the distribution and sales system you select.

Let's examine the alternatives just mentioned. First, when should you use a company sales force, and when should you use independent sales agencies, independent reps, or a broker? The terms are interchangeable. Different industries have different names for those individuals or groups of individuals who cover a given geographical area on a commission basis, usually handling compatible products going to specific market segments. Regardless of what they are called, they generally offer the manufacturer the following:

Advantages:

1. An existing sales force.

2. Quick market penetration.

3. Specialized sales and marketing knowledge.
4. Knowledge of their marketplace and customers.
5. "Clout" or entry with their customers.
6. A fixed cost to sales ratio.

Disadvantages:

1. Lack of control.
2. In an up market, they may cost less than a direct sales force. (In a down market, they can cost more.)
3. Can't move them around into different territories.
4. Customer loyalty is built first to the independent agents, then to the manufacturer.
5. Some customers do not like dealing with independent reps.
6. They need the leadership of strong management people who understand independent agents.

When deciding whether to use a direct sales force, keep in mind the training, turnover, and time and cost it will take to develop a company-owned force. Sometimes it is wise to use reps in certain market segments and key account or company salespeople in others. Some territories are better served by company people, others by independent reps. Ask yourself:

1. What is the custom and practice in each market segment?
2. How much time do I have to penetrate the market?
3. How long will it take me to field a company-owned force?
4. What are the costs involved?
5. Do I have the right management team?

Should you go one step, direct to retailer or end-user, or two step, through a distributor? Perhaps selling direct to the consumer as Avon does might be best. Or, as in the automotive aftermarket, you may have to sell through warhouse distributors to wholesalers to jobbers to the end-user. Figures 1, 2, and 3 show three different industries' distribu-

FIGURE 1: Selling the Volume or Mass Market

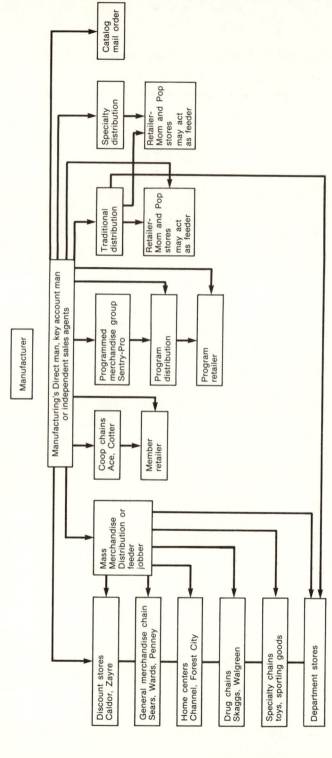

FIGURE 2:   An Overview of Automotive Aftermarket Distribution

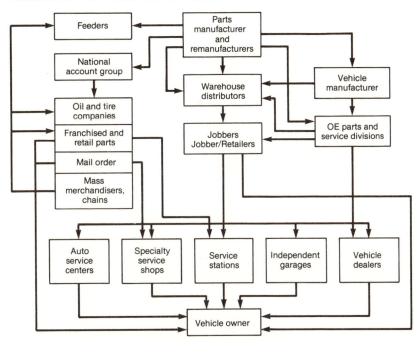

tions network. In today's marketplace, none of the three charts are absolutely correct for every vendor; changes and segmentation proliferate, so it is hard to nail down the absolute flow of goods. The charts will serve as a guide, however, demonstrating the various alternatives. What is important is to recognize the alternatives so you can match them to your goals and needs and to the dictates of the market.

It is even wise to develop distribution curves as you would a life cycle for the new product, so you can trace the effectiveness of your distribution in each market segment. By doing this, you can tell which segments need more attention, when they are maturing, and when they are beginning to decline. This can indicate shifts that take place in the market.

Should you start the new product off with selected distribution or try to saturate the market? When production is limited, there is no choice but to select a small number of

FIGURE 3: Channels of Distribution—Electrical Products Manufacturer to Consumer

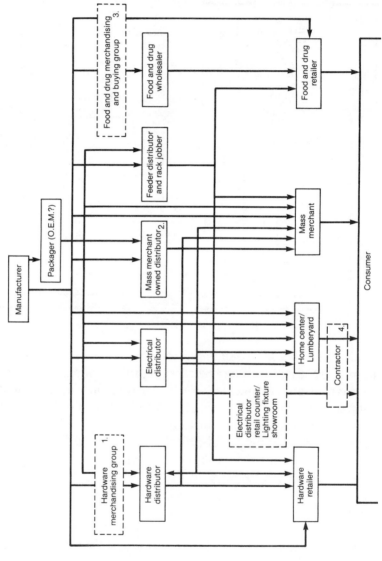

customers whose needs you will be able to fill. The alternative is to ship anyone and everyone and make them all unhappy by failing to completely fill or, more important, refill their stocks. It is best to give the quotas to the sales force and with them pick the key targets in order to control the distribution. If, however, there is an abundance of product, you might want to sell all comers as much as you can. Of course, product availability is not the only factor for choosing either course or going to a franchised-type distribution or authorized distributorships. The nature of the product, quality control, the need for service, and other factors may dictate a selected distribution strategy.

Once you have selected the distribution patterns and the type of sales force that will implement your plan, it is time to think of the tools they will need to sell the new product. In some companies, all the tools are supplied by marketing; in others, it is a joint effort. There are times when it is solely in the hands of the sales department. Whatever the system, it is important that you and your sales executives be involved. It is up to the sales executives to reflect the needs of his or her sales force and the marketplace so that the sales tools developed won't be developed in a vacuum. It is vital to develop selling tools that will be effectively employed. Only by interacting with the sales force and the marketplace can you select tools that will be put to best advantage. In a very real way, the total marketing plan provides all the tools that the sales force will have available, as well as all the tools that distribution will have in order to move goods through. These include:

1. Incentive programs for the sales force, distributor's salespeople, or retail salespeople. Contests, spiffs or "push money," awards, and recognition.

2. Samples—carrying cases or sample cases that show the new product in the best light as well as protect and make the showing of samples easy. Sometimes these sample cases are designed to take the sales person through the presentation step by step.

3. A program of sampling to salespeople and the trade could be appropriate to your product line.

4. The handling of distributor trade shows as well as national shows can be effective tools.

5. A system for supplying leads and providing follow-up and measurement.

6. The proper catalogs and "leave-behinds."

7. Audio-visual support.

8. Presentation or methods for developing presentations for buyers.

9. Training in both product and program for:

    a. Sales force.

    b. Inside support, customer service, telemarketing people.

    c. Distributor sales and service people.

    d. Retail or end-user training, if appropriate.

    e. Telemarketing.

10. Clear targets, communication of targets, and means of measuring achievement.

There are other sales tools you can employ. Some may be unique to your situation, and others may be traditional to your industry. You should test whatever tools you choose and obtain feedback. Sometimes secrecy is critical, so the tools employed can't be tested. The input of a trusted rep council or distributor council is most valuable. Checking the concept or prototype of the sales tool with your rep council or distributor council will not only give you information about the usefulness of the tool and it's viability and acceptance, but it will make the important people you selected to serve on your council or advisory board feel that they are part of the development of the tools they will use. They will "own" your sales plan with you. That is why having a rep council, rep advisory board, distributor council, or customer council can be so valuable. Setting up these councils or boards by selecting the 20 percent of the sales force or customers who are most likely to give you 80 percent of the business can be a valuable selling tool and provide a good testing ground and feedback.

With your goals set, your sales force of choice being developed, your distribution plan worked out, the sales tools selected, training established, and the management team in place, it is a good idea to clearly define the responsibilities and authorities of the management team. Not only job descriptions but exceptions and personal job-related goals should be committed to paper. Part of the sales plan is the deployment of those who will lead the effort to implement the plan. Only if they are clear on what is expected of them and the job they have to do can you expect everyone to work in the same direction. Communication of the plan with clear understanding of who is doing what is vital. In addition to the management team all working toward clear goals with agreed-on strategies, it is important to have good methods of keeping score.

The right kind of data processing reports or even hand-kept records are needed in order to know where you are in achieving the new products sales plan. You have to decide what you want to measure and report on. Too much data won't be reviewed. Striking the right balance of information and frequency of receiving this information will let your team know just where it stands. Measure the cost of getting the information against the need—often the "nice to have" data is costly, and the added paper flow obscures what is really important to monitor.

Putting together all of the elements of a sales plan for a new product is not simple. The time of grabbing the new product prototype and booking orders may not be totally gone, but it is at its sunset.

Clear goals, thoughtful strategies, and people who can make it happen are needed to optimize the success of the new product. It is the exceptional product today that can be sold without a complete support system. And the written sales plan, properly communicated within the company, pulls together all the resources into a support system that sells the new product in a way compatible with the company's resources and the market's needs.

19

The Role of an Advertising Agency in Marketing New Products

Raymond D. Hehman
BBDO, International

INTRODUCTION

To determine the role that an advertising agency should play in the new product development process, two questions need to be answered first. These are:

1. When should an agency get involved?
2. What role does advertising play in a new product development and launch?

   To answer the question of why a marketer would want an agency to get involved or when an agency should get involved, let's look at what role advertising plays in the success of a new product. First we look at a product idea after it has gone through technical/feasibility exploration and after it has been consumer tested as to concept and product use tests. Then we look at the marketing job that's required to launch a new product. Moving from a tested idea to national marketing requires at least 10 basic steps or tasks (see Figure 1).

FIGURE 1:　Basic Marketing Tasks/Decisions for New Product Development

	Premarketing		*Marketing Communications*		*Marketing*
1.	Name/Package products			**6.**	Test market selection
2.	Define benefits/features	**5.** Develop communications program		**7.**	Researching of the marketing program
3.	Price the product			**8.**	Evaluation of results
4.	Establish marketing budgets			**9.**	Expansion planning
				10.	Rollout

1. *Naming the product.* Perhaps the most difficult job and one that often holds the key to success for the product is giving it a name that fits the product's positioning and that attracts consumer interest and attention; i.e., Lean Cuisine from Stouffers.

2. *Defining the benefits or features.* Every product has a number of features, benefits, and potential appeals to the consumer. It is important in launching a new product to hone in on the key benefit or feature so that the communication concerning the product is singularly aimed and so the consumer can come away with one solid idea about the new product; i.e., Tylenol's pain relief without asprin's side effects.

3. *Pricing.* Determining where in the marketplace a new product's price point should be is another key marketing decision. Do we take a premium pricing position versus alternatives? Do we take a parity pricing position? Or would a value comparison be appropriate, like

Purex's positioning of name-brand quality at a value price?

4. *Marketing budgets.* Determining the funds that are available to market the product and then segregating these funds into the various types of marketing programs; i.e., advertising, public relations, sales promotion, trade promotion, etc., constitute a rather substantial undertaking.

5. *Consumer communications.* Having defined the benefits and having obtained some idea of the communication funds that are available, the next step is to develop and refine the actual message about the new product and the context of the message to the consumer.

6. *Test market selection.* Here the job is to find markets that will be representative of national marketing and yet allow the brand or product to learn without paying the heavy penalty of marketing throughout a broad area of the United States. (Nielsen has put together a special service for monitoring popular test markets.)

7. *Designing a research program to monitor test market results.* It is important that the product be evaluated from more than just a sales and profit standpoint. Consumer awareness, trial, and satisfaction are key measures to determine the viability of the product over the longer term. A research program must address at least these as a minimum. It would, of course, be useful to know what the new product is being substituted for and what share of market the product is achieving.

8. *Evaluation of test marketing results.* Once the product has entered the market, the marketing program implemented, and the research taken, we have to evaluate not only the marketing results but the potential financial success of the product. Test marketing can be a long and extensive marketing laboratory. Initial results may be off-target, but often insights into the marketing mix can turn an apparent failure into a success.

9. *Expansion planning.* Assuming the success of the product in test market, the plans for expanding the

market area must be laid—bearing in mind the production and financial limitations.

10. *Rollout*. This is the actual implementation of the expansion plan in which the product eventually achieves national distribution and is then treated as an ongoing product rather than a new product.

As can be seen by the above semisequential listing of jobs, the advertising agency certainly should be and normally is involved in steps 5 through 10. The question is, should the agency be involved in steps 1 through 4? Being involved in steps 1 through 4 could be tagged as "early involvement" in the new product development process. Let's examine in the next few sections what usually occurs in premarketing and what the drawbacks and advantages of early involvement are.

PREMARKETING OR EARLY INVOLVEMENT OF AN ADVERTISING AGENCY

As noted before, the premarketing phase involves putting together all of the key elements leading to the formulation of the communications program that ultimately supports the new test product in test market. The new product process begins with a product idea or concept that has either come out of consumer research or out of research and development at the company's laboratories. Quite often the decisions that are made about what to do with this product idea or concept set the tone for its eventual marketing success or failure. These early decisions involve the key elements in what is being offered to the consumer—name, package, benefits, and price. And these are the very same elements that are the heart of the message in the communications program.

The most difficult assignment is often naming the product. Selecting a name involves analyzing or reviewing three factors:

1. Positioning of the product; that is, what does the product stand for? What are we really offering the consumer?

2.   What are the brand names of close competitors and acceptable substitutes?

3.   The availability of trademarks that will fit with the positioning and within the competitive environment.

It is, of course, helpful to have the advice of those who are expert in communication when trying to pick a brand name. In the course of the marketing life cycle of the brand, many elements will change. The one constant element will be the brand name, and this makes its selection a critical decision relative to the new product. For example, Tide has been reformulated and/or repositioned a couple of dozen times in its life.

The next area to be culled down and focused on is product benefits. Almost every new product is composed of many benefit areas, improvements, and refinements in comparison to other items that the consumer might buy as a substitute. Concept testing is often utilized to determine which benefit or which group of benefits should be used in the communication process. In-home placement of the product is another method of getting feedback from the consumer. In particular, concept test results are often compared to actual (in-home) use test findings to see which is stronger—the product idea or the product performance. These types of research projects often call for creative thinking as well as counsel and advice on the design of the research. After the product and/or the concepts have been tested, it is desirable to have an analysis of the results prepared by someone other than the client marketing organization. Ultimately the marketer and his team will select a key benefit or two to receive the major emphasis in the communications program.

After naming a product and singling out a key benefit, the product must then have a package. Package design is a very specialized activity, and it is not normally the province of an advertising agency or client graphics department. The package is the most universal communications medium that the product has. It should reinforce the positioning, make the name of the product clear, call attention to itself on the shelf, and, if possible, accentuate or highlight the benefits or features of the product. Usually there is research involved here too in terms of shelf testing and consumer testing of various designs. To ensure a close connection between the name, packaging, and benefit, it is helpful to have some input from the advertising agency. The agency will also ensure that there is a wide range of alternative presentations for the product packaging.

The next key element in the process is the intertwining of price and financial planning for the brand. While there are many different approaches to determining a product's pricing, one of the more important considerations is the adequate funding of a marketing effort. The question involves how high the price can be before the volume is adversely affected, thus decreasing the total gross margin available. This type of analysis cannot be done with pinpoint accuracy, but certainly the product can be tested at various price levels and estimates of market share can be made based on the results. If the price is set too low, there may be insufficient margin for funding marketing activity. If the price is set too high, there may be too low a sales volume (even though the per unit margin is high), and this will result in less-than-adequate funding of the marketing program. Somewhere in the middle there is a price at which the brand will achieve a substantial share and yet generate a substantial margin for marketing investment. The analysis and review of financial plans or their development can be accomplished by the advertising agency—thus giving the company a check on their own estimating capabilities. Management is given more encouragement to believe the projections when they are developed independently by both the marketing group and the agency—that is, if the estimates are fundamentally in agreement.

The premarketing phase of the new products marketing process determines all the key elements of the communication program. While these elements can be changed as the process moves along, the time and costs involved can escalate significantly. Certainly any team is capable of developing the new product's program and overseeing its function. The management question should be, How can the team be structured to raise the probabilities of success for the new product? While there would appear to be a productive role on the team for an advertising agency, some objections are often raised about having the agency get involved early on.

POTENTIAL PROBLEMS WITH AD AGENCY INVOLVEMENT IN PREMARKETING

There are five major areas of concern that marketers often express or experience when involving agencies in new product development process.

1. Advertising Agencies Are Not New Product Specialists. Rather, they are set up to handle major ongoing brands. To a certain extent this is true, but it overlooks the central role of the advertising agency, which is to be the expert in communications with the prime prospect. It so happens that most of the assignments an agency has are for ongoing brands—thus the basis for the feeling that they are specialists only in continuing or expanding the success of an already established brand. However, as most of us have observed over the years, major brands often have line extensions and spinoffs that are usually handled by the brand's current agency.

Most agencies have a research department or access to research talent to help evaluate the new product situation, which has some different facets than monitoring ongoing brand marketing. Furthermore, the agency has the ability to look at a new product more objectively because there is usually a wide cross-section of marketing experience in the agency research, account, creative, and media groups. The agency, in effect, can become a consumer panel to set forth more clearly what the product offers and to whom this offering will appeal. Therefore, while it may be true that advertising agencies are not new product specialists, they have the talent and ability to aid the client in marketing the new product and in helping shape the communication message and media needed for success.

2. New Product Work Is Not Profitable for an Agency to Handle. In general, this is true, and it may lead to several undesirable actions on the part of the agency. These actions include, but are not limited to:

a. They may not deliver work on time.

b. Junior people may be assigned to the project.

c. Those working on the new product may be distracted from the current ongoing brand's needs.

When the agency is given a new product assignment, it is up to the marketing company to ensure that the agency is properly staffed to deliver the assistance the new product project requires. The client must determine that the members assigned to the team have a sufficient depth of experience to enable them to render judgments and suggestions in the premarketing activities. In other words, if the client spells out ahead of time what is epected of the new product development team, the agency will not be prone to taking shortcuts. Discussions with brand managers will elicit whether those working on current business can handle new product assignments or whether new people will be required for the team.

The problem of agency profitability can be dealt with by constructing a fee or remuneration system that covers the agency's costs. Most agencies that have profitable ongoing brands will be willing to forgo profit markup on staff time to aid the client in the new products effort. If clients want the best results from the agency, they should certainly compensate the agency for the use of the staff and facilities. A payoff for the agency (and this must be positioned by the client) is the budget levels and ongoing income that will result if the product is successful. Of course there is the implied promise that additional assignments will be given to the agency that can prove a successful track record with the current new product assignment. The fee arrangement avoids problems of not covering the costs of staffing.

3. Advertising Agencies Cost Too Much. Advertising agencies, depending on their location and management structure, do have a high cost per man-year relative to smaller new product operations. The key question is, What is a good idea worth? Utilizing the services of an advertising agency in the premarketing phase, may be looked on as an insurance policy relative to the success of the new product venture. In other words, are we willing to pay a little bit more to raise the odds for success. If we are, then the cost issue should not be overly burdensome.

The costs associated with an advertising agency are, by and large, people costs. The costs are high relative to other professions because of the training, experience, and valued advice given by those who work at the agency. The talent is paid according to its ability to contribute. The costs are somewhat controllable by the client in that clear direction and crisp criticism of work done will minimize overall time spent by those on the new product team. Smoothness and efficiency are certainly possible in dealing with advertising agencies. Costs are usually higher when there is uncertainty as to what should be done or indecisiveness in terms of reaction to alternatives that are presented by the agency.

In summary, therefore, a new product client will get full value for his invested dollar from utilizing an agency in the premarketing phase. If many alternatives are to be explored, it will cost more than if there is a clear concept of what the product is, what the message is, and what the budget levels are. So while agencies are more costly on a man-year basis, there should be efficiency in terms of access to resources and ability to distill alternatives to a manageable number. Recommendations and thinking should reflect the experience levels of those contributing to the new product development.

4. Lack of Secrecy about the New Product.   Advertising agencies are usually more fluid or in more of a state of flux relative to personnel than are client organizations. Keeping a new product team together for a year or two is admittedly more difficult on the agency side than on the client side. There is often more openness at the agency in terms of communication within departments and communication between departments. The great advantage that an agency has over a client organization is the ability to discuss marketing situations with a variety of individuals whose backgrounds and prior experiences differ significantly from each other. Therefore, the idea of keeping something very secret is more difficult at an agency than it would be at a client organization.

Sophisticated marketers, however, do not need to be informed about projects via advertising agencies. Registration of trademarks and patents, SEC filings, court documents, and compliance with government requirements for information often give clues as to which direction a company is heading in its new products development program. There are, of course, many other sources of possible leaks about a new product project as a company begins to deal with outside suppliers who implement parts of the marketing communication program. The best way to ensure that secrecy is maximum and leaks are minimum is to insist on:

a.   A very restricted team for the new product project.

b.   No communication about the project with other members of the agency except in a disguised form.

c.   Work being done in a secluded area of the agency or behind closed doors.

5. Agencies Have a Built-in Bias Toward Commissionable Media versus Utilizing Marketing Funds in Other Programs.   Since most agencies receive income proportional to advertising expenditures, this could bias the agency toward regular media. However, an agency's long-term success depends on the client's long-term success, and this is even truer when it comes to a new product launch. To start the whole process of getting consumer sales, awareness of the brand must be established. Normally the most efficient way of doing this is to utilize advertising, but other forms of marketing communication may build awareness at a lower cost and may also induce trial at a lower cost. Some examples are free trial sizes either handed out by professional samplers or sold through stores at special prices, publicity events including the involvement of charitable organizations, direct mail, couponing, etc.

The basic way to avoid a commissionable media bias on the part of the agency is to ensure that their compensation is geared to costs rather than percent of billings. Fee structures that cover costs and give a percentage of profit are common enough in the industry and certainly have enough application to the new products assignment. While an agency may be willing to invest staff time without a profit during the premarketing phase, certainly in the marketing phase, the agency would like to be on a normal, profitable basis. This can be accomplished with a fee structure that marks up costs to provide a profit margin.

As can be seen from the above, there are several drawbacks to involving an agency early in the developmental process, but each one of these drawbacks can be taken care of through proper planning and communication with the advertising agency. If these drawbacks can be neutralized, then it makes sense to involve the agency as soon as possible. In the next section of this chapter, we will examine more closely the benefits for the advertiser when there is an early involvement of an agency in the new products process.

ADVANTAGES OF AD AGENCY INVOLVEMENT IN PREMARKETING

There are five major benefit areas that marketers should enjoy when involving agencies in the early stages of the new product development process.

1. A New Product Marketer Is Able to Acquire a Consultant without the Need for the Long Learning Phase Associated with Hiring Most Consultants.   Advertising agencies are generally able to assemble teams to help in the development of the marketing program. These teams are familiar with the category and can quickly be brought up-to-date in terms of the "uniqueness of the new product." Agency personnel take on the task of analyzing initial research and development work and plotting that against their knowledge of the category and the consumer needs within that category. This can be done in a relatively quick manner. The agency is therefore able to appraise the work done to date and to suggest additions or changes in a relatively short period of time. Since the agency did not develop the new product or idea, they can take on the role of fresh eyes and review all of the developments and thinking leading up to the time that the agency is asked to be involved. Therefore, the new products team is able to get the advice of a consultant within a relatively short time frame.

2. A More Involved and Committed New Product Launch Team Will Be Guiding the Destinies of the New Product. The sooner that those responsible for the new product marketing activity are involved in the formulation of the plan, the better. This avoids the "not invented here" syndrome where prior decisions are questioned and decisions are reversed because a new group is involved. If the new products launch team is responsible for the naming of the new product, then there is a reasonable certainty that the group will be able to closely link the name and positioning. Similarly, if budgets are set with the agency's input, it is reasonable to expect that there will be sufficient funds to generate needed awareness levels for adequate trial. In other words, if the team is assembled in the beginning and is held responsible for the outcome of the new product launch, they are more likely to come to better decisions regarding the premarketing activities than if those premarketing activities are determined by only part of the group. Early involvement fosters a stronger commitment on the part of the product launch team to the product success.

3. Greater on Time Scheduling Will Occur as Response Time Will Be Quicker to the Developmental Needs of the New Product. In the premarketing phase, there is often a need for research and, within the context of this research, a need for communication of concepts, packaging, etc. By having a committed team at the agency who will look on the new product as their responsibility, the client is usually given a quicker response time than would be the case if there was no commitment. Far from being last on the list, the new product development program takes on a higher priority. There is a sense of involvement and a sense of creative fulfillment by allowing the launch team to get involved early on.

The essential situation that has been created by early involvement of the agency is to give the agency team an opportunity to shape the final product offering in the marketplace by input in the developmental process. This sense of involvement not only brings about quicker response time, but often it is the agency that pushes the client in the development of the new product. This can indeed shorten the total response time from the inception of the new product idea to the marketplace launch.

4. There Is an Increased Likelihood of Financial Success for the Product.   One of the major goals of any new product is to create awareness in the market and, as a function of that awareness, to gain trial. As we all know, there is a cluttered environment in terms of media communication to the consumer. Therefore, budgets are a primary concern in getting out the message about the new product. The advertising agency certainly has an understanding of the media environment and the cost of doing business in terms of using media. One of the key elements that will be looked at very closely in shaping a new product plan will be the funds available or the funds earmarked for advertising and promotion.

To become a viable new product, a brand must attract a sufficient consumer following to generate the sales required to fund that initial payout period. In constructing theoretical financial plans, there is often a temptation to shorten a payback period and thereby make the proposition more attractive to management. The usual outcome of shortening the payback period is to reduce the marketing funds available. This inevitably is a shortcut to disaster because the brand never has a real launch in terms of consumer awareness. It will certainly, therefore, be a prime contribution of the agency to discuss fully what the budgets can achieve in terms of consumer awareness, gross impressions, etc. And this input will remove the new product from a theoretical budget to an actual marketplace performance/specific program on which some judgments of practicality can be made. When the level of marketing expenditures necessary to launch the product are put into a practical context, then management can decide whether spending those sums is worth the reward in terms of payout period and eventual profit contribution of the new product.

5. A More Unified Marketing Communications Program Will Evolve from the Agency's Early Involvement. The major elements of the marketing communications program are:

1. Product name.
2. Product packaging.
3. Product message.
4. Selection and use of media to deliver communications to the consumer.

If any one of these elements is not optimized, then the probabilities of success are diminished. Incongruities in name and package or in message and media make the job of introducing the new product much more difficult. On the other hand, if all elements are working together and are reinforcing each other, a cumulative impact is generated usually with a smaller budget.

The agency's mission and assignment is to aid in the communications area. This, as we've stressed before, is the key element to the success of the new product—a clear, meaningful communication delivered in a media mix that builds awareness leading to trial. Individuals who have to write a commercial or develop a print ad are faced with transforming a multitude of product facts into an understandable, focused, and motivating message. If the product name and the product package blend, the communication is easier. There should be no need to waste time explaining to the consumer why the product is priced higher than the consumer thinks it should be or that the product name does not complement the benefits that the product delivers. The creative people charged with developing the communications are quick to realize when there are inadequacies or inconsistencies between the various elements in the product mix. Therefore, the sooner that you can get these people involved in product development, the sooner you will achieve consistency in key elements of the new product program.

Ultimately, new product success depends on the marketing communications program. The more unified that program is, the harder the invested dollars put into the program will be working. This clarity of communication will be based on two factors:

1. A consistency in all of the product's elements that go into the marketing program.
2. The clarity with which the message is delivered, both in terms of actual creativity and media environment.

Both of these elements can be and will be addressed by early involvement of an advertising agency in the new product developmental process. The result will be a stronger, more unified communications effort, which then heightens the probabilities of success for the company launching the new product. This key advantage of a more unified marketing communication program (and thus the greater likelihood of success) seems to outweigh any of the earlier drawbacks that were discussed relative to early involvement of the agency.

While we are on the subject of marketing communications and the budget level necessary for success, it would be appropiate to review a computer modeling technique that a major New York agency has had significant success with. This agency is the one I work for, BBDO, and their new products computer marketing model is called "NEWS,®" which stands for New Product Early Warning System.

NEW PRODUCTS COMPUTER MODELS

Computer modeling of marketing variables to predict sales of new brands can be traced back at least to Fourt and Woodlock in 1960. These models usually involve brands that are inexpensive but frequently purchased (i.e., packaged goods). For an unbiased but nevertheless favorable review of NEWS, read the *Journal of Marketing* (Winter 1983). In an article by C. Narasimhan and S. K. Sen, nine computer models are reviewed and compared. The authors conclude:

> If the test market model is expected to evaluate the new product's marketing mix in addition to providing a sales forecast, the TRACKER and NEWS models appear to be the preferred choices. Both models are complete in terms of modeling all stages and including marketing mix variables. Yet, they are not so complex that they are difficult and costly to implement. Both models provide good diagnostics, predict well. (p. 19)

As detailed in the Winter 1982 issue of *Marketing Science*, NEWS is based on a mathematical relationship between *brand awareness, trial, repeat purchase, usage,* and *brand share.* These key output measures are defined as follows:

1. *Awareness*—Awareness of the brand name is measured on an aided and unaided basis among prime prospects.

2. *Trial*—The first time a consumer actually spends money for the brand.

3. *Repeat Purchase*—The second time the consumer pays for the brand.

4. *Usage*—The proportion of prime prospects who purchase the brand during any given time period.

5. *Share of Market*—The percentage share of the category sales that a product (brand) will achieve.

These measures of marketing activity are forecast by the model based on 12 key inputs.

1. *Prime Prospect Universe*—How large is the category user population?

2. *Purchase Cycle Length*—What is the average time between category purchases (i.e., two weeks, six weeks)?

3. *Initial Trial Size*—What size is the new trier of the brand likely to buy?

4. *Purchase Volume*—What is the average purchase size

amount (i.e., one-pound can, six-pack, etc.) that a user buys?

5. *Media Weight*—Gross rating points against the prime prospect.

6. *Promotional Activity*—Any sampling, couponing, or other trial-stimulating devices are analyzed in terms of reach and impact.

7. *Distribution*—What is the anticipated initial distribution level, and how quickly will this All Commodity Volume (ACV) distribution increase?

8. *Initial Awareness Levels*—Premarketing studies are taken to see what if any level of awareness exists. For the model to be effective, the brand must have less than 25 percent initial awareness otherwise the product is not considered to be new to the consumer.

9. *Brand Registration via Advertising*—A measure of what percentage of viewers retain the brand name after exposure (can be obtained from most commercial/ad testing services).

10. *Awareness to Trial Rate*—Can be gotten from concept testing results (i.e., how many of the prime prospects want to purchase after they are exposed to the brand's concept/positioning).

11. *Trial to Repeat Rate*—A measure of satisfaction with the product in terms of repeat purchase interest after use which can be obtained from in-home use tests.

12. *Loyalty*—How loyal are consumers in the category to a brand (i.e., how often do they change brands)?

NEWS has proved extremely useful and effective for many BBDO clients. Figure 2 is a recap comparison of predictions to results.

NEWS or other computer models should be extremely helpful in:

1. Formulating budget levels for introducing new products.
2. Finding the influence of various marketing mixes on sales.

FIGURE 2

Product Area	Predicted Market Share	Actual Market Share	Predicted Share Minus Actual Share
Beauty aid	0.6	0.7	−0.1
Health care	0.9	1.1	−0.2
Beauty aid	2.5	2.2	0.3
Health care	5.7	2.2	3.5
Health care	2.2	2.5	−0.3
Food product	3.8	3.3	0.5
Household product	2.4	3.8	−1.4
Beauty aid	4.2	5.4	−1.2
Beauty aid	4.7	5.5	−0.8
Beauty aid	5.6	5.7	−0.1
Beauty aid	6.1	6.1	0.0
Household product	6.4	6.2	0.2
Household product	7.9	6.5	1.4
Food product	7.3	7.1	0.2
Food product	4.7	7.9	−3.2
Household product	10.0	9.0	1.0
Beauty aid	9.0	10.2	−1.2
Food product	10.5	11.0	−0.5
Household product	10.0	11.0	−1.0
Household product	12.6	12.7	−0.1
Mean			0.86*
Standard deviation			0.97*

* Calculations are based upon the absolute values of the deviations between predicted and actual share.
Source: "NEWS: A Decision-Oriented Model for New Product Analysis and Forecasting," *Marketing Science,* Winter 1982.

TABLE 1:   NEWS®/Market Unit or Case Sales Validation*

Product Area	Predicted Sales	Actual Sales	Predicted Sales Minus Actual Sales
Food product	5.2 M	5.8 M	−0.6 M
Food product	19.3 M	22.1 M	−2.8 M
Laundry product	100.2 M	100.5 M	−0.3 M
Food product	153.7 M	146.5 M	7.2 M
Food product	1.2 MM	1.3 MM	−0.1 MM
Food product	1.0 MM	1.4 MM	−0.4 MM
Food product	2.4 MM	2.3 MM	0.1 MM
Food product	2.3 MM	2.5 MM	−0.2 MM

Note: The above examples involve NEWS/Market, which uses early test market data to project yearly results. News/Planner can be used for premarket analysis.
* Market share measures are not available for these NEWS applications due to difficulties in defining the relevant market.
Source: "NEWS: A Decision-Oriented Model for New Product Analysis and Forecasting," *Marketing Science,* Winter 1982.

3. Setting goals or targets to aid in analyzing early results from test markets.

4. Instilling confidence in management as to the brand potential.

Whether done by model or by the new products team using traditional market planning, the forecast is critical to ensuring adequate funding for communications. The involvement of the agency to formulate as well as implement bugets leads to more likelihood of new product success.

CONCLUSION

This chapter has explored two questions about new products: When should a marketer involve an advertising agency, and What role does advertising play in the development and marketing of new products?

After examining early involvement of an advertising agency from both the pro and con sides, the conclusion reached was for involvement as early in the developmental process as possible. This helps sharpen the positioning focus and better coordinates the intertwining of the market mix elements. The building of a committed team from the start will not only speed the process but, more importantly, will avoid costly backtracking. The greater the breadth of experience the company utilizes early on, the greater will be the scope of issues explored and the analysis of options— and thus the confidence of management in the team's recommendations.

Advertising generally plays a pivotal role in the success or failure of a new product. It does so in two areas:

1. Was there a sufficient level of advertising to break through the clutter or general noise level surrounding the prime prospect.

2. Was the message motivating enough to create brand awareness and to induce purchase. If the media level of activity is too low, awareness and trial may build too slowly causing financial losses in excess of plan goals. If

the message is not memorable and/or meaningful to the prime prospect, trial will also be below goal.

As part of the generation of awareness and trial, we can also view advertising as the brand itself. Many products have little or no discernable physical/performance difference. What separates them for us is the advertising approach each brand adopts. Advertising not only becomes the only point of difference, it also adds to the enjoyment of our purchase or use. Advertising is therefore a value added to the physical product. Thus advertising, in some new products, may be the only rationale for that brand's existence. Especially in these circumstances, early involvement of an agency would appear to be critical to ensure that all marketing mix elements complement the brand's positioning (the advertising appeal).

20

Legal Considerations
The Ownership and Protection of Innovation*

Robert Alan Spanner
Beckford, Spanner & Kelley

This article discusses how the law of trade secrets protects—or sometimes fails to protect—one's right to exclusive use of commercial innovations.

The logical starting place would be to define what is meant by the term *trade secret*. Unfortunately, there is no universally accepted definition. What's more, it is not uncommon for two judges to apply the same legal principles to similar facts and arrive at exactly opposite conclusions as to whether or not something is a trade secret. Needless to say,

---

* Excerpted from Robert Alan Spanner, *Who Owns Innovation: The Rights and Obligations of Employers and Employees* (Homewood, Ill.: Dow Jones-Irwin, 1984). Copyright 1984, Robert Alan Spanner. All rights reserved.

this uncertainty makes it difficult for companies to plan and allocate resources efficiently. For instance, a company may invest substantial amounts of money developing a technology which it believes to be proprietary, only to learn later on that anyone else can use the technology with impunity. Or a company may be unwilling to exploit information developed by someone else for fear that the information is a trade secret, when in fact it is not.

Nevertheless, there are some factors which are frequently used to determine whether or not something is a trade secret. These include: (1) the extent to which the information is known outside the business; (2) the extent to which it is known by those involved in the business; (3) the nature and extent of measures taken to protect the secrecy of the information; (4) the value of the information; (5) the amount of time, effort, and money expended to develop the information; and (6) how difficult it would be for others to properly acquire or duplicate the information. Roughly speaking, a trade secret must be valuable (that is, confer a competitive advantage) and must be a secret (not known to or accessible by the public).

As will be seen below, courts also consider the relationship between the competing parties. For instance, an employee usually has a duty of loyalty to his employer, which includes a duty not to misappropriate the employer's trade secrets for his own use or benefit.

WHAT TYPES OF INFORMATION CAN QUALIFY FOR TRADE SECRET PROTECTION

Certain types of information are generally recognized as being proper subjects of trade secret protection. Examples are devices and machinery, processes and methods of manufacture, and formulations and compositions of substances. Data relating to these types of information—e.g., research and development analyses or performance data—are also usually protectible.

Depending on the type of information at issue, a court may issue an injunction (i.e., an order requiring someone to do something or to refrain from doing something) to protect a company's trade secret. For instance, a court might enjoin a competitor from manufacturing or selling a product that was developed by misappropriating trade secrets. Or a court might order an ex-employee who has misappropriated or exploited the company's trade secrets to turn over the fruits of his misappropriation and to return any confidential materials he might have taken from the company.

Computer software can also, in principle, be a trade secret, even where, as is usually the case, the techniques used to write the particular program in question are all well-known.

It should be noted in passing that nontechnical aspects of a company's operations may also qualify for trade secret protection: for instance, personnel files and other personnel information, particularly salaries and performance evaluations; competitive bids and bidding practices; financial information, such as profit and loss statements, price and cost data, capital spending plans; market research; operations manuals and other operations information; customer lists; and identities of suppliers.

KEEPING TRADE SECRETS SECRET

Fundamental to the concept of a trade secret is, not surprisingly, secrecy. Traditionally, before information can qualify for trade secret protection, it must have been kept secret. This means that the owner of the trade secret has to show that he took reasonable security precautions. Otherwise, the judge may well find that the trade secret has become public knowledge and is no longer "secret"; or he may decide that, if the owner of the trade secret couldn't be bothered to protect it, the judge should not be expected to either.

However, this does not mean that companies have to turn their premises into microcosms of the Pentagon. All that is required is that the company adopt security measures which are "reasonable under the circumstances" and which would make it difficult for others to discover the company's proprietary information without the use of improper means. Virtually any well-thought-out security program will pass legal muster, and the more thorough it is, the more it will help convince a judge or jury that (1) the company really does believe it has valuable proprietary information known only to itself, and (2) the information probably has not become public.

The first step for a company wishing to develop a security program is to perform an "information audit," to decide what information should be protected from unauthorized disclosure. It is *not* a good idea for a company to attempt to protect every single piece of information in its possession—for, aside from the high costs of doing so, such an overbroad security program may boomerang by suggesting that a company really has no idea *what* information it really considers to be secret or valuable. Also, such an effort will be perceived by employees as hypocritical, and they won't help protect *anything*.

Once a decision has been made as to what information should be protected, the next step is to determine where that information reposes. Obviously, it makes no sense to lock and guard research and development files if a copy of those files is freely accessible in the president's unlocked file cabinet. Usually, the decision as to how widely to distribute documents containing confidential information should be made either by whoever created the document or by whoever is responsible for transmitting it. For highly sensitive documents, management might create a log to record distribution or make it company policy to restrict distribution. At the same time, the company should pay particular attention to what information goes outside the company. The professional staff needs to understand what types of information should never go out the door, and what types of information may go out only under particular circumstances.

Once a security program has been developed, it is essential to enlist the support of top management in its implementation. Otherwise, the program will be doomed to failure: if upper management ignores or bypasses the security procedures, so will everyone else, and the whole program will become little more than a sham. From a legal perspective, tolerating breaches of a security program may be worse than not having adopted it in the first place. Judges sometimes view this as evidence that the company did not regard the information as confidential at all, or that the company does not deserve the benefit of the court's protection because the company itself did not take the trouble to protect its information. Therefore, it is better to have a modest security program that is enforced than an elaborate program that is honored more in the breach than in the observance.

It is also important to elicit the support of employees—particularly technical and management employees. This means educating employees about why a security program is important and why it is in their best interest to adhere to it, thus preserving the company's ability to compete and prosper.

Indeed, some companies make a practice of having the employees themselves develop the security policy. On new product developments, the staff submits a security program for approval along with the R&D program, marketing plan, etc. When the security program has been devised by the employees themselves, they are more likely to comply with it.

The particular measures that might be adopted as part of a security program are too numerous to list and will vary with the circumstances. In addition to such obvious measures as physical barriers and locked cabinets, there are numerous other possible safeguards. Some companies have visitors sign log-in sheets on which is printed a confidentiality agreement. Confidentiality agreements may also be obtained from other third parties, such as manufacturers and suppliers of equipment, customers in possession of proprietary material, and outside consultants and sales prospects. Another technique that has met with success is obliteration of identifying characteristics, part numbers, or manufacturer's identification of component parts before delivering the final product to the customer.

Confidential information stored in computers should also be kept secure. It may suffice simply to restrict access to computer terminals and other peripheral devices. Other techniques include: use of passwords, software "keys" and data encryption; putting "fuses" into software to detect unauthorized access and to stop or erase the program if such unauthorized access occurs; using unusual formats to record data on disks or other media; and imbedding firmware in epoxy or other material that is difficult to penetrate without damaging the firmware.

SECURITY PROGRAMS AND EMPLOYEES

The typical trade secret dispute involves an employee or former employee of a company, who is accused of having wrongfully appropriated the company's confidential information. Sophisticated managers attempt to head off such disputes, or at least place the company in a more advantageous position should a dispute arise, by using some or all of the following security techniques:

1. Having employees sign confidentiality agreements prior to commencement of employment; at the same time, informing them what information is considered confidential.

2. Conducting an audit for each departing employee to enumerate what information the company considers to be confidential, to ensure that the employee has returned all materials that might contain confidential information, and to extract from him a pledge that he has done so.

3. Requiring employees to document R&D so that a record of the information they had access to and the information they participated in developing is readily available.

4. Monitoring disaffected employees or employees who have given notice. Such employees will sometimes regard as fair the review for their own edification and memory of confidential material to which they have had access.

5. Using noncompetition agreements. In most states, such agreements may be used by a company to prevent a key employee from going to work for a competitor. However, some states do not permit such agreements because they may tend to prevent or restrain people from working in their trade or profession.

MARKETING PRODUCTS EMBODYING TRADE SECRETS

When a product goes on the market, there are a number of things that can happen to cause the loss of trade secret protection. Some companies have found, to their chagrin, that their own efforts at publicity and promotion caused their products to lose their trade secrecy. Examples include a company that invited a trade journal to photograph its allegedly trade secret production line and prepared a trade movie showing the production process; a manufacturer of a camera for taking pictures of the cornea that disclosed its alleged trade secrets in its catalog; and a software house that asserted that its customer list was a trade secret even though it listed many of its customers in its advertising brochures. Other pitfalls include demonstrations at trade shows, technical papers delivered at conferences or published, and sales demonstrations to customers.

Further problems arise when the product is put on the market. Frequently, the features of a product are obvious to, or can be readily ascertained by, any purchaser. If so, those features are no longer considered to be trade secret because what anyone can see is not a secret. However, public sale of a product will not be deemed to disclose the process by which it was made or the tolerances for its components for the simple reason that that type of information cannot be readily ascertained from inspection of the product.

A harder question is this: Suppose that the product has features that are not readily ascertainable by inspection but that can be derived by reverse engineering, perhaps at considerable expense and with considerable difficulty? If a competitor actually does reverse-engineer the product, the original creator cannot do anything about it (unless, as discussed below, he has a valid patent). However, what frequently happens is that the competitor, rather than reverse engineering the product, uses a shortcut—for instance, hiring an ex-employee of the company that created the product and using his knowledge to duplicate it. When the first company sues, the second company claims that it or anyone else could have reverse engineered the product (even though it chose instead to take a shortcut) and therefore that the product never was a trade secret in the first place.

There is no hard and fast rule to predict who will win in this kind of situation. Judges will consider how many units have been sold, how difficult it would have been for a competitor to obtain a unit, and how difficult the reverse engineering process would have been. Judges also consider how heinous the competitor's conduct has been. For instance, a competitor that engaged in industrial espionage or stole blueprints would have a hard time evoking the judge's sympathy by claiming that it could have legitimately duplicated the product by reverse engineering and therefore the product ought not to be considered a trade secret.

A company should consider ways to make reverse engineering more difficult. For instance, if specification or tolerance data would be helpful for reverse engineering, such information could be withheld from the company's literature or be made available only on a confidential basis. And, as mentioned above, identifying marks may be obliterated from components, or fragile components may be encased in resin, epoxy, or some other material that would make access to the interior of the product more difficult, or assembly may be organized so as to conceal secret arrangements between the components. It may even be feasible to have each customer sign a confidentiality agreement under which the customer would agree to take precautions to prevent public access to the product or to the documentation accompanying the product, such as manuals or design drawings.

Another way to protect against reverse engineering might be to obtain a patent. However, this procedure has its drawbacks. The holder of a valid patent has the right to prevent other people from duplicating or using his discovery for 17 years—even if they duplicate it independently without even knowing of his product. But there is an associated cost: full and complete disclosure of the discovery. In other words, the inventor discloses his invention to the world, thereby adding to the fund of human knowledge, in return for which he receives a monopoly for 17 years. Thus, an inventor must choose between keeping his invention a trade secret or obtaining a patent; he cannot do both, for one is incompatible with the other.

There are a number of relevant considerations in deciding which course to take. A patent is expensive and usually takes years to obtain. But the greatest risk in applying for a patent results from the fact that, once the patent is granted, the description of the product becomes public knowledge. One of the following things may then happen.

1. Competitors may read the product description in the patent application and then use information from it in a somewhat different way without infringing the patent itself ("inventing around" the patent), thus forcing the patent holder to compete with himself.

2. Even if a competitor infringes the patent, it may be very difficult for the patent holder to do much about it. The patent holder may never even learn of the infringement, particularly if it occurs in a different geographical or technological area than the patent holder's own business. Patent litigation is also extremely expensive. This is particularly true for the small entrepreneurial company, which often will have expended considerable sums to develop the product and must price the product high enough to cover those costs. By contrast, patent infringers do not have research and development costs to amortize and may be able to undersell the patent holder or force the patent holder to sell at a lower price at the same time that the costly patent litigation is going on.

3. Another serious problem with obtaining a patent is that a competitor who infringes (or wishes to infringe) the patent may attack the validity of the patent—usually on the ground that the product is not "original" enough. The mortality rate of patents subjected to this kind of attack is quite high— more than half the patents challenged in court are found to be invalid. And, of the patents that are held valid, only about half the time is an infringement found. These are not good odds. If the patent is found invalid, not only will patent protection be lost, but trade secret protection will no longer be available, because the product will already have been fully disclosed when the patent issued.

Of course, eschewing patent protection in favor of trade secret protection also has its risks. Trade secret protection is effective only against improper use or disclosure of the secret. If someone independently discovers a company's trade secret, he could use it with impunity, or disclose it to the world and destroy the secret altogether.

COMPETING RIGHTS OF EMPLOYER AND EMPLOYEE

Most trade secret cases involve a clash between an employer and one or more employees (or former employees). A company that spends large sums of money developing products or information usually considers that information as its own property. But an employee who arrives at the same knowledge in the ordinary course of his employment responsibilities, and who perhaps contributes to or enhances its value, will tend to regard the information as being part of his own employment experience.

This conflict has implications for public policy. Should we protect information an employee develops for a company on the theory that this will enhance R&D spending by encouraging companies to develop new products without fear that an employee will then be able to take that information elsewhere? Or does such protection of company information discourage technological innovation and new job creation by preventing the formation of start-up companies by employees wishing to compete with their ex-employer? In one landmark case confronting this policy dilemma, where employees who had themselves developed certain software for their employer left to form a competing company, the judge ruled that their use of the technology they themselves had originated did not constitute a breach of confidence because under such circumstances "the employee may then have an interest in the subject matter at least equal to that of his employer." Other cases have followed this line of reasoning, although this outcome by no means represents a consensus.

However, the situation is different when the product is the result of joint development—that is, where the employer has devoted substantial resources to a development effort in which the employee has participated. A common example is the participation of a particular employee in a major research and development program. In this situation, it would be extremely difficult to separate the employee's contribution from the contribution made by the rest of the company. In addition, companies just aren't going to make sizable R&D expenditures if any employee participating in the project could then walk out the door with the fruits of that research. Thus, whenever there has been a substantial contribution by the employer to the creation of a new product or process, employees usually have not been permitted to use the information contained therein for their own benefit, even when their contribution may have exceeded that of any other person.

CONFIDENTIALITY AGREEMENTS

It is routine nowadays for employers to require each employee to sign a confidentiality agreement and an invention assignment agreement, which are usually contained in one document. A confidentiality agreement requires the employee to keep confidential and not to disclose or use the company's proprietary information. An invention assignment agreement requires the employee to assign to the employer (i.e., transfer) any rights he may hold in inventions or discoveries, whether patentable or not, which he developed during the course of employment.

As discussed above, the law forbids an employee from misappropriating trade secrets and confidential information whether or not there is a confidentiality agreement. One might therefore wonder why employers consider confidentiality agreements to be necessary.

The answer lies in the practicalities of trade secret litigation. In most disputes between companies and their former employees over rights in information, a central question is whether the information was confidential in the first place. Not all information learned by an employee in the course of his employment is confidential to the employer; employment "experience," consisting of the acquired knowledge, skill, and information that any employee would have picked up in a similar position, is not proprietary to the employer; nor is information already known in the trade. It might be very difficult for a judge or jury to assess whether information learned by an employee is proprietary to the company, is simply a natural product of the employment, or is already known in the industry. A confidentiality agreement helps remove this uncertainty, by specifying what the employer and employee themselves agree shall be deemed confidential to the company.

There are further benefits from an employer's point of view. If an employer sues a former employee for misappropriating confidential information, the judge may want reassurance that the company isn't just trying to oppress ex-employees or stifle legitimate competition. A confidentiality agreement signed by the former employee may help convince a judge that protecting proprietary information has been a long-standing company policy, not just something thought up after a valued employee left to join the competition. In addition, once an employee has signed a confidentiality agreement, he will not be able to claim lack of awareness that he held a position of trust and confidence.

The best time for a company to have employees sign confidentiality agreements is before they start work. This allows new employees to reject the terms of the agreement at the outset, should they so choose, and look for other opportunities. A confidentiality agreement signed after an employee has started work may not be upheld in some jurisdictions if, at the time of signature, the employee did not receive "consideration" (i.e., a quid pro quo). Thus, knowledgeable managers faced with the need for an employee's belated signature on a confidentiality agreement would be advised to offer the employees something in return. For instance, signing the agreement could be a condition of a promotion or a raise.

Sometimes employers go overboard and require that everyone sign confidentiality agreements covering everything. Such an indiscriminate approach can be self-defeating; if the agreement attempts to label as confidential things that obviously are not confidential, a judge may refuse to enforce it at all. To be effective, a confidentiality agreement should cover only information that is in fact confidential and should be signed only by employees with access to such information.

Typically, a confidentiality agreement will include the following types of provisions:

a. It will state that the employee will hold the company's proprietary information in trust and will not use it or disclose it except as necessary in the performance of his duties for the company.

b. The agreement usually states what the employer is giving the employee in return for a signature—e.g., an offer of employment.

c. The agreement will define what information is proprietary, either by describing it or by listing categories of such information.

d. Often, companies require new employees to state that they have not taken anyone else's proprietary information. This is for the company's protection. If it turns out that the employee *has* taken proprietary information belonging to, say, a former employer, the company cannot be held liable for having used that former employer's trade secret if it was unaware that the information was someone else's trade secret.

e. The employee usually promises to return any written materials or other physical embodiments of information upon termination, and not to remove such material from company premises without permission.

f. In the event that the employee leaves for other employment, the agreement may give the company the right to contact the subsequent employer and alert it to the company's claimed rights in information learned by the employee while he was on the company's payroll.

g. The agreement may also contain a noncompetition clause, under which the employee agrees not to work for a competitor for a specified period of time after leaving employment with the company. Such clauses are disfavored by the courts because they limit an employee's right to earn a living and they hamper competition. Indeed, in some states, noncompetition clauses are illegal. Even where they aren't, judges scrutinize them at length to determine whether they have "reasonable" limitations on duration, geographical limits, and types of conduct prohibited.

INVENTION ASSIGNMENT AGREEMENTS

An invention assignment agreement gives a company the rights to any invention or discovery developed by an employee during his employment. It is usually contained in the same document as the confidentiality agreement.

If an employer and employee have not entered into an invention assignment agreement, the law assumes that the employee owns any inventions that he has developed—with two exceptions. First, if the employee has used the resources and facilities of the employer to develop the invention, the invention belongs to the employee, but the employer may use it without paying royalties. Second, if an employee was hired for the specific purpose of invention and development, the invention belongs to the employer.

An invention assignment agreement changes all that. Such agreements usually include three things: a promise by the employee to disclose all inventions and discoveries, the employee's assignment to the employer of all rights to any such inventions and discoveries, and the preservation of the employee's rights to inventions and discoveries made before his employment commenced.

Companies sometimes attempt to require employees to disclose and assign inventions and discoveries created after their employment has terminated. Judges are sometimes unwilling to enforce such a provision, except to the extent necessary to protect the company's confidential information.

CONCLUSION

This article has attempted to discuss the most frequently occurring problems in trade secret protection of new products. Once a company has identified a particular area of concern—for instance, what internal security procedures are appropriate, whether to seek a patent, what commitments to seek from employees—the next step should be to have a capable lawyer review what the company proposes to do.

By recognizing and dealing with trade secrecy issues at the earliest possible stage, developers of new products can substantially decrease the dangers of losing their right or ability to exploit their products commercially to the best advantage.

21

New Product Development

The State of the Art and The State of the Action

Volney Stefflre

To provide an overview of the new products function, it is useful to compare what goes on now with what went on before and what will probably happen in the future. It is also useful to compare what goes on routinely—*state of the action*—with what we are capable of doing at a particular point in time—*the state of the art.*

About 25 years ago, there were a number of things that were obvious about the new product development function in the consumer products area.

The first of these was that, technically, using the market research methods and practices available at the time, companies simply could not do very well at forecasting the demand for products as yet unbuilt. Second, also technically, there did not seem to be a great deal of optimism about radical improvement on the market research side of the then available state of the art. Third, more managerially, it was widely assumed that new product development was part of general management and the skills relevant to running an ongoing company were about the same as those needed to successfully introduce a new consumer product.

On the state of the action side, there was something of a consensus that around 98 percent of new product projects did not develop into successful new products in the national market. But there was considerable enthusiasm on the part of marketing and general management about the new products function, and at times there was a fairly serious effort to live up to the apple pie and motherhood notions of letting future earnings potential influence current management decision making.

Research methodology consisted of having consumers sit in groups and discuss various product ideas and/or product prototypes. The somewhat ambiguous data that resulted was then used creatively to (a) help move ahead or hold back particular new product projects and (b) facilitate the development of exciting new product prototypes and positionings.[1] Concepts and prototypes were in turn evaluated by methods that included recycling to snap discussions with more refined stimuli, and/or moving the product into some form of product test that measured paired comparisons and/or average preference, or asking some individuals whether they would purchase the concept or prototype, and asking individuals why they liked what they liked.

Results of these investigations (plus perhaps judgments of a panel of experts and a few assorted executives and their spouses) were then processed in idiosyncratic ways by local management, and influenced by the local organizational and political exigencies. Eventually, the product was (1) recy-

---

[1] The term *positioning* has been around for much longer than we have known how to measure its meaning. Messages sent to France on BBC prior to D Day were *positioned* so as to let the French underground know the event was in the offing but to avoid stimulating them to premature action that would destroy their later effectiveness. A neat communications problem.

cled to some stage of the above for further development, (2) dropped (perhaps to be rediscovered later when things had changed), or (3) introduced into test market in some town selected partially for its demographic composition, partially for its convenience, and, to be fair, partially for its weather. (There is, after all, much to say for Phoenix in the winter and Rochester in the summer.)

At each step in this traditional process we have technical problems. Using focus groups to evaluate market potential has a bit of a problem in that, due to the interdependent nature of consumer responses, 13 groups of 20 people behave more like 13 people than 260. Groups may be helpful in (1) helping individual managers learn how consumers talk about their *widgets*, (2) eliciting ideas (though not evaluating them), and (3) providing managers with an ambiguous data base that allows maximum use of their creative capabilities (e.g., maximal malleability so they can interpret the data to benefit their own careers).

Paired comparisons and averages, like focus groups, are useless at predicting how many individuals (what proportion of the market) will purchase a given product or try a given product concept and what the product's sales volume will be. People are not particularly good at verbalizing *why* they like things. As a result, researchers are unable to predict what modifications in the product will produce what modifications in preference among which individuals.

An even more amusing fact of nature is that a test market in a particular region may or may not enable one to predict the performance of that particular product in another test market and/or in national rollout.

The problem is a quite simple one in many categories (e.g., foods and beverages)—regional differences in taste are major (e.g., 300 percent) and unpredictable as a function of the other demographic characteristics of the populations involved.

Pool, Abelson, and Popkin (1964) showed years ago that if one used people types constructed from demographic data to inhabit states formed of populations matching voter composition you could estimate fairly accurately which states would tend to vote for which candidates. Their largest errors occurred in candidates' home states because people tended to overvote for local boys in comparison with what was expected from their demographic composition.

For many markets, the situation is more like the local candidate phenomenon than like a nice linear function of demographic factors. The categories to which these irregularities are relevant seem to be an empirical matter, so one cannot assume that they will not occur in a market one does not know.

I have addressed test marketing in more detail because, even in contexts where the product rolled out was the product tested, the rollout implementation matched the rollout plans, and competitors did not muddy the evaluative waters, the failure of test marketing to forecast national demand accurately had important consequences.

First, a number of companies developed a corporate market research culture along the following lines: "Since we cannot even predict what happens when we take a product whose performance has been measured in a test market and accurately forecast what will happen when we roll it out nationally, let's get quickly out of the forecasting business and talk only about the reliability of our data, about the quality of our sampling, and about the statistical significance of our results. Let's not stick our necks out and actually forecast what will happen, what will happen next, and/or what will happen if, in the new product context."

Second, a much smaller number of companies decided that an appropriate solution to the regional variability problem was to run multiple test markets in each of the major sales regions. In this way, regional variability was included in the initial tests rather discovered later during national expansion.

These market research obstacles to successful new product development in the traditional context are dealt with in more detail in Stefflre (1979).

If we move backward in the new product development process, by 1967 it was clear that survey research, if done correctly, could roughly estimate the potential for a particular new product idea (if consumers saw the product as fitting the idea evaluated earlier). Some of my work in the early 1960s used this approach for new products we had under development and for testing the demand for new products competitors were about to introduce. The 1967 NICB report noted that this type of concept test did a fairly good job of estimating volume potential but that market researchers had not yet developed a generally acceptable and working final evaluator and forecaster for the total product bundle (product, packaging, advertising, etc).

The method by which this was achieved was obvious—to test product trial and repeat in a national sample to evaluate the new item's performance potential against the current competitive array (or some surrogate for this).

This type of device was used to base forecasts on the proportion of respondents in a survey who preferred the advertisement to the competitive array of advertising, and preferred the product to the competitive array of products, and this intersection of respondents and their purchasing potential being roughly the volume potential of the product.

A number of other individuals and organizations have developed devices of this type using a national sample and simulating trial and repeat to evaluate new product entries, and the average error of this type of forecast seems pragmatically adequate.[2]

If things are executed more or less as planned and forecasts are moderately conservative, errors based upon product underperformance should occur only 1 out of 10 times.

In general, then, in the old days, companies' success rates were not very high, there were problems with the research methods most widely used, and there was considerable interest in, and lip service to, the notion that new products should be an important contributor to future earnings. America was seen as the most advanced industrial economy in the world and our management style was considered second to none.

If we switch from our before scenario to our after scenario (1984–85) we find ourselves in a situation where the state of

---

[2] Urban and Hauser (1980) review one tradition; Wind, Mahajan, and Cardozo (1983) provide a more eclectic review and my own work is discussed in Stefflre (1979, 1985). Mauser (1983) examines the applicability of this approach to political campaigns.

the art has moved ahead considerably, but the state of the action has not changed greatly—though how people think about the nature of the problems involved has changed.

If we start upstream in the new product development process, the heuristics used in developing new product concepts and prototypes do not seem greatly improved over the heuristics used in the old days. A number of algorithms have been proffered for developing an optimal new product for a particular market, but none of these seem to be up to turning out a stream of winners.

Recently, I have had fairly good results with a quick and dirty method for screening prototypes (20–30) from around the world, other distribution systems, R&D, etc. I give these prototypes to a small number of families for naturalistic use at home, seeing how they describe these products, their uses, and their similarities to other products and an ideal product. From these verbatims, I develop various product concepts and then test these concepts in a 300-person sample, tagging on a repeat purchase test among concept preferrers for products and concepts that look interesting. This gives us the ability to select from simulated trial data, for a large number of positionings (50–60) of a fair number of prototypes (20–30), those concept prototype couplings on which we wish to obtain repeat purchase data and fairly precise volume estimates.

The thing that is most interesting about this quick and dirty version is that an analysis of the 30-person product preference data generally allows a reasonably rough estimate of the final outcome of concept test (and the concept test plus repeat purchase version)—a situation that would not have been expected, until it happened a few times.

In general, then, given that we can forecast awareness from advertising expenditure, and distribution and availability of the product, the current state of the art in forecasting trial and repeat from estimates is quite good. Our heuristics for hypothesis generation may not be so good, but our evaluation techniques work just fine. The best are now *valid* in the pragmatic sense that if A tests better than B, A will perform in the market better than B (usually).

Another improvement in the state of the art is the use of

field experimentation more systematically to fine tune the continuous marketing variables, price, advertising expenditure, size, etc. Since people, when asked about money, tend to tell the interviewer who they want the interviewer to think that they are, these verbal responses do not fit well with actual experimental data on price elasticities.

It has also become clearer to the survey research community that most of the error in forecasting is not sampling error but rather the error of using research instruments that do not forecast what will happen, and what will happen if, in the marketplace.

Given all the progress in improved devices for making valid forecasts of what ifs in the new product market, one would expect the success rate in this area to have increased over the last few decades.

On a superficial level, this seems to be the case for 2 percent success rates that are no longer discussed. Now, counting begins after a successful test market so 50 percent and/ or 66 percent success rates during this *commercialization* phase are talked of. However, if one counts the careers of products introduced into Nielsen records in traditional package goods areas (like foods) relatively small percentages appear to achieve moderately high sales ($15 million).

Solving the problem of new products' high failure rate by changing the calibration of measuring instruments would be fine except for three problems.

1. If the new product success rates were high in the 1980s, then a lot of funds spent on other attempts (not counted) were added into overhead.

2. The high success rate in new products did not carry with it an increase in earnings.

3. Foreign competitors that approach the problem of innovation a bit differently made massive inroads into consumer durables in the United States and around the world, and consumer package goods may follow.

Basically, then, we have comparable performance, better rationalized now than in the 1960s. It is more generally recognized to be a managerial problem relating to coordinating often feuding functions and treating tomorrow's external corporate realities as seriously as today's internal career realities.

Corporate managements in mature industries seem to have given up on new products for growth potential and/or as devices for diversification—acquisition is the tool of choice. Having tried new products and found that they did not work, many managers are focusing on short-run (often franchise-destroying) promotional and push activities that temporarily alleviate the symptoms of strategic marketing problems.

In general, the state of the art has moved ahead considerably in the last 25 years. The state of the action in the technical arena remains about the same, however, with *focus groups* and *averages* still brand share leaders in market research and Rochester still sold as a test market (representative of the United States demographically). I have collected a variety of incorrect forecasts from the business press, so, on occasion at least, things appear to be as badly done as ever.

On the other hand, American industry's performance over the last 25 years has raised some question about whether our management practices and principles are the best we can do, and some organizational principles have been suggested that might facilitate our ability to innovate successfully.

If I try to predict the future, some things look as though they will remain the same.

1.   New industries will be formed by small companies betting on major technological breakthroughs (as happened when Haloid developed Xerox).

2.   A number of technologically driven growth markets will shake down, and the many smaller companies that create a constant stream of innovation will be replaced by a few big companies savagely fighting for market share as their earnings and organizations ossify and foreign competition provides an external stimulus (the position Xerox currently finds itself in.

3. On the new product side, a few companies will automate, some companies will ossify, and some companies will attempt to use intuitive entrepreneurial skills.

Some very successful companies may utilize fully automated and constantly updated computer simulations of consumer markets that allow simulations of what will happen *if* various types of new products are introduced into the market, various current products are seen in certain different ways, and/or various aspects of consumer preferences are modified in specific ways.

The first of the widely validated versions of these simulations (running on micro- and/or minicomputers) are just starting to appear. Of interest, is Allan Frost's *Scribe,* used fairly widely in Europe and Japan. Frost (based in London) has a procedure for a large sample that measures ratings of a number of products along a wide variety of carefully selected scales, respondents' placement of ideal products along these scales, and respondents' preferences for and use of various products in various situations. The program then does an intra-individual product map, segments the market into like segments, and measures the effects of moving products along scales in terms of implied movements along other scales and shares of purchases captured from various individuals. It segments by any move specified and estimates what will happen if new products exhibiting specific profiles are introduced into the market (in terms of forecasting the shares they will receive and the effects of their introductions on competing products sales). And it will search for and select the optimal profile for a new product to exhibit within the current market structure. (*Optimal*, in this case, means the attribute configuration that gives the manufacturer the largest share new product, or the largest increment to corporate market share.)

Frost's simulation has been validated through pre- and postmeasurements before and after advertising campaigns and through field experiments designed to test its predictions, and it is used as a strategic planning device by some of the livelier firms in Japan.

The continued updating of simulations like these through rolling samples (continuing insertion of new information in the files) allows one of these simulations to provide, ready-made, much of the information often required of a market research department.

A second type of simulation that will greatly aid many better companies is the one described by Akoff (1978) as being used by a major beer company. It breaks the company into regions, estimates the effects in various regions of various advertising and promotions expenditures, and helps set budgets for these activities.

In both of these areas, I see the simulations initially used as hypothesis generation devices whose forecasts are then tested in field experiments before serious implementation. But, if simulations are validated and time is important, one may see a move directly from simulations into implementation.

Since the cost of developing and maintaining these systems is high in terms of both talent and dollars, one might expect to see some companies choosing not to participate, others reallocating much of their usual market research budgets toward these centralized data bases, and others selling access to large category-specific data bases and simulation models as an information resource, with access leased by several companies on a yearly basis.

On the other hand, other companies, realizing that use of a whole brain may be better than use of half a brain, may start allowing and rewarding successful usage of executive intuitive marketing capability to a greater extent. Some people are simply better at imagining what other people want in some markets. Whether this makes use of the individual's experience, the individual's creativity, the individual's unconscious, and/or the individual's psi powers is an open question. But what is clearly true is that some individuals, at some stages in their careers, have been imaginative enough to help create new industries and major companies.

Other individuals, equally capable, have been in organizational contexts where their intuitive capabilities were seen as odd quirks and therefore troublesome. Successful exploitation of this type of talent will be a major factor in stimulating the growth of many American industries. Along these lines, some firms may attempt to motivate and reward their executives' creative and entrepreneurial talents.[3]

My own view is that the types of approaches used by organizations is a regular function of where they are in their corporate life cycle. In the beginning when they are full of pizzazz and close to the consumer, they have some good ideas, try them in inexpensive ways, and go with the winners to create a big new firm. Then some failures occur, checks and balances set in, and form becomes more important.

As covering one's back with paper and justifying one's behavior in the organization short run becomes more important than the effects of one's behavior on the firm's performance longer run in the market, the firm's corporate performance falters.

For the first type of situation, cheap, effective heuristics and tools that validly measure demand are used. In the second place, larger-scale more systematic, conventional devices that may or may not work (but that have long histories of hallowed usage) seem appropriate.

I wish that I could provide the young manager who looks into *The New Product Handbook* with a quick recipe for producing successful new products.

Two factors complicate this simplicity. First, differences between types of research that validly forecast demand and those that do not hinge on subtle matters of data collection, analysis, and interpretation—issues more technical than seem appropriate in this context. Second, and more important, whether a manager's company is serious or not serious about the new products function is often difficult to determine (for part of general management is talking a good game in this sector).

---

[3] Business education is heavy on analytic skills and weak on creative skills. The role of intuitive factors in decision making and the possible role of psi in major industrial innovations, are just starting to be examined. Since these abilities appear to be fairly widespread and learnable, interested readers may wish to examine Dean, Mihalasky, Ostrander, and Schroeder (1974), whose work was partially funded by Chester Carlson, inventor of Xerography and Bartlett's (1981) partial update.

On the market research side, since details of execution make such a difference, managers should try to determine what kind of record the devices used in the research actually have in forecasting sales volumes.

On the organizational side, younger managers may wish to focus on external consequences of strategic marketing in the marketplace and/or internal consequences of their actions on their careers.

If you are in an organization that tilts toward the short-term internal reality, and, in pursuit of long-term external strategic advantage for the corporation, you challenge the windmills, you will probably be punished (even if you make a long-term external success). But you will be learning about real marketing. If you play the inside game well in an organization that plays this way, your career will glow, but don't try to become an entrepreneur.

My own recommendation is to go for external strategic advantage for the company. Even if the company doesn't appreciate your efforts, you can often exploit your capability in a more entrepreneurial fashion in other contexts.

However, this is a matter for the reader to choose after looking at the organization, the project, and what he or she wants out of life.

The serious manager in pursuit of external long-term corporate strategic and competitive advantages is constrained to some degree by what is internally possible in the short term. He or she should prepare for a complex set of trade-offs in which what is externally desirable in the market but organizationally impossible gets bartered into what is organizationally possible to implement and externally satisfactory in the market.

An optimal new product is one that satisfies the strategic need and happens, rather than a strategically optimal product that does not happen and/or an organizationally optimal product that fails in the market.

So though the industry leaders may make innumerable minor innovations in the products in a category, outsiders (small firms, foreign firms, and/or firms in other industries) will still tend to be the ones that make the radical innovations that transform a market, an industry, and/or an economy (Stefflre 1985a, 1985b). But that is another story.

REFERENCES

Ackof, R. L. *The Art of Problem Solving*. New York: John Wiley & Sons, 1978.

Bartlett, L. F. *Psi Treck*. New York: McGraw-Hill, 1981.

Crawford, C. M. *New Products Management*. Homewood, Ill.: Richard D. Irwin, 1983.

Dean, D., J. Mihalasky, S. Ostrander, and L. Schroeder. *Executives*. New York: Prentice-Hall, 1974.

NICB. *Market Testing Consumer Products*. New York: National Industrial Conference Board, 1967.

Mauser, E. *Political Marketing*. New York: Praeger, 1983.

Pool, I. S., R. P. Abelson, and S. Popkin. *Candidates, Issues and Strategies*. Cambridge, Mass.: MIT Press, 1964.

Stefflre, V. "New Products: Technical and Organizational Problems and Opportunities." In *Analytic Approaches to Product and Marketing Planning*, ed. A. Shocker. Cambridge, Mass.: Marketing Science Institute, 1979.

―――. "Organizational Obstacles to Innovation." *The Journal of Product Innovation Management* 2, no. 1, 1985a, pp. 3–11.

―――. *Development and Implementation of Marketing Strategies*. New York: Praeger, 1985b.

Urban, G. L., and J. R. Hauser, *Design and Marketing of New Products*. New York: Prentice-Hall, 1980.

Wind, Y., V. Mahajan, and R. N. Cardozo. *New-Product Forecasting*. Lexington, Mass.: D.C. Heath, 1981.

Index